D1601125

Those Several Summers

Summers

...that led to difficult decisions

A Memoir

Jackie Davis Martin

Those Several Summers . . . that led to difficult decisions
©Jackie Davis Martin

All rights reserved. This book or any portion thereof may not be reproduced or used in any manner whatsoever without the express written permission of the publisher except for the use of brief quotations in a book review.

Print ISBN: 979-8-35094-414-3
eBook ISBN: 979-8-35094-415-0

Our doubts are traitors

And make us lose the good we oft might win

By fearing to attempt.

William Shakespeare: Measure for Measure 1.4.86

I was a-trembling because I'd got to decide forever
betwixt two things, and I knowed it.

Mark Twain: Adventures of Huckleberry Finn

There is no correct decision waiting to be made.

Ellen Langer: The Mindful Body

CONTENTS

The Summer of 1984

Portland, Oregon   2

   1   *At Harrington's, Friday, June 29*   2

   2   *The Greek Festival, July 1*   14

   3   *Cannon Beach, July 5*   21

   4   *Life Before Portland*   32

   5   *The Green World*   38

   6   *Ashland and Elsewhere*   45

   7   *Nearing Seminar's End*   50

Two More Weeks   55

   8   *Not Alaska, But-*   55

   9   *Last Days*   69

   10   *In Flight, August 18*   73

Cherry Hill, New Jersey   77

   11   *Home Again*   77

   12   *The "Affair"*   82

   13   *The New Doug*   93

   14   *The Old Me*   97

   15   *Torn*   105

Tension   107

   16   *Ringing Phones*   107

   17   *Riddles*   117

   18   *The Ticket*   123

New Old Doubts   134

   19   *Christmas, 1984*   134

   20   *Us Again*   139

   21   *Forward and Reverse*   151

Moving In, Moving On   157

   22   *Arrival*   157

23 *Oliver! and More*   164

24 *Intrusions*   172

The Summer of 1985

Shifts   **181**

25 *"Home"*   181

26 *Gone and Back Again*   185

27 *December Reflections*   193

28 *Preparations*   203

The Summer of 1986

One Goodbye   **208**

29 *The Chaos of July*   208

30 *Garage Sale*   217

31 *Walking Away, August 1, 1986*   220

Crossing the Country   **223**

32 *Advent of Adventure*   223

33 *Some Surprises*   228

34 *Final Days*   236

Adjustments and Discoveries   **239**

35 *Arriving in San Francisco*   239

36 *Coping*   250

37 *Vacillations*   257

The Summer Of 1987

San Francisco, California   **263**

38 *Opportunities and Agonies*   263

39 *The Letter*   270

40 *Finale*   276

Two Photos: Early and Late   **280**

Epilogue: What Became of Everyone in This Story?   **282**

About The Author   **284**

The Summer of 1984

Portland, Oregon

1   *At Harrington's, Friday, June 29*

I'd taken a bus from the Reed campus and headed to downtown Portland. As I walked to the museum, the "Harrington's" sign surprised me. The book I'd bought in Powell's, *Being Single in Portland*, had a section about places "to meet people," Harrington's being one of them. I was far from home and lining up things to do to keep me entertained for whenever our seminar wasn't meeting. I'd noted Harrington's as a place to eventually check out, but when I saw the sign at street level, I thought I'd take a look right then.

Halfway down the wrought iron staircase that led to the underground restaurant, I hesitated. I could see a man in a brown leather jacket sitting at one end of the long bar, drinking a beer. He looked to be in his forties, as I was. I liked his moustache, his glasses, his seeming pensiveness. Would it be too absurd to take a seat near him, maybe talk to him?

I'd met men this way before. I would appear self-contained, but glance their way and make eye contact, maybe strike up a conversation. A social hour at Harrington's promised to be a place that would promote such a scene, although it was only three o'clock, too early. Still, the interesting-looking man was alone, and I debated. Should I continue down the curving staircase and take a seat near him? Or find the Portland Art Museum? I started back up the stairs—then stopped, looked down again.

The man in the leather jacket seemed tall—a feature I found appealing. I'd order something simple, perhaps talk, perhaps not, and be on my way. I knew no one here in Portland. My seminar didn't meet on Fridays, which was what today was, so I'd spent the morning alone, studying *Henry IV*, taking a walk around campus, and now, heading to the museum.

On the staircase I debated: down-up, stay-go, which one?

Oh well, what difference did it make to talk to that man who was alone? I was already here, wasn't I? I descended the curving steps, pulled out a stool two seats away from him. He turned to me when I did that, and I smiled slightly. He nodded his head in acknowledgment, smiled slightly also, and turned back to his beer. His height was apparent in the way his legs extended out from the barstool, his back broad beneath the brown leather of his jacket. I ordered a club soda and took out a pack of cigarettes from a carton that my rather uncommitted boyfriend back home, Doug, had given me as a send-off gift. I left matches in my purse. "Do you have a light?" I asked the man.

He turned toward me, pulling a lighter out of his pocket, and looked pleased to have been asked. His eyebrows matched his moustache; his hair, although thinning, needed a trim. I was dressed up for a city museum visit: a black linen suit, bone-colored pumps. The man extended his arm gracefully toward me and lit my cigarette, shaking out one of his own to join me before tucking the lighter back in his pocket. The smoke drifted upward. On the sound system a piano played softly; it sounded like Gershwin. "Biding My Time," I said.

He laughed. "I guess I am, too. Right now."

Was he deliberately playing with the pun? I gestured toward the loudspeaker. "I meant the music, that song. I'm on my way to the art museum."

He listened briefly to the music, studying me. "It's a great museum," he said. "A few blocks from here." His eyebrows lifted a bit in inquiry.

I must have seemed different—a woman alone in the afternoon going to a museum and stopping in a bar to order a club soda. I admitted to him I was new to Portland; it looked to be a beautiful city. "Do you know the Michael Graves building?" I asked. "I read about it on the plane, in the plane's magazine."

The man turned fully toward me; he had to move the middle stool a bit to make room for his legs. He lived in Portland and knew all about the building, as well as the planned statue of "Portlandia" that would eventually adorn it. He'd been a city planner for ten years before he quit to open his own business—long story—but it had failed. I heard the words "live in Portland" and "city planner" and was thrilled, feeling that I'd walked into an information source—something to share with my seminar fellows in getting to know them.

The man said he was once again looking for a real job and selling cars in the meantime. His wide shoulders shrugged an apology, and he paused a moment. "What are you doing here, all the way from—?"

"New Jersey," I filled in. "I'm studying Shakespeare. At Reed."

The word "Shakespeare" sometimes caused strangers to pull back, but he seemed pleased with that information. "That's great. Reed's a great school. Is there a summer program?"

I was still absorbing the candor of his admission of failure and felt, absurdly, that I was now boasting. But I explained. Yes, there was a program, a National Endowment for the Humanities, for a six weeks' study. "It's for high school teachers—we apply for it. I mean, I teach high school English, Shakespeare." I shrugged, took a sip of my club soda. He was still turned toward me, seemingly with interest. "I arrived two days late," I continued. "Long story there, too—and found out our seminar doesn't meet on Fridays. I think the others probably already made arrangements for today."

I didn't tell him I was the only participant who had asked for the one available studio apartment and so been granted it. Several had opted for the communal dorm; a few brought families and rented houses. Since I'd been a single mother of teenagers for years, I loved the idea of my own place. When a cab took me from the airport to the apartment, I was so happy to be there that, even though it was three in the morning, I poured a glass of whiskey from a bottle of Canadian Club that Doug had also given me. Actually, Doug had suggested he might visit me in Portland, and so I'd also accommodated that possibility, remote as it seemed.

"But I bought a book about Portland yesterday," I continued to the man at the bar, "that praised the Art Museum—and also mentioned Harrington's. I saw that sign up there at the top of the stairs—"

"I saw you come down," the man said. "You turned around and went up and came back down."

I blushed. I think I blushed. "I bought a book on Shakespeare criticism, too," I said.

He laughed. "I don't even know why I'm here today." He said he got off work—the car lot—early and went to the Virginia Café, but for some reason didn't like it and thought he'd try something different. "I haven't been here in Harrington's in years," he said. His eyes behind the wire frames were direct.

We continued to talk, this man in the leather jacket and I, nursing those drinks along. Whatever we touched on we seemed to have in common. I was single—divorced a while back—with children in college; he was in the process of a divorce with one son who had just graduated from college, another son still there, and a third son living with his almost-ex wife.

The ambient sounds of people beginning to mill around alerted me to check my watch—it was after five o'clock. "I think I've missed the museum," I said.

He agreed. "Let's get something to eat. Do you like jazz? There's music and great pizza at the Jazz Quarry, around the corner."

That sounded like a good idea. Why not? What else was I doing?

When he stood, I saw his great—to me—height. Doug, whom I'd been dating, was tall to me at six feet. This man—I asked—was 6'4", a full foot taller than I. Together we ascended the staircase where I had initially vacillated into the street, the man I just met behind me.

His name—Bruce Martin—I asked that too—sounded made up, and I said as much. Of course, my own, Jackie Davis (the last name an acquired one), sounded equally false.

"It's not," he said matter of factly and didn't question mine.

Still, I suspected he might be a sham; he was too agreeable, too bright, too altogether interesting to me, and oddly comforting in his size, his angles. He had a wart on his cheek, faintly disheveled hair, and, behind his glasses, clear hazel eyes. I couldn't put him together.

At the end of the block he suddenly turned to me. "Maybe you don't want to do this," he said. "I mean, I can pay my share, but I don't have enough money to pay for both of us. I'm sorry."

I looked up at him. I'd never been told such a thing. It was 1984, and through my dating over the past nine years, I had not picked up a single tab. Either it was the standard of behavior then or

I was fortunate. My last two relationships—spanning as they did the past six years—had spoiled me: always dinners out, performances, trips. But this man from Harrington's was baldly admitting that he could not pay for two. I shrugged it off. Of course I'd pay my share. He nodded but looked uncomfortable. Then he smiled and indicated the Jazz Quarry, a few doors ahead. As we entered, a small combo of middle-aged men was playing "Sweet Georgia Brown," and I commented that the old sax player looked like "an Elk." I loved that he laughed, getting my little joke. We took a table—rustic, as I recall—somewhat away from the music. The pizza was good; we drank wine; we continued our stories.

I revealed that there was someone in New Jersey I had been in love with and hoped to reconcile with. He listened, tracing an unlit cigarette around his lips, thoughtful. There was another man, too, I'd been dating for a while, I told him. I didn't want this man, Bruce Martin, to think I was needy. I did not think I was.

Those were shaky relationships, I knew. And besides, why was I out and about to begin with? A question he no doubt posited to himself about me as he traced those lips—nicely shaped, I noted—and a question which, frankly, I didn't want to answer. I'd suffered a big rejection before I met Doug from a man I'll call Sam. With Sam I thought, after five years, I had a relationship that was fairly permanent. Emotionally I was still clinging to that doomed situation and thus was willing to accept Doug's guardedness. Both of these men made more money than I did as a high school teacher; they didn't have to support, in addition, two teenagers. By the time I met Doug, my son John was away at college and my daughter Susan, although at home, was attending a local community college. I was in grad school myself and rather "free."

And yet. I still felt, contradictorily, both at the apex of my attractiveness and a self-conscious failure, approaching middle age and unsure if I could ever rely on any sort of relationship. I remember looking at all the beautiful people in the streets of Portland and thinking, why can't I belong somewhere? What does it take?

Bruce Martin, sitting across from me at the Jazz Quarry, knew what it was to be responsible for children, for income. He briefly summarized his failed business venture that resulted in an in-process divorce of a marriage dissolving anyway. He was now selling used cars just for some money. I can't believe I'm talking to a used car salesman, I thought, amused and appalled. Obviously, this is a lark, a one-evening thing. I was already shaping up the evening into an anecdote that might amuse the other seminar members as I got to know them.

But, remembering the seminar and Reed, I was jolted. I looked at my watch: it was quarter to 9. "I can't miss the last bus!" I said. "I've got to go." I put down some bills—my share—on the table and stood up.

Again he looked uneasy, tentative, as though he wasn't sure how what he had to say would be construed. "I have a car," he ventured. "It's up the hill, in the garage under my apartment building. I can take you back to Reed."

I hesitated again. It was getting dark, and I'd have to find the bus stop. The man—Bruce—had been straight forward, easy to be with. I agreed.

"These are the Park Blocks," he said as we walked up a park— on each side of which was a street, a sidewalk. The park featured sculptures, benches to sit on, even a rose garden, and, as its name announced, block after block of park bordered by sidewalks. The evening was warm and smelled of grass and roses, dusk now fading into night. I'd learned more of his life, too, on the way.

I considered: if he'd had twenty-five years of marriage and was now in the midst of divorce, he had to be older. He didn't seem that old.

Unexpectedly, coincidentally, he asked me: "How old are you?" My age was an embarrassment to me. Dating the younger Doug had made me conscious of it. But what difference did it make at this odd occurrence? "Forty-three," I said.

"That's great," he said, surprising me again. What was great about forty-three?

"I started young," I said, by way of explanation.

"I'm forty-four. I started young, too."

I'd already explained that I was here in Portland for six weeks and being paid for the seminar. I explained that I'd left my two kids—21 and 19—to their summer jobs, sharing my car, and living together. I'd never done that. I didn't tell him that the man I'd been dating for eight months, Doug, suggested he'd come out to visit.

"This is it." The man named Bruce stopped. We were standing in front of an apartment building much like others on those long blocks. I followed him to the underground garage, suddenly overcome by a sense of caution. What was I doing? The fact that I'd traveled 3,000 miles from home and arrived in the night straight from a faculty weekend in, of all places, the other Portland, in Maine, to arrive at the Reed apartment and drink at three in the morning, then to cross a strange campus a few hours later to meet strangers in a seminar room—seemed odd, even reckless. The reckless summer. But how reckless?

He indicated a small red Fiat, a charming little sports car in a garage space that was mildly claustrophobic, and as he moved to the driver's door, I approached the passenger side. He stared at me across the top of the car, holding the door handle, looking nervous again. "Do you want to come up for a cup of coffee?" he said. I relaxed. His tone suggested he thought he was being ungracious to just get into a car in an underground garage. Or, as though he'd weighed an invitation against what might seem aggression. I said No, I'd just as soon get back to campus.

We drove into the night. Having been a planner, he knew all of Portland, and, since he'd tucked away the convertible's odd roof, I could take in the buildings he enthusiastically pointed out as we drove through the city streets. "Reed's on the East side of town," he said, "but before we cross the bridge, let me show you the view close to the river." He turned the wheel abruptly and the car seemed to plunge down a hill right toward the water. I held my breath. I knew it! I was heading into disaster—the man was a stranger, and how did I know what he had in mind? I watched that shimmering water come into view, the warm air streaming over my head, and thought this might be *it*.

He braked at a boat ramp. The river undulated calmly before us. He leaned back, sighed, looked at me. "It's beautiful, isn't it," he said.

I exhaled deeply. "Yes." What had I feared? That there must be a catch to the evening, that the ease with which we'd related to each other had to have a "catch" to it? It didn't. It just was.

He—Bruce—it was difficult to assign him the name—drove me back to the Reed campus and pulled up in front of "my house," a typical suburban brick house behind a sidewalk, a green lawn.

"I can get out," I said. "My apartment is around the back."

He leaned forward, cradling the steering wheel. "You're here for a while? I'd like to see you again. How would I get in touch with you?"

"There's a phone," I announced. "In my room." I'd been there only two nights, but of course I'd called my kids, given them the number of the phone there on the apartment desk. I would have to pay for my calls. "Can you memorize?" And I rattled off that number.

He watched as I walked around the brick house, and I waved into the dark. Well, I thought, inserting the key into the lovely little apartment: that was something, wasn't it? I don't think it sank in completely how much I had enjoyed myself.

There was a note under my apartment door. Alan, a man from Philadelphia and also in the seminar, had a brother who taught at Reed. The note asked if I would like to join him, the brother, and the brother's wife, to drive to the Columbia River Gorge tomorrow, Saturday? He'd stop by in the morning and see.

Life was suddenly shaping up, wasn't it? An engaging Friday with a stranger in Harrington's, and now another date with a group to see the sights. I glanced at my row of Shakespeare books in the small rack I'd purchased at a garage sale that morning, surveyed my room with its sofa and bed and huge desk, and felt an enormous sense of smugness and pleasure. Who knew life could be such an adventure?

"You went out with a stranger?" Alan said Saturday morning. As though he were not. But he and I were both part of the same seminar, a family of sorts for the next six weeks. Walking to the brother's house, he and I compared notes about our "free Friday." "You met him in town?" He sounded vaguely jealous, which was odd. The brother—actually Alan's twin, making things even odder—drove us to Columbia River Gorge for a picnic his wife had prepared. I remember the wife's frosted hair, her sucking in her stomach, thin as she was, and smiling a lot. The brothers even had identical glass frames and haircuts, although they lived on opposite sides of the country. We had a cordial enough afternoon, though. I was dazzled by the magnificent river flowing well below our picnic area, the mountains in the background scalloped across the horizon. The great trees cast lacy patterns on that very green Oregon grass, and we sat high aloft the river, eating the cheeses and fruits and wine the couple had brought along.

Coming from Pittsburgh's industrial steel town setting of my youth and the subsequent clean flatness of New Jersey, I was overwhelmed at the beauty and variety of our setting. And yet our conversation was the ordinary banter that would take place anywhere. Alan told them, laughing, about my "date" of the night before, a laughter with some pride behind it. That had been my second evening here, Alan pointed out.

I laughed too. "The previous night I wandered into that garden right down the hill from the campus," I said, reframing what had been lonely restlessness that first evening into a sense of adventure. "And talked to a man who lives in town. He said there was a Rose Garden in Portland. A famous one." I didn't add it was some old guy; I wanted to keep up the image they were assigning me. It was truly a wonderful Rose Garden, they said. Alan got excited: perhaps we four could go together? There was pleasant, noncommittal agreement. We had the summer, didn't we?

No sooner had I returned to my little apartment late in the afternoon than the man from Harrington's called. Did I want to walk along the riverfront the next evening? He had to work during the day—Sunday—but there was a Greek festival going on that I might like. He could come and get me.

"Yes," I said. "Yes, I would like that." My reaction was mild, disguising the fact that I was quite thrilled that he wanted to see me again, that he had indeed memorized the phone number. I added that I was attending a Chamber Concert on the campus lawn that evening, Saturday. "That summer series?" he said. "It's supposed to be really good. I've heard about it."

I admitted I'd purchased the series while in New Jersey, fearing I'd be lonely so far from home. So I did have the six concerts lined up. I didn't add that I'd also signed up, my first day on campus, for modern jazz dance lessons and for the same reason: the fear of not belonging.

The next morning, Sunday, I called my kids. Susan missed me and complained about John. John complained about Susan. The summer had only begun. I tried to assure them that they'd work it out, hoping that my assurance would ease my own anxiety.

Then I called Douglas, to let him know my phone number. "Two hours a day, four days a week?" he said. "I've always wanted that kind of a job."

I had to admit it was heavenly. To justify this luxury, I spent the Sunday reading up on criticism and interpretations for *Henry IV, Part 1*, planning to be super-alert for the next morning's seminar session. Then I showered and got ready for what I saw as a real date that evening.

When the man from Harrington's pulled up in his red Fiat in front of the house at 8 p.m., his tall lanky frame unfolding from that small convertible, I ran out like a teenager.

2   *The Greek Festival, July 1*

That night:

At the festival we walk the Willamette waterfront—balalaikas, maybe, flutes—in the background, lights festooned across booths that feature Greek grilled meats and salads. The air is bright; the stars, the river, shimmer in reflection.

We walk along sharing a gyro, taking turns with the bites— about as intimate as anything I've done. I grip his wrist as he guides the sandwich to my mouth, our eyes meeting over that gesture. I like his square hand. His physical appeal is enormous—the way his tall body leans expectantly toward what I say, the way he touches the small of my back briefly as we pause at a stand. We buy a Greek salad, settling ourselves on the grass to share it. When he takes my hand to assist me up, he doesn't let it go. His arm, clutched against my own, feels solid, strong. We walk, we talk, we wander the waterfront.

The night is beautiful—clear and warm, as, actually, all the Portland nights will be hereafter, totally unlike the stuffy, humid summer days of New Jersey. I don't want the evening to end. Am I falling in love with the setting? Does his height give me a sense of security? His arm folded in mine?

The festival booths are packing up when he suggests we go to a Jazz Club in town where Art Blakey is performing that evening. He thinks I'll know who that is. I am not sure, but I can tell my son, who will know these things. I wonder about Bruce not having money to pay for our drinks, but surely he wouldn't suggest such a thing if he didn't have the money? Maybe he'd just gotten paid. Why does it matter? What is on my mind is staying with him, extending the night.

The night moves on as we nurse whiskey-and-waters, listening to the combo, talking, sitting close to each other in a round leather booth, our thighs touching, a physical contact I am reluctant to relinquish. The last set finishes, and, as the musicians leave, he sighs. "I have to take you back to campus," he says. "I know that."

I look at the angles of his face—feel the pressure of his body so close to mine—and I plunge: "I guess we have two choices. You take me back. Or you take me to your place."

I know this surprises him.

Our eyes meet for a full two seconds. "Let's go," he says.

In the car, riding up the Park Blocks to the garage I'd been in before, I think, How crazy can I be? I've already been to bed with Doug this week in my New Jersey life—how many nights before this one? I just claimed I missed Doug (I *had* called), suggesting a loyalty to him he hadn't actually demanded, but I felt I should volunteer.

Still, I am burning for this new man, this large, graceful and angular man, with his easy wit and intelligence and. . . well, if I had to find a word, it was acceptance: his acceptance of what *is*—himself, me—of possibilities.

It is around one or two in the morning when he parks the Fiat in the garage where I stood only two nights ago, and we take the elevator to his apartment. What a surprise that is! I can still picture that apartment, can still see its barrenness. We enter through a short interior hallway (closets on either side) to a large room of hardwood floors with corner windows that face the park blocks that we walked along that other night.

A red easy chair sits next to a short bookcase overflowing with books and in front of that chair a red hassock. More books—several by Hermann Hesse, *Magister Ludi* opened, I remember—are scattered on the floor. That's it! Those are the furnishings. The rest of the large space is just that—space. Along a wall near the kitchen sits a card table and two folding chairs. I am surprised and impressed by the new electric typewriter the table holds and comment on it. "For job applications," he says. "A slow process; I don't really type."

He offers coffee (he has instant, he says) or water. It occurs to me that that is all he has there, and I say water will be fine. He starts down the adjacent hallway, indicating the bathroom to the right, the bedroom to the left, and, when I call out a remark, he turns and says, "You'll have to speak a little louder. I'm a bit hard of hearing."

Good grief, I think, are you kidding? You have nothing here and now you're going to admit to a handicap as well? I don't know whether I am appalled or impressed. Clearly a divorce—or whatever he was dealing with—left him with little, or he took nothing. The bedroom is furnished with a child's chest of drawers, animal decals intact, and a futon on the floor. When I use the bathroom, I wash my hands with a sliver of Ivory soap and dry them on a very thin white towel.

So: here I am at a scene for a tryst with a stranger from town, as Alan—whoever Alan is—described him. Bruce, propped on an elbow as we lie on the Futon, runs his hand over me, over my body, as though he has been presented with a gift, as though he wants to just touch it, savor it. I am aware of my own body too, of its fitness from dance, its bikini tan.

"Are you safe?" I asked in the car on the way there, perhaps trying to indicate that I was not so forward all the time, although that was not, technically, true.

He chuckled from deep within. "Am I safe," he said softly, with irony. "Yes. I am safe." I gathered he hadn't slept with a woman for a while.

He is a gentle and easy lover, unlike Doug's more energetic style, but simply folding me into him, satisfying me, the greatest of surprises.

I stay the night. He takes me back to Reed in the morning so I can shower and change and report with my *Henry IV, Part I* book in tow, eager to discuss the play again. I also carry to the seminar a mug of coffee I'd made with the coffee maker I brought along, as well as my confusion about all that I experienced the night before with the man named Bruce.

In that new bright morning I assume the identity I am there for: one of a group of crisp and shiny scholars gathered around a table on a lush campus to talk about a play—*Henry IV, Part I*—that involves a prince, a king, a rebel and a buffoon. Although I taught the play several times as a high school Shakespeare elective, and also re-read it on the overnight flight to Oregon, I felt in some ways that my inclusion here might have been a mistake, that I wasn't as bright as the others. I wanted to be a good participant, and I'd already joined late. Walking across the campus that bright Monday morning I also tried to shake off the dalliance of the previous evening—-that had nothing to do with my real life at all—neither here nor back home. Here was the seminar group before me, and I could participate at their level, surprising myself. I would live this new life moment by moment, take it as it came.

The discussion of *Henry IV* veered into various topics, including one about Falstaff at the battlefield. After a beautiful speech about "honor," and asking himself what honor really is, Falstaff is found on the ground and declared dead. When others leave the scene, he gets up again. He has feigned death to avoid being killed, justifying his idea of "honor" as being self-preservation. The audience, if they hadn't read the play, would be surprised to see Falstaff get up from his "death." Our question in the seminar was: Would the audience's reaction to Falstaff's "death" be different if they knew Falstaff was only *pretending* to be dead? This elicited various responses. I argued that it does make a difference if the audience knows he will get up again. Knowing he will get up, that he is only pretending, we can't take his "death" seriously. I cited an anecdote I'd read about the restaurateur Toots Shor, who, at the intermission of *Hamlet*, when everyone was out on the street smoking, said to his friends, "I'll bet I'm the only s.o.b. here that doesn't know how this play is going to turn out!"

Robert Knapp, our leader, loved the story.

But the word "pretending" had penetrated. Was I pretending to have had a good time the previous evening, and did I rise to reality this morning? Or had desiring Doug, or Sam before him, been the pretense, the sort of union I thought I wanted, when, if I looked around, I'd realize it wasn't? What was real about those men and my relationships with them, and what was not? And what did that answer have to do with me?

A few days later I call home to ask about bills that might have arrived.

"The Gas and Electric," Susan says. "And the phones. Mom, I really haven't been on mine much." She knows I still resent, seven years later, the fact that her father "gifted" her with a phone that had to have its own landline and never paid for it, so I had two phone bills. I never had the heart to take her phone away. In 1984 there were only landlines, contracted individually, and any calls made outside a local area commanded high charges. Like the call I was making on

18

this third account in Portland, temporarily mine. I tell Susan to put the bills in one of the stamped envelopes I left behind.

"John sat out in the driveway last night again," she tells me. "In the car. It's really stupid."

John is 21 and has a job working with construction and painting. "He's probably tired," I say, wondering about the marijuana I once discovered in a box on an end table. "You probably don't want to open that, Mom," John had said. He'd been sitting across the room then. I didn't.

"Is he there now?" I ask Susan.

"No. I dropped him off this morning. I have to go to the college for records. And to get light bulbs. Why don't we have light bulbs?"

"Forget that porch light," I say, remembering with a pang. "It needs some electrical work. A new bulb won't do it."

She asks about the light out back. It doesn't seem to work either. I ask why she needs it. I dislike having my halcyon life interrupted with such mundane details.

"Mom, tell him to empty the cat box. He has to take a turn. It's disgusting. It's his cat, too."

I say I will, and she has further directions to tell John: the dishes he neglects. He does too much laundry. Her job at the local ice cream shop demands doing laundry, too.

"Are you having a good time?" she asks. "It's hot here. We have the air on all the time. You said we could."

Fine, fine, I say, adding up those dollars in my head.

"How many weeks are you there again?"

"I'll talk to John," I say.

A few days later I call again, at a time I assume John will be home, and he is.

"Mom, can you do something about Susan?" he says. "Tell her to stop playing that ridiculous music. Do you know she's had a group of friends here for a party? They stayed here until almost one with that stuff. I have a strenuous job to get to."

The entertainment section of the *Oregonian* sits on my desk, and I see an ad for the group Manhattan Transfer. "It's the music, then? Are they drinking, too?"

He doesn't think so. Maybe a few have a beer. Yes, it's the music, their stupid voices.

"John—you can say that. You can tell her to turn it down. I don't see the harm in her having some friends over."

I wonder if Bruce would like to go to the Manhattan Transfer concert, if he could pay his share.

"She doesn't listen. And—she let the car almost run out of gas, driving to see Denise or someone on her day off. In Reading, Pennsylvania?"

I ask about the car. A four-year-old Toyota Tercel, it seems to be holding up.

"But I had to fill the tank," he says. "Pay for it. And she used it up." I think of reminding him of all the tanks of gas I've purchased, but don't.

"How is it there?" he asks. "Are you having a good time?"

I say I am, that the people are great, that I met someone in town that I've been having a good time with. He can translate that.

"I'll talk to Susan," I say before we hang up.

3   *Cannon Beach, July 5*

He pulls up in front of my studio/house at noon where I am waiting at the curb. I'm toting a change of clothing and a bag with wine and cheese and crackers I bought when I hiked to the Safeway up the hill. He indicates he has a picnic bag as well. I'm wearing my pink striped blouse and pink cardigan and pink sneakers—all purchased from L.L.Bean a few weeks back. "You look edible," he says, as he opens the small trunk to tuck our bags. The remark surprises and pleases me.

The Fiat's roof is again somehow tucked into its hood, so we're open to the sunshine. I'm going to see the Pacific Coast—my first time. I am going with this man who makes me feel wonderful, at ease. After less than a week I don't know him, really, but know how solid I feel with him.

I'd spent the past eight months wondering about Doug, what would be likely to happen next. He seldom made any plans from one weekend to the next, waiting until the last minute to call and check my availability. Of course, I was always available. I felt that if I'd said I was "busy," he'd never call again. I assumed his pattern, although I didn't like it. Our relationship, if one could call it that, never seemed to be more than just one date after another, a getting together for dinner and crossword puzzles, concerts and reading Shakespeare to each other—an activity I really liked—and sex. There would be morning coffee, more reading, and more sex, never with any commitment, but sometimes some verbal sparring: *What do you want? Probably the same thing you want: nothing. Don't get serious. I won't, I'm not.*

Preceding that had been the five years of dating Sam before being told that I didn't "value" him enough, that he didn't love me anymore, and why didn't we take a "break" for a year or so. I translated that to mean "never" and, as he drove me home that final evening, I cried and pummeled his arm in anger. "How can you do this to me? How? You said we had a future—we've been together so long!" He kept his eyes on the road, endured my punching. "Now I'm five years older! You've used up five years of my life!" I'd sunk back in my seat, sobbing, exhausted. For weeks I became so numb with that rejection that Susan had worried about me. "Mom, are you all right?" she kept asking. I wasn't.

Riding along in the Oregon sunshine that July afternoon, I glanced at the man behind the wheel: I was no problem so far, here. There was no "relationship" to analyze, no tension; all those judgments were somewhere else. The summer was a lark, a reprieve, an escape from my life. It wasn't my life at all. It was the life of a woman in pink confection colors who rode among green mountains in a red Fiat convertible. I'd even said goodbye to the Reed Campus, thinking: *See you all—I'm off for the day!*

I had no need to escape. Reed and the seminar people were enough in themselves to create in me an inordinate and unusual happiness. Of course, I got to know the participants, loved their variety, their ideas, their laughter. We'd had a barbecue out on the Reed lawn the day before, the real 4th of July; someone had produced Halloween masks, and we took turns wearing them and taking pictures. Toni was an actress from New York; Jane, from Indiana and recently re-married, was my counterpart with college-age children. George, gentle and sedate, from Colorado, and Frank, wiry and animated, from Texas, both married, were a pronounced contrast to each other but both equally witty, involved. There were eight men and seven women, and we were all around the same age. We were rather astounded at first at how much we had in common until we realized that, in addition to being selected by Robert Knapp, we were pretty much self-selected in that we'd chosen to study Shakespeare in Oregon. Their reasons were similar to my own: they'd taught various plays of Shakespeare in high school—indeed, we shared lesson plans and project ideas—and were attracted to the immersion of study of the four genres, as well as the promise of Oregon, an exotic destination to all of us except the guy from town, the one "local."

On my journey to the Pacific Ocean that afternoon, I was saying goodbye to one pleasure as I embraced the next.

He—Bruce—narrates our coastal ride, as he narrates everything. He points out landmarks. We stop at a shady grove of trees for a picnic and continue on our way. Over the crest of a mountain I suddenly see the horizon of deep blue ahead and I gasp, causing him to almost drive off the road. "It's the Pacific Ocean! I saw it!" We find a motel room on a hilltop overlooking that ocean, make love. Being with him is natural, satisfying, and, since we can anticipate returning to the room and each other, we get back in the car so he can take me to more Oregon coastal sites.

Later, at the neighborhood bar downstairs from our room, we have sausage sandwiches, and he tries to show me how to play pool, but I am lousy at it and don't care to learn. What I am learning is something I didn't know: how lovely it is to be touched, as though I am part of a familiar couple, as though someone genuinely cares about me. We've known each other six days. Close to midnight we walk along the sandy beach, getting our shoes soaked. I wear his leather jacket and am reminded of walking the beach at the other ocean, the Atlantic, wearing Sam's leather jacket and my sense of enchantment then. I am seized with fear and tell myself, as I stare at the profusion of stars, so wholly visible out here, that I don't want

23

to be hurt again. I have only . . .what? four or five weeks? This is all temporary.

When I wade into the water's edge, Bruce says, "Well, now you can tell your friends back East that you got to the other coast." I venture a few steps into the water. "And then some!" he calls out.

In the morning, over breakfast, we are both agitated. In my case, in spite of my resolve of the previous evening to not care, I start to wonder what will happen next. I feel that I have entered the all-too familiar territory of anxiety, even as I prepare to return to academics after this romantic tryst. Bruce seems upset. He says little. Then he announces, as though it's a conclusion he's come to: "I want to make you happy."

Surprised, I say, "You do make me happy." He looks away, troubled. Riding back to Portland through the mountains again, we are quiet, holding hands, thinking our own thoughts. I don't know what his are, but my own go along these lines: What do I do if Doug calls? He said he was going to come out. And what will I do with this man? And who exactly is this man, this large, gentle man, pensive at the moment?

I think Bruce might be anxious about having to go to work, and I suggest I return to his apartment and take the bus back to campus. There I watch him change into a sports jacket and tie. I study him: all angles of face, his profuse eyebrows, his scholarly glasses. "You look handsome," I say.

"Thanks," he says, amused, eying me. I'm cross-legged on the futon because there's nowhere to sit in that room. "You look beautiful."

Beautiful. I don't see myself as "beautiful," although, years later, when I see pictures of myself from that summer, I can see that I was attractive; I just never felt "pretty." I take the bus back to the campus, which is silent since it's Friday, and wonder that so much has taken place—in me—and in only twenty-four hours. So much. What has gone on? Why do I feel different?

I've invited him to come over after his shift on Saturday, and he showers in my shower. I drive his Fiat up the hill to Safeway to get wine and a wine opener and then walk across campus to buy him a ticket to the Saturday night chamber concert, part of that series I already have. Tonight's program features a group Bruce is familiar with called "Free Flight." The purchase of a ticket for a man is a new experience for me, as has been paying my own way. He buys dinner; he keeps it even, always. Still, I feel strangely burdened at this arrangement and a little resentful that he hasn't the money.

Dinner—set out before the concert on the Reed campus lawn—consists of gourmet hamburgers and salads, which we eat at white-clothed tables on the grass, like a country club. Conversation is easy for us; this time we are talking about non-conformity. I am feeling again stereotypically rigid in my pants and blouse, always ironed and matching, with my perfectly cut short hair. I tell him, as though to qualify for being somewhat of a free spirit: "I had long hair twice and didn't look good."

"How could you not look good?" he asks.

The concert engrosses us both, and the rhythms of the pieces seem to resound with physical pleasure. Between songs, he leans over and whispers to me, "You're terrific."

"Really?" I turn to him. "You were just telling me how uptight I was and how loose you are."

He looks upset. "I never said that."

"No. I guess I just felt it."

"It's not true. In fact, neither of those is true." He laughs, loud at first, then instantly settles down. He always seems too large for the space, yet somehow folds in. I feel an overwhelming, confusing desire for him. I place my hand on his leg briefly. He grasps my hand in his, holds it.

At his apartment, which we return to, I see he's added a used sofa someone gave him to fill its space and to keep the one chair company. We're back on the futon, for which he has a thin blanket and no top sheet.

In the morning I wake to him staring at me. He says, "You really have to go back to Pennsylvania?"

"New Jersey."

"Same thing."

"Yes."

He serves us instant coffee in delicate teacups that rattle in their saucers and spill on the floor, which we're close to on that futon. (Where would he have gotten such a silly set of dishes?) But when he reads me a theater review or something from the paper, we laugh at the exact same words. He is sardonic. He is messy.

He discovers his car battery is dead and he has to get to work. He can get a ride; I'll take a bus back to campus. As I walk the streets of Portland on that sunny Sunday, I wonder why I feel so good when I am with him. He owns nothing; even his underwear has seen better days. And yet he has opinions about everything; he is kind and easy and loving and I climb happily onto that silly sleeping arrangement he has and try not to question how different and yet real this situation is.

That day I stop for coffee and carrot cake at a sidewalk cafe, and I think: I am happy. It is a startling revelation. This is what *happy* feels like, I think. I get it.

It's just that this "happy" is not based on reality.

But it's summer and it's Portland, and this life with him is as irrelevant as all the hours I do not spend with him talking about Shakespeare. Shakespeare is irrelevant to my New Jersey life, too— at least so much of it, although I do love it all. Our seminar group moves on from *Henry IV* to *As You Like It* and, in the evenings, a cadre of us gets together in the living room of the main dorm where we take parts to read *Cymbeline* or *The Merchant of Venice*. I report to these readings sweaty and breathless, direct from the jazz classes I'm now taking.

The jazz sessions, twice a week, are torturing. I signed up that first day on campus thinking that, aside from something to do, to report to, I could learn new techniques to share with the dance classes I'd be teaching in the fall. The sessions are taught by a tall, willowy Black man who wears a shiny white body suit that outlines his muscles, his tautness. He is an athletically beautiful Accomplished Dancer, and I want to please him. The barre work is extremely strenuous, legs lifted awkwardly, body straining forward and back, and he often pulls my leg higher on the barre or pushes my back into arches that are painful or forces my foot outward. The group of us leave the barre for floor work combinations, but I don't really see the others; I concentrate only on this tall body in spandex, the haughty toss of his head, his black and white form, driving us on and on. I try desperately to keep up with the rapid step combinations he recites as we move across the Reed gymnasium floor to the rhythms of a Rastafarian drummer who sits to one side with his bongos. The pace is beyond me and certainly beyond the scope of what I teach. Yet I keep going to these sessions; I sweat it out.

I have my rewards: the group members who marvel at my exercise, the man I barely know who marvels at me.

I don't neglect the seminar, not in any way, nor the friends I'm making there. One day three of us: Alan, of the double-date to Columbia, and Jane, the woman who's become my good friend, and I rent a "Rent-a-Wreck" cheap convertible and drive to Mt. St. Helens, which had erupted a few years before. It is a moon-crater of a place, a wasteland that makes us gasp, and we take pictures of each other, posing among the fallen charred trees, the ashes. Another time four of us hike through Forest Park, one of the many verdant parks of Portland. We have lunches together; we study together, sprawled on the lawns.

I spend hours reading the plays on my own, particularly ones we discuss in class, but the ones we plan to read at the dorm as well. I read the critics we're all reading: A.C. Bradley, Northrop Frye, Jan Kott. Our seminar leader, Robert Knapp, wants us to write reactions to our readings and submit the writings to him. These assignments I truly love since we're encouraged to give a personal response to the plays. I argue against feminist criticism, saying it's overdone, that Lady Hotspur—like Lady Macbeth—is a totally believable female creation. I argue against an interpretation of Ornstein's that Hal is a good and loyal friend, citing a number of quotes from the play to show Hal's wariness. I admit—on paper—that I get weary of every-one citing the critics, of reading the critics, quoting the critics! I liken the reading of critical interpretations to checking the answers to a crossword puzzle when one has merely glanced at the definitions. It's more fun to work through the text on one's own, I say. There are no consequences or grades for my opinions. I can think freely. I pound away at the typewriter I've rented for the summer. I acquired the typewriter on my first day here, when kind George offered to take me to a shop that had such things to rent. George remains my favorite seminar member, next to my close friend Jane. Individually and together our group is immersed in Shakespeare.

And yet he—Bruce—lives there in town, and I report to him at every other turn; he calls, he picks me up. Laura, another participant, comments: "Where did you find him, that Marlborough Man?" This is an allusion to a popular cigarette commercial featuring a mysterious, craggy-featured cowboy on a horse. "And you look so cute in that red convertible with him!" The fact that we're a collective image, an impression on others, makes me feel good. We're a couple, in a way, for these weeks.

These weeks. These happy weeks.

I can't resist thinking in those phrases after reading *Henry V* and the king's urging his small army to fight on St. Crispin's day. He notes that his men will be able to tell the tale about their victory. They will be the few who have survived, have conquered. "We few. We happy few."

My old life intrudes as well, reminding me that I have a job at the high school I will have to return to, two children to rescue from each other, bills to pay, a home to take care of. Even Doug might be waiting in the wings, I think, although I'm not sure. He seems to be. He calls and is wavering about a visit here to Portland, one that has been delayed because he's being sent to Rome.

I feel a sense of envy over the phone, as I always do when I talk to him, of all his accoutrements and opportunities and say, "Oh, you'll see the Villa Borghese, the Sistine Chapel!"

He says, "Yes. But you have already been to Rome." I pick up a minor but distinct clipped tone.

He asks if I will be around—be home—in August. "I have all these extra airline miles," he says. "I can purchase trips for both of us." Really? It's a thrill to think that Doug would include me in European travel, provide my airfare, commit to that much time with me. Is that what he is suggesting? In spite of the thrill this offer evokes, I say nothing.

Another old boyfriend, actually a former neighbor, Paul, whom I'd had a brief affair with before he moved away, divorced now, calls. He has found out from my kids that I am in Portland and asked for my number. He's calling because it occurs to him that I might like to go to Aruba with him in August. What? I think. This offer goes beyond absurd. I say such a thing is unlikely; I try to be kind; I like the man.

I've always wanted to be wanted and now it seems I am. But the longing I feel is perhaps something else, too. Not so much a longing for Doug's largesse or Paul's offer, but a longing to stay in the world I am in, to keep it forever, as absurd as that wish is. Here I've been accepted for who and what I am. I can't be too "smart" among scholars; I've never considered myself super-smart, or an intellectual, although others have reacted to me as though I did, as though I am. And with Bruce there are no contingencies—it's just us in this playland called Oregon—and he seems to accept everything about me. The Shakespeare Seminar is scheduled to end on August 2, and I have a ticket home for August 3. And it is absurd, isn't it, this world of Shakespeare and Bruce?

One day we all discuss illusion versus reality in *As You Like It*. The characters, disillusioned and betrayed by their royal positions, take refuge in the forest of Arden where they assume another life-style, other identities. The question then becomes: which is their real self and which the identity they've been playing? Or, as Jaques asks, Is "[All]the world a stage and [are] all the men and women merely players?" We in the seminar take sides: Which is more the illusion, court or forest? Which the real?

It's great fun; however, I can't help but see the debate as a meta-phor for my own experiences at the time. In my life there is certainly the "reality" of home and kids. The seminar, with its finite date, is also a reality. And illusion? A man named Bruce in Portland? Is my feeling of happiness with him illusory? What is really real?

4   *Life Before Portland*

Three months earlier, by March of that year, 1984, I'd dated Doug for five months and felt pulled by him in two directions. Those were: Come Close but yet Not Too Close. I saw him only on weekends. Still, he would accompany me to school events, attending the play I'd co-directed, my faculty Christmas party, the musical I was in charge of, all of which were also on weekends.

This arrangement sort of worked as I was so encompassed with my own life. My kids were important. I fought with Susan a lot, but of course loved her and was concerned with her education, her future, and, in many ways, relied on her. My son John was witty and literary and fun to be around, but he was away at college. We three were all in college: Susan at the community college not far from our house, and me at Rutgers, in graduate school.

For most of that school year, prior to leaving for the Portlands, I spent those evenings when I didn't have grad school with Janet or Barbara or a few women I'd met during a previous summer course. We often made dinners for each other. I studied for my courses. I took two courses each semester at Rutgers in Camden, a twenty-minute ride from my house, working toward my M.A. in English. That semester the courses were on Yeats and Joyce; I wrote papers. I worked on the musical *The Music Man*, choreographed the "Show Choir" that Hazel, the vocal teacher, and I had put together. The Show Choir consisted of eight high school students singing and dancing together and was, basically, her idea. "Bo Jangles" and "Birdland" were my favorite numbers. I taught my classes: two of English and one of dance. I was responsible for the department, small as it was in members, but huge in import, involving the orchestra, the concert band, the choir, all music lessons, the plays. I was extremely occupied all of the time, and yet I welcomed Doug and his bright company. I loved his precise good looks, the way he'd banter with me, his music choices—classical and jazz; loved going to bed with him. I waited to see if he'd call, if he'd want me one more weekend. And he seemed to, every weekend.

Then he'd summon me on Friday afternoons—and take me out to dinner and we'd make love later. Sometimes we listened to jazz, or we'd take parts in a Shakespeare scene. We liked, particularly, watching *Richard III* or *Hamlet,* which he'd later quote from, and we'd have a great time together. Other times he'd be moody and, although he'd made the date, make me feel as though I were intruding on his life. Sometimes he didn't talk at all, and I felt I was just waiting around, waiting for something to happen, for a cue on how to behave.

He committed to nothing, not even the next date, and I would be back to myself for days on end, my friends, my books, papers, responsibilities. Susan was still home and a comfort and a conflict, depending. John called enough that I felt he was there, too. So: what on earth was I missing? I felt I was missing something in life. I think at that time I was a mixture of confidence and insecurity. I felt fairly confident about my job, my A's in grad courses. From this stance of confidence I viewed others' marriages and relationships. How did some women find husbands who were responsible, loving, attentive? I mean, I frequently saw myself as superior to such women, in talent, often in looks. But I also was conscious that I was basically alone; a woman who had failed—or had others fail her—several times.

The adults at the high school, many of them, bored me. They did not seem to measure up to the challenge that being with Doug offered me, a challenge that I anguished over even as I constantly craved it. We never seemed to get tired of each other physically. I also worked very hard at school and my courses. Once Doug said to me, "Do you realize how many books you've screwed your way through?" That was funny; there we were fine.

He traveled a great deal during the week; I had all those responsibilities. We collapsed into each other, demanding nothing and yet, by that very not-demanding state, were wary of one another's not demanding anything. It was hard to explain. As long as we stayed at some stage of remove, we sort of functioned. He was always happy to see me, often said he missed me, but seemed wary. There were moments of warmth, such as when we went to a bookstore and he insisted on buying me the leather Globe Shakespeare volume. Or the time I mentioned the ads in *Philadelphia Magazine*—the singles section, how people presented themselves—and he was curious. "It's funny the way people summarize themselves in an ad," I said. "A brief statement of who they are—or think they are—then a 'desire line.' I wouldn't know what to say."

I continued. "The most common is "Tom Selleck look-alike seeks woman for walks on beach. Object: long-term relationship." I grimaced.

"Hmm," he said, regarding me, thinking for a moment. "How about 'Woman with Shakespeare coloring book desires to meet man with colored pencils. Object: illuminated manuscripts.'"

Of course I had to laugh. He knew I had the "coloring book," an amusing gift from a student. It was Doug's quipping that sort of thing that kept me going back to him.

At school my accomplishments were noticed. "That Jackie Davis! How does she do it?" That's what my friend Barbara told me she'd heard from others. My principal assured me, "You certainly lend a note of class to this organization." I felt I was barely "doing it," and the routines of coming and going to that building for sixteen years often bored me. I felt pressured by the responsibilities of the department, of grad school, of the kids, my home. I yearned for something and didn't know what. When the principal told me I would be going to Portland, Maine, in June, with other department chairs for a weekend conference, I experienced a boost of hope: *Something different is happening!*

That same month, in mid-April, I found out I'd been accepted to the NEH Shakespeare Seminar in Portland, Oregon. My acceptance was acknowledged by a personal phone call from the seminar leader, Robert Knapp, at Reed College. I was wild with pleasure over the prospects. I'd taught an elective in Shakespeare for eight semesters, teaching myself as well, appreciating more what Shakespeare was doing each time through. I had a system: read the play once to get a feeling for it; read it again to sense the characters and plot development; read it a third time to understand the imagery and theme. Then: teach it. I'd ordered records so that students could listen to the play being performed. I'd devised games—little boxes of quotations, teams to answer essay questions. We'd work our way through a few histories—*Richard II* and *Henry IV*, then a few comedies: *Twelfth Night* and *Much Ado About Nothing*, then the tragedies of *King Lear* and *Antony and Cleopatra*. We'd end the semester of Shakespeare with a Shakespeare party. Often I would draw and color characters from the plays on paper plates—an enjoyable but time-consuming exercise that I ultimately abandoned. One year a student brought in a cake with the First Folio drawing of Shakespeare replicated in icing. I'd gone from classroom to classroom that day trying to find someone with a camera, but no luck. Back in those days that's the way it happened: one either deliberately brought a camera or did not.

In spite of this great enthusiasm I had for Shakespeare's plays, I knew that the competition for the NEH seminar would be tough.

NEH rules permitted a teacher to apply to only *one* choice, although they offered around thirty, so the odds of being chosen were great. And I'd overcome them.

Two nights after the acceptance phone call, Doug summoned me to meet him at the RB that Friday afternoon. The RB, short for Rhythm and Blues, was a popular bar and restaurant, one that offered a lively social scene on Friday afternoons and music on the weekends. I was delighted at his reception of me. "You look so pretty!" he'd exclaimed. He admired my dress. He often admired what I was wearing—a gesture I found greatly pleasing. "It's so good to see you," he said. He announced his upcoming trips, to Chicago, to New Orleans. He ordered us drinks. I was happy to also have good news and told him about studying Shakespeare in Portland, Oregon—my acceptance to the six-week summer seminar. His expansiveness seemed to shrink a little, but he mustered a smile. "Congratulations."

"It'll be Portland to Portland," I said, explaining the department chair conference the same week, amused by the coincidence. "I'll have to fly from Portland, Maine, for the department chair thing—that's only a few days—to Portland, Oregon, for the Shakespeare Seminar. For six weeks." Doug nodded an acknowledgment and looked away, lit a cigarette.

The next weekend Doug beckoned me again with his usual last-minute Friday phone call, and in his bed Saturday morning, with our customary carafe of coffee and boxed pastries, we had an actual conversation, a rare thing. He told me I made him nervous; he said I demanded too much of him; he said that I forced him to talk about significant things. He couldn't relax around me.

I listened in tense consternation, trying to take in this unexpected protest. I didn't know what I'd done other than try to be interesting to him. Sam had always told me I did too much, he had to keep competing with me; it was an old and appalling argument. Although I was impressed that Doug confided these misgivings to me, I was aware that I had once again affected a man with my very being. "But I like you," I said to Doug in a weak defense.

"Yes. I like you too, you know," he told me, his eyes scanning my face, as though he was asking why.

We were both quiet for a while. He suggested a break. I said nothing, thinking: *A break from. . . what, exactly?* I wondered. The idea of a "break" suggested that there was a wholeness or together-ness that was capable of being "broken." Was there? What was he protesting? I didn't know what to say.

After a beat of silence, where he seemed to be mulling over his own suggestion of a "break," he assumed a new tone: "Okay, why don't we do something this evening? Get in trouble in Philadelphia?"

I breathed a sigh of relief, imitated his sudden casualness: "Good." I smiled. "I'll wear my new spring suit."

"Why don't you wear your new spring suit?" He kissed my cheek. "I'll pick you up at 7."

And there we were. Or were not. And so we continued in this push-pull relationship until I left for Portland Number One.

5   *The Green World*

In *As You Like It* all the characters revert to Arden Forest, which they call "The Green World." Reed Campus is literally the green world with its vast stretches of lawns and shrubbery and gardens. And we fifteen participants are also "green" in the metaphoric sense of having been paid to study.

The world gets greener when Bruce drives the two of us to Multnomah Falls along the Columbia River Gorge. His idea, after we've run out of riverbank to hike on, is to wade up the actual river—not very deep—to the top of the falls and picnic up there. Wade? The river is maybe three feet deep, but I'm wearing jeans and the hiking boots I'd had the kids mail to me. I protest: I can't wade in *jeans.* "They'll dry out," he says, gesturing to the forever-blue sky and intense sun. "It's hot."

Wet jeans?

"Well, take them off and carry them," he says, stepping into the river, fully clothed.

Is he insane? I stand there, debating. Then, I remove the big boots one by one, take off my jeans and wrap them around my neck and pull on the boots once again. I stand there in my underpants, in bare legs and boots, aware of the varicose vein popping on my left thigh. I try to imagine, for a moment, Doug's reaction to such a scene. He'd called just that morning and said he was finally on his way to Rome—maybe he'd fly out to see me when he returned. I picture Doug in an elegant hotel near the Coliseum and me in my underpants fording a stream.

For I've stepped into the water next to Bruce, who's carrying the picnic basket on his head like a woman in *National Geographic,* and we wade on to the top with its spectacular view, as he'd promised.

There we pour wine, eat our deli sandwiches. "You're great," he says, and, for a change, I feel I've earned the praise. I feel smug in my underpants up here, the falls gushing nearby, the sun bright.

Still later, thoroughly dry, we drive out to Timberlake Lodge at Mt. Hood where we have a drink at their bar.

"If I had my druthers," I tell him, surprising myself with this thought: "You know what I'd really like?"

"What?"

"To just take off and live here and there and maybe get a job when needed. Live out of a suitcase." I'm not sure where this comment has come from. I've been totally responsible for myself and two children for over twenty years. Was it the freedom of wearing jeans around my neck? Was it this man's simplicity and acceptance and sense of fun? Or just an awareness of how far from my responsibilities I'd strayed?

"You could do that," he says. "*We* could do it." His big laugh. "I have nothing to give up anyway. Certainly, the kids—all of them—could do without us."

Outside we throw snowballs—we're at Mt. Hood!—and then stop for strawberries and cream on our way back to the city. He always "knows a place."

We have our last picnic of the day on his futon before sleep, but he kisses me goodnight and holds me.

"I can't believe you happened to me," Bruce says.

Doug calls. I ask him how Rome was. "Hot," he says. "And it's like touring a parking lot. Everyone had four wheels attached."

But he offers nothing else.

I tell him I'm having a good time—the plays, the hikes, the readings, the playmates.

"You're going to be insufferably expert," he says.

Insufferably? I translate that to mean, *I am jealous.*

He says, "I guess you're not going to come home." How would he know that Bruce has already suggested I extend my stay in Portland beyond the seminar? "Oh, I have to," I say. "Eventually." I attempt to sound offhand, airy. "It's so nice. We call it the Green World."

There is silence.

"I miss you," I say. And, actually, that is somewhat true. There is much I miss of him: his exactness (which appeals to me more than I like to admit) and his buying me dinners and tickets to things. I miss his success, his stability. His furniture.

"I miss you, too," he says. And, since my response is qualified, I wonder whether his is. Maybe he has found someone? I think that's probably not true. He is inherently shy; a woman would have to approach him—and he knows I'm such a woman. We had originally started talking when I walked up to him at the RB and said something about Hamlet, the character. He had smiled with pleasure and said what a rare thing it was to "talk Shakespeare" at the RB. He took me to dinner that very evening and—well, we'd been involved with both each other in that off and on mode ever since. When I think about it, that narrative was about the same as the one I'd experienced with Bruce: meeting at Harrington's, talking, the dinner later. This thought surprises me because I don't *feel* they were similar.

"I still haven't made plans to come to Portland," he tells me. "Although time is running out."

Now the silence is mine.

I'm not sure where we leave things. Doug is perceptive and no doubt suspects something different about me.

Bruce calls, too, from the used car lot where he works, saying he misses me. I tell him I miss him, too, aware that it's the second time I've said such a thing within an hour. And it is also true. I am beginning to miss him even while I am here at the seminar, even though I recognize that "we" will be over when the seminar is over.

I tell myself that what I do with Bruce has no connection to Doug, to my life 3000 miles away in New Jersey. I will return home and feel intact. Bruce is like Steve and Jane and George and Frank and Margaret and the others in my seminar—all of whom I "love" while I'm here with them all the time, our own family. We read and drink and talk and hike together and they all mean everything to me. And, ultimately, nothing.

I will go home.

We're encouraged to do projects about *As You Like It*, and I spend a happy afternoon putting together a booklet of costume designs and quotations that reference clothing in the play. My idea, I think, was that the characters were all assuming "costumes" of identity. The language itself points to that interpretation. The women, Rosalind and Celia, are, in fact, disguised as pages in boys' clothing while in the Arden Forest. My little drawings are such superfluous fun—adaptable, I think, for my high school students, a booklet such as the one I have crafted.

Excited by my costume work, I walk up the hill above Reed to a clothing boutique I've spotted, one whose prices seem beyond what I usually pay. That day I purchase a fitted khaki-colored denim skirt, a fluttery off-white sleeveless blouse and a wide hemp belt that circles my waist in definition: I feel it's the costume of a liberated woman.

The seminar discussions move from the frivolous green world of *As You Like It* to the disturbing landscapes and issues of *King Lear*. Studying *King Lear* sets me spinning about my life.

First there's the role-play we do in the classroom where we take parts (as we've done informally during evening readings in the dorm), but with a sense of purpose here. How does it feel to be this character? How does Goneril—whose part I am to read—feel when she's talking to Lear, her father? I thought: that's easy. I've taught this play several times; I can't stand Goneril; she is such a selfish, mean bitch. She mistreats Lear, betrays him. But—here's the thing: playing Goneril, dealing with what Lear, her father, was saying and doing, the way he was making peremptory orders and demands, I became sympathetic to her, angry with Lear.

When I had to stand opposite George, whom I liked, who was playing Lear, and listen to Lear demanding that Goneril maintain a hundred knights in her castle just for his pleasure, I really get angry, insist he and his knights could all leave. He says, fine, he'll go to Regan; she'll take them all in. As Goneril, I knew I had to get to Regan first and warn her: dad's mad!

How odd—to be against old King Lear.

I'm not sure this exercise has any greater meaning beyond the obvious two sides to every story, but it was enlightening to me. I would have my students assume parts thereafter and talk about how they "felt" when they were reading those lines. This role-playing was a great tool of insight into characterization.

Another result of this exercise is the question I ask myself: What are my roles? What role do I play at home? What role here?

Some answers are obvious, serious: mother, teacher, scholar. But girlfriend? Lover? Which is the real one? What am I?

I was given the opportunity to combine my Portland identities, of "fellow" and bedfellow. Our seminar leader had acquired the VHS of Olivier's performance of *King Lear* and we participants were going to gather around a large TV monitor one afternoon in one of the Reed classrooms to watch it together. I asked Bruce, who had expressed an interest in *Lear*, if he wanted to join us. I asked the group if they'd mind—no, they wanted to meet him. So: Bruce, off for that afternoon, sat around with us and followed *Lear*. I realized he actually knew the poetry, a fact that of course impressed me. On another day, when I was sitting in Bruce's apartment, I was trying to remember the final couplet in a sonnet—lines I couldn't get quite right. "I have them," he said, "the sonnets." And he went to one of his closets and handed me a book of Shakespeare's sonnets.

One of the critics we talk about in the seminar is Stanley Cavell, and again I am excited. John, my son, had raved again and again about Stanley Cavell, a professor he had for a philosophy course. I loved that these pieces of my life overlapped. Cavell's essay "The Avoidance of Love" suggested that what triggered Lear's tragedy was trying to avoid love. Cavell suggested that being loved or open to love is equal to self-recognition, self-revelation, self-sacrifice, none of which Lear has until the end, when it's too late.

This thinking was a revelation to me to even consider. I wondered about Doug, about Sam: were they avoiding "self-revelation?" What did either of them ever sacrifice? How much self-recognition was I capable of? Did I just run from myself, seeking what I thought I should be wanting? How much of me was I willing to "reveal?" Self-revelation seemed a risky business.

Of course that led me into thoughts of Bruce: his acceptances of his failed marriage, his failed business, his present stupid job. The principal characters in *King Lear* are the wise man, the fool, and the madman. Lear, seemingly wise as a king, behaves foolishly and goes mad. Lear is accompanied on this terrible descent into madness by both his own Fool, who spouts more wisdom than anyone else in the play, as well as the man who ultimately saves them all—Edgar—who is disguised as a madman.

So: this man that I was so deeply attracted to, who had lost all, foolishly, one could assume—certainly it was foolish to be 44 years old and have nothing but a Fiat convertible and an electric typewriter (yes, I saw them as equal!)—what was he? It seemed that his lack of "worldly things," his coming to grips with who he was without them, paralleled a theme in the play. I felt a wisdom about him, too, a sense of solidness. His spontaneous ideas and lack of inhibitions didn't qualify him as mad, but he certainly was an example of "unaccommodated man." I felt a wisdom about Bruce, a sense of solidness.

But reading *King Lear* perplexed me even more about him. Wise man or fool?

6   *Ashland and Elsewhere*

During our fourth weekend at Reed our seminar group travels in various cars from Portland to Ashland, to the Oregon Shakespeare Festival. I knew about the festival from Doug. Initially surprised that I had been going to Portland to study Shakespeare, Doug had done some research. "Do you know there are books about Shakespeare in Oregon?" he'd asked me. No, I did not, but I was learning. The Shakespeare Festival in Ashland, Oregon, with plays in repertory in three theaters, was a big deal, and we seminar members had purchased, ahead of time, tickets to three performances. Those of us without spouses (I think we number twelve) stay in the Southern Oregon College dorm, where we gather on the fire escape late at night as though we are teenagers, although most everyone seems to be 43, including me. I buddy around with George, the married guy from Denver, whose graciousness and wit are welcoming and comforting—as is the vintage Scotch he takes me with him to buy and insists I try. He pours the whiskey into paper cups in the hallway before we dress for dinner—all of us dining enmasse at Omar's Seafood, down the hill from the dorms. That afternoon we saw *Troilus and Cressida*, which we're all talking about, and that evening we're heading for a performance of *The Winter's Tale*—our next reading project. Back at the dorm, late that night and again on the fire escape, we celebrate with a birthday party for Alan. I give him a bottle of Jack Daniels, purchased that afternoon with George.

And I, for the first time in my life, find myself to be—using an adolescent term—"popular." These men at the seminar are enjoyable, intellectual companions, and they want my company. We are all at our best.

And yet I yearn for Bruce. "What does he do—that guy of yours?" people ask. "He sells used cars," I say. And they don't know what to say next except "Oh." I debate qualifying it all—saying he has a master's degree in city planning, and so on, but what's the point?

The summer is the point. And the guy from "town," Bruce, is hiding nothing that I can see. His shortcomings are right out in the open. Everything about him is open. I'd said to him once that he seemed "unreal" to me. What did I possibly mean by that? Perhaps that he was so without guile that he made me suspicious? He'd scoffed. "Oh, I'm real enough," he said.

I'm part of George's carpool on the way back to Portland and we detour by prior mutual agreement to Crater Lake, a site I thought I wanted to visit, but now I am impatient to return. When we pull into the parking lot at the large stone Visitors Center and the others declare "Let's each do our own thing," I am more than annoyed. I look forlornly at the paths that disappear into trees. I can see the shimmering lake beyond, but I don't want to hike by myself. I can sit in the sun and read, but I don't want to read *Lear* one more time. I want to get back to Portland: he is waiting for me. I want to scream it to them: *he is waiting for me, I can't dawdle away my time seeing scenery!* But I am here at Crater Lake. I walk around part of its rim, taking in its beauty, its grandeur, then find a spot to spread my jacket and sit, waiting, watching others go by, including Jim and Margaret in our car-group, and George, who pauses to take my picture. "You look like Thoreau would melt in your mouth," he says. I have no idea what the remark means, although I smile and wave an acknowledgment, and he moves on.

Crater Lake is stunning in its color—the purest turquoise—and its size—a circumference that seems impossible to get around; that lake and the ride before it along the Deschutes River are beyond anything I've ever experienced—but what do I know—with my background of steel mills and flat southern New Jersey. The landscapes of snow-capped mountains and rushing waters—and now this enormous jewel of a lake—have all left me gasping with wonder.

But I still want to go back to Portland.

Finally! It's close to 9 p.m. when the group makes our final stop at a roadside café south of the city and I rush to a payphone to dial Bruce's apartment where he's been waiting for me to call. George agrees to drop me off, although taking me to the Buffalo Gap bar and restaurant necessitates a slight detour on their way back to Reed. Outside the restaurant I see the red Fiat and hop out, waving goodbye to my friends. Bruce is indeed inside, waiting. We embrace in the joy of being together again.

We have drinks, which I pay for this particular evening, noting that irregularity once again. He has purchased an odd piece of jewelry for me at the Saturday market—an ear cuff, which both delights and puzzles me. What pleases is the fact that he sees me as an adventurer, someone who would wear this odd piece of jewelry, like a ring that one fits on the rim of the outer ear. I put it on, smiling. But it seems to announce a freedom I don't feel I truly have.

He also delivers an announcement: he has quit his job. He needs the time to look for a real one, as a Planner. I'm not sure how to interpret this move: is it indicative of his not taking anything seriously? Or, does he see a future with the two of us, one he cannot entertain unless he is back in his own career, earning a substantial salary? I dismiss my concerns, happy once again to be with him. We make love that evening and the following morning before he takes me back to campus for my seminar. At five o'clock he returns to my studio apartment, and, as he sits at my desk chair waiting for me to change, my phone rings.

It's the former neighbor, Paul, the one who asked me to go to Aruba. Paul wants to find out what two weeks could possibly work out for me to visit him, or perhaps to travel somewhere else. "Can you talk?" he says when I don't immediately respond.

"No." Maybe I add "not now" or "sorry." I put down the phone, aware that Bruce is watching me. "An old friend—who lives in Florida," I tell him, turning around. I'm sure my voice is not steady. "He wants to know if I'll vacation with him." I add: "it's absurd."

Bruce stares at me from the chair. There's a beat of about three before he says. "I see."

The two words strike me as though they'd been delivered across my face.

We say nothing for at least a full minute.

"This seems to be your year," he says.

But he says nothing else, and we go about our plans for a picnic at Selwood Park, gathering a blanket, picking up sandwiches, and later, stopping for late drinks and our usual animated conversation before we return to his apartment.

"And what did you decide about Florida?" he asks, turning on the lights as we enter and signaling to me that he's been wondering all evening.

"He's a friend," I defend, deflecting the implication of more, which had once been true. "Like Jean." Jean is a woman who is merely Bruce's friend. I've met her and I can see they're just friends. "I haven't seen him in years." That part is true. "No," I say. "I guess, no. How could I?"

I had been asking myself that question all through the evening. How could I? How could I, why would I, have suggested such availability to several men at once? Was I really that insecure? And: what is it about this particular man that makes me aware of what I am doing?

7   *Nearing Seminar's End*

It's too soon to start counting, anticipating, even dreading, but that's what we do: we have two more weeks. The weekend of Ashland and the Shakespeare plays meld into the next-to-last week of the seminar. Bruce is now free at all times, and so we'll start with an afternoon walk around Portland's Pioneer Square or Yamhill market before having dinner, going to his place.

The seminar people, particularly my friend Jane, are aware of how involved I am with this "man from town," which sometimes sounds like "man from Mars," an idea foreign to others, insulated as a group here on campus. Jane questions what will happen when the seminar is over. "A summer romance," she muses. "You wonder." She and I have become confidantes and have already made plans to somehow visit one another after the seminar ends, although Indiana and New Jersey are nowhere near each other. Alan, whom I regard as my first "friend" in the group since he invited me to the Columbia River Gorge that initial Saturday, still seems to be attracted to me, or confused that I've been "taken"—unfairly, to him—by someone not even in our seminar. One evening he walks me back to my apartment after a late play-reading in the dorm and actually moves forward to kiss me.

I pull back, trying not to insult him, but I am annoyed. Did he think I was open game? Maybe. There had been that early incident—one that I felt a little embarrassed about. It was one of Bruce's and my first dates, when we'd had dinner in a Greek restaurant in town, a sudden whim of his on a Wednesday afternoon. I'd gone back to his apartment afterward, and he returned me to campus early the next morning—maybe 7 or 8—before he went to work. After he drove away, I discovered I didn't have the key to my apartment.

Where had I left it? At the restaurant, I was sure; I remembered setting it on the table as I got out my wallet to pay my share, as usual.

What would I do? How could I get into my apartment? How could I change my clothes? Get my books?

We'd been assigned a Reed College assistant, but he, too, was living in the Woodside dorm along with the seminar members. I couldn't call him anyway, even though I'd memorized his number, since I didn't have access to a phone—unless there was a payphone in the college union, if that building was open, which was unlikely at that hour. I couldn't possibly walk up the hill to knock on our seminar leader's door to explain that I was sorry—but I'd spent the night in town and now couldn't get into my apartment—did he have another key?

Finally, I just walked to the dorm and banged on its door. Alan answered. He was up and dressed and having breakfast. "Well!" he said, seeing me in the dress and heels I'd worn the previous evening when he'd waved to me as I was getting into Bruce's car. Alan managed to rouse the assistant, who had an extra key, and I rushed across the lawns to change into khaki pants and sandals and gather my book and notebook for class. But Alan *knew*—and I felt he saw me as promiscuous, stoking his own desire to make this seminar worthwhile in more ways than one, prompting, no doubt, his liberty in trying to kiss me.

Actually, if there was anything going on among the others, I was not aware of it, nor did I care. I could see they all accepted me, and, if anything, viewed me as more exciting, I think: a risk-taker, a free spirit. I liked the feeling.

In those remaining weeks Bruce divides his time between getting together with me and working on applications for serious jobs, so he is unscheduled except for his family. Early on he tells me that his youngest son, Preston, is accustomed to coming over on a weekend. I realize that the reason Bruce found the sofa some-where—it's actually a nice sofa—is so Pres would have somewhere to sleep if I am there, although I am careful that we do not overlap. Apparently, Bruce would share his only bed with his son every other weekend. I also meet Bruce junior who has just graduated from col-lege. Handsome and taller even than Bruce, he's loud and confident and engaging. But he's on his way elsewhere so it's just a brief get-to-gether in the apartment, as it is with Scott, who also stops by to see his Dad, meet me. I am impressed by Bruce as a father even while I resent the sons taking time and energy away from him because—because it's time that we are running out of.

I call home regularly and it seems that John and Susan are managing—both their lives and jobs, if not each other. They report anecdotes from work (John: "He had us pushing those wheelbarrows of bricks from one site to another. You should see my biceps." Susan: "This guy came in and wanted a half-scoop each for a three-scoop cone—that was six different ice creams! And of course no tip.") And their usual complaints about each other. They're aware that time is moving toward August 4, my return.

As are Bruce and I. We take advantage of the time we have. There are the Tuesdays' Jazz at the Zoo, which are a delight to report to. We can take snacks and wine and walk through the park, past the zebras and giraffes and gazelles to the grassy lawn with a stage at its end to listen to music. The stars are always out, the air is always warm and clear but never too hot. It doesn't rain. Bruce says it rains all winter in Portland, steadily, but not in summer; thus, the lush greenness. On our afternoon walks around Pioneer Square or the Willamette River front, musicians always seem to be in concert.

There is constant food and drink and color and excitement. But the summer closes in on us.

It closes in on our seminar, too. We have one more group outing, this time to Lewis and Clark College to see *Two Gentlemen of Verona*, and another cookout on the Reed lawn, but we feel the end approaching. One day we get our leader—at the instigation of Henry, from town—to ransack a storage room where graduation gowns and mortar boards are kept and arrange ourselves on risers for a group "graduation" picture. "Your tax dollars at work!" someone quips since we are being funded by the NEH. In spite of the fun, the mock-ceremony of robes casts a shadow of finality.

In the seminar sessions we're discussing *The Winter's Tale*—with its complications of jealousy and betrayal and death. Yet it has the fairy-tale ending of a statue coming alive, of a miracle happening. The middle of the play shifts to an Arden-like green world of shepherds and shepherdesses and peasant-dancing, as well as the absurd stage direction that ends a bucolic scene: *Exit Antigonus, pursued by a bear.*

The phrase becomes what we say to each other as we leave a room, and, ultimately, "Pursued by a Bear" becomes the title of a newsletter one of our members, Chuck, will publish after the conference on a duplicating machine at his school in Fresno. All I am thinking is *Exit Jackie, pursued by. . . what? Regret? Longing?* A love that she had to abandon because she has a real life she has to get back to? Like the kids, the house, the job. Perhaps, even, like Doug.

He calls once more, still hedging about whether to come Portland. Of course, I give him no encouragement and am fairly close-mouthed about what I am doing. I have a sense of discomfort, realizing he must be hearing between the lines things I am not saying. I suddenly remember the piece of paper he gave me before I left that morning for the first Portland, with his credit card information on it, and the phone number of his secretary, who would be able to reach him. I wonder if I—a person he held at arm's length emotionally—is now letting him down, or even hurting him. I wonder also if he regrets that he has reneged on his own intent or not been more forthcoming earlier. In any case, Doug knows that the seminar will be over August 4. I am scheduled to leave, to exit.

But why? Why must I leave this almost pastoral life of being happy? And who will I be after I leave? It will be over—the summer, the seminar, the man named Bruce. It has all been irrelevant, and it will be over.

Exit Antigonus.

Exit Jackie.

Two More Weeks

8   *Not Alaska, But-*

One afternoon with the seminar's last week closing in on us, Bruce says, "We could go to Alaska."

"What?" I laugh. We're sharing a huge cinnamon bun at Rose's restaurant.

He takes another pull of sticky dough; his eyes meet mine. He is serious. "We could take a trip together. Drive to Alaska."

I stare at him, incredulous, yet he sets off a spark in me. I picture us on the road together, driving somewhere exotic, together. Staying together a while longer. "Seriously? You can drive there?"

He says not easily, not in the Fiat. "I don't know. I don't want you to go back."

"I don't want to go," I say. He nods. We're both thinking, finishing our coffees.

Then as we walk out onto the Portland sidewalk, he says, "Maybe not Alaska, maybe somewhere else." I've been gone six weeks; what would a seventh week mean to the kids who, in their own way, are holding down the fort? I don't dare think of Doug and any expectation he might have. I stop and turn to Bruce. "I can change my ticket," I say. "A week."

Our outlooks are considerably brightened: we'll take a trip!

"We'll go to Canada," he says. "Banff. Lake Louise."

I don't know those names. I shrug, agree, of course. We begin to plan.

Well, he does, mostly; he's the Planner. He knows Oregon; he acquires maps and shows me routes that I can't follow. We need to consider how much money each can contribute, which we determine to be $300. I'm not sure where he has gotten his share. I don't ask. I had been given the NEH endowment money, but I also had the airline ticket to purchase, the apartment to rent, and all I've been spending on entertainment and books. So: we agree on $300 each. He says he owns a tent.

"A tent?" I make a face. "You mean as in camping? I've never done that."

He laughs. "You'll love it."

"No I won't."

He points out that we'll be gone a week and maybe a few camping stops would save money between motels. "Besides, it's all beautiful," he says. "It'll be beautiful; you'll want to be *in* it."

I am not so sure, but I go along with him. At the Army-Navy store we each buy a sleeping bag, a maroon and a navy. He finds his tent in one of those closets that I begin to see hold a lot, including boxes of books, Ken Kesey, Knut Hamson, Robinson Jeffers, Dylan Thomas. The folded tent looks totally inadequate, and I can't picture how it will house us. He determines our route through Oregon to Montana and into Canada. The scheme is wild. We might as well be driving to Alaska it is all so foreign. At the same time I am genuinely excited at the thought of seeing more of the West and, above all, continuing to be with him.

On the evening of our final seminar morning, a Thursday, the group has a big cookout at the home of our seminar leader—Robert Knapp. Some of us have volunteered to find "Shakespeare farewells" to share with the group. These we've written in thick pen or crayon on manilla folders to hold up to the group.

Frank holds up the practical "My necessaries are embarked—farewell!" from *Hamlet*, and several note that they haven't finished packing and don't want to.

Jane contributes the sad and hopeful wish of Brutus to Cassius: "If we do meet again, why, we shall smile; / If not, well then, this parting was well made." Others protest: "parting is not 'well made' at all!" and "Let's see if we can have a reunion—we have each other's addresses, right?"

Toni and I have chosen *Romeo and Juliet*. Mine is the simple "Parting is such sweet sorrow," since that's what's so much on my mind, in several ways, and hers the more despairing "Farewell! God knows when we shall meet again."

George stands and waves his folder. "Mine's on meeting, too." His does a take on *Macbeth*: "When shall we fifteen meet again?" We groan at the adjustment of number. "In thunder, lightning or in rain?" Jane reminds us that we just agreed to try to do that and why not in Indiana, where she lives? She has a big house, near a lake.

Robert Knapp gets the final word, producing—most fittingly—Prospero's farewell: "Our revels now are ended." He says it again, sinks down in his lawn chair, nods his head sadly.

We are all quiet a moment until Laura, the youngest among us, says, her voice thick, "I don't want our revels to end. I can't believe it's over already. I can't believe we're going home!"

I take this opportunity to announce proudly: "But I am not." They turn to me and I continue, "Going home. Bruce—my 'town friend'—and I are going to travel for the next week. I'm not going home. Yet."

Alan shoots me a look. "Don't you have kids at home?" He's already reminded me that he lives in Philadelphia, close to my New

Jersey house, so maybe we can get together. I had called the kids and told them I was staying another week. "But Mom!" Susan protested. "Have fun," John said, then added, "It sounds a little crazy."

"They're fine with it," I say.

What I remember most about that afternoon (where I am wearing my newly-purchased silk blouse and straight skirt and espadrilles) is George's hug. George: one of the few who has a car to shuttle us around, who took me into town that first day to rent a typewriter, who took us to Powell's books where I found the guide to Harrington's, who introduced me to single-malt scotch and drove us to Crater Lake. "Goodbye, Lovely Lady," he says. I hear those two words as though they are a title, a name, and I treasure them.

Goodbye, goodbye! Our revels have indeed ended. We are all off to somewhere else.

My days have consisted of the now and the now and the now, and I cannot imagine them ever coming to an end. I have prolonged the one "ending," the conclusion of the six-week seminar, by rear-ranging my ticket home to be with him another week. It's an exten-sion of time, and it's what we do not have except for this slim week.

I must pack up my studio apartment and shift my clothes and possessions to Bruce's. He has to borrow his friend Jean's car so I can fit everything in. We don't mind any of this.

Now the challenge is How do we both travel for a week in that little Fiat?

He figures it out. The car's hood opens to what is a shallow area above the engine. In that we lay a few pairs of pants and tee shirts and underwear: two or three changes each. There is a small trunk, about a foot high and foot deep and the short width of the car. Into that area we stuff his tent, our sleeping bags, my coffee maker and hairdryer, and whatever toiletries we need. In the area behind our front seats (the only seats) there's room for maybe a bottle of wine and two of his thin towels, a jacket each. All we need! We've known each other for five weeks, and now will have one more.

We set out on Saturday morning, August 4. He says we'll head toward Canada, maybe get as far as La Grande, Oregon, that first night. I'm along for the ride. My communication that day consists mostly of "My God!" again and again, as I exclaim over pine forests and deserts and mesas and mountains, the gold rolling hills and plains. The weather is hot, as we both are, all the time.

To my relief, we spring for a motel this first night. I realize at some point I must "camp" (I am totally unfamiliar with what that verb entails) to save money, but tonight I don't have to think about it. Having driven in the sunshine all day, found an air-conditioned motel, made love, and showered, we go to a pub called "The Long Branch," a name remote from any identity I thought I had.

"You're the greatest fun," I say. We're drinking beers in a pine-paneled front room. The lights flicker off and on erratically for a minute or so. He leans forward to kiss me. "I think *you're* the greatest," he says. We fold into each other in bed, get up at the same time to another day of sunshine.

"We'll be going through reservations today," he says as we drink the coffees I've run across the street to get. "There's a gondola that goes over the mountains. You'll like it. "

"I like everything," I say. I feel that I'm participating in a Hemingway novel.

On Monday morning I wake up in a tent at Flathead Lake in Montana; I've actually "camped" one night. I crawl out of our zipped-together sleeping bags (placed directly on the thin bottom of the tent, which is on hard ground) to inhale the purest air I've ever breathed. I cannot get over the big sky of Montana; the cliché proven true in the way the sky forms an enormous blue canopy over the teal-colored lake, the mountains beyond. Even the air is redolent of fresh water and pine. My personal horizon of experience, already stretched beyond anything I'd imagined by the likes of Columbia Gorge and Crater Lake and the mounts St Helens and Hood is stretched even further.

Bruce crawls out of the tent awkwardly. He twisted his back yesterday and now he curves decidedly to one side, like one of those Gumby dolls the kids used to have, bendable. Except Bruce can't straighten. It hurts me to look at him twisted that way.

He joins me at the picnic table, and I wince on his behalf. We gather the few things we brought for the journey—a towel, soap, shampoo—and head together to the camp's bathrooms. I'm also carrying my small coffee maker since I'd seen an outlet there yesterday, and, since there's only one woman in the facility, I manage both to shower and make coffee. "Well, I'll be damned," the woman says as I roll up my bathing things, then balance the coffee decanter on the towel. I think maybe I've committed a camping *faux pas* and try to shrug an apology. But she adds, "Now why didn't I think of that? Smells great."

At our table in front of the tent—where I want him to take a picture of me since my friends back home might not believe I did such a thing as camp—he sits atilt, unpacking the peaches we bought yesterday. We breakfast on these, sliced, and cheese and brown bread and our coffee and it's about as splendid a meal as I've ever had—in this remarkable setting.

Leaning to one side, my man-tower-of-Pisa, says, "Are you still glad you came?"

"Yes, of course."

"Even with my bad back—to look at?"

"Yes!"

Yes, is what I have said to everything this summer. Yes to every idea he's had, yes to not going home. Yes yes.

But it's not the only thing I've said. Last night, as we were zipping together the sleeping bags for the first time, with his leaning, crooked back, and my period starting, I blurted out "I love you!"

"I love you, too," he said, looking directly at me. "You know that."

I nodded and tried to lessen the significance of what I felt was a commitment I shouldn't be making—it was too unwarranted and useless, considering the circumstance—and I hastily explained: "I didn't mean to say that! I was just—I don't know—thinking aloud."

"I know," he said.

There was an afternoon that was unsettling, even terrifying. It occurred in Jasper, Canada, in a laundromat.

I'd never heard of Jasper, or any of the places we'd just been to, but as we drove in his little car that day, the mountains became higher and craggier, the road narrower as it wound through and around those mountains, and we became increasingly dwarfed by the setting.

The Rocky Mountains in Canada overwhelmed me. As they rose in size and bulk and jaggedness, my own sense of who I was and what I was diminished in proportion. That day, driving from Lake Louise to Jasper, had been the ultimate shrinking of me in the presence of those monumental mountains, the narrow highways that wound around themselves. I could see a car or two creeping along a mountainside up ahead, the car the size of a small bug inching along a tendril, and think, could that be us, in proportion to this setting? Could that be me, in this vastness of space? If so, if I am then infinitesimal next to this vast setting, well, then, what am I? Who am I? And who is this man sitting next to me?

In late afternoon when I was driving, the top down, the sun bright, the vistas invisible beyond the next skyscrapers of mountains, Bruce, in the passenger seat now, relaxed with a plastic glass of wine. This in itself was not unusual or alarming; he certainly could have a glass of wine after hours of his turn at the wheel. But my inner tensions and fears were such that if I glanced at his ease of bearing and then took in the enormity of the mountains we were traversing, I became more tense. It wasn't a matter of losing my direction: there was nowhere to go but to stay on that road; still, because of feeling almost annihilated in that vast setting, I resented his having a good time. At one point he reached over and patted my leg, commenting, I think, on wasn't it all wonderful.

I'd been lost in thought. Well, that's an understatement. I'd been lost in *being*. I felt erased, obliterated, by this landscape, and my memory of what I'd referred to as my "previous life" appeared as mythical as a mirage in my head. I'd never felt so displaced in time and sense of self before. Was there a house somewhere? Were there children named John and Susan in it? What was that place called "high school?" Had there been a "seminar?" Who was Shakespeare that I had been drawn to think about? And where? Some city, some campus.

And men! In my mind I paraded them forward, again questioning their reality. Sam, so important to me for years, and the more recent Doug: who were they in the scheme of things? In those Canadian Rockies I was a speck of no consequence.

The man next to me basked in the afternoon sun, his legs stretched in front of him. He never napped. He tousled my hair; he was clearly happy.

I was quiet. We knew we had to camp that evening since we'd spent three times our usual motel allowance on one night at Lake Louise. I'd agreed with him that it was the most romantic place I had ever been—one which he had been insistent I see—and I had not minded the splurge at all. The splendor was beyond all imagining, the stay there a fairy-tale world on top of the unrealities piling up one on top of another. So: I was sort of a veteran camper now, having tried it three times, and willing to sacrifice this coming night to have had the luxury of the one before.

However, as we got closer to Jasper the campsites in the forests along that winding highway were few, and those that existed were marked with a sign: "Filled. Sorry."

"We'll find something," Bruce reassured me.

I was still behind the wheel when we entered Jasper, a bustling resort of a town as it turned out, surprisingly, perched high in the mountains. The last campsite we'd passed also had the "Sorry—Filled" sign out, and now we were distinctly out of camping possibilities. We conceded: one more motel; we had no choice. But, as we drove through the streets of Jasper, unbelievably crowded with summer tourists, every motel or hotel we drove by had "No Vacancy" signs displayed.

We drove down a street with a laundromat and I suggested it was a good opportunity to do some laundry. Bruce said he'd take over and drive around town, continuing to look. He'd pick me up in. . . what? A half hour? An hour? We set a time. I gathered our few clothes and towels and he drove away.

It was in that laundromat in Jasper that I experienced fear, doubt, anger at myself, almost to the point of tears.

It had been the otherworldliness of the day, the afternoon. He was the only thing real in this setting, and in that laundromat I wondered: What if he didn't come back?

He'd been in an easy mood; he was too confident, I thought, since reality pointed to such a grim situation: no room at the inn or even on the ground. And where would we go beyond this cute little place plunked in a wilderness of mountains and trees and rocks? He had our last travelers' checks and I had only a few dollars in my purse—plus my driver's license and a BankAmericard.

I'd acquired that "BankAmericard" two summers before, where I'd used it for the first time in Norway with Sam to buy a heavy sweater for myself and ski caps for the kids. It had taken me a while to pay off that bill since I never had any extra money. Even my Macy's and Gimbel's cards I'd used sparingly at home, not charging more than I could immediately pay off, thus keeping my credit score high. I hesitated to charge a large hotel bill—which surely in this resort town such a hotel would cost—but was weighing that possibility as well. Bruce and I could not squeeze such an expense out of our travel money. I knew he didn't have a credit card, or any means of procuring an expensive room. And: suppose he took off and left me here—where could I go with these few things? How would I ever get out of this place—a laundromat in the wilds of Canada? What would become of me?

My mood was the culmination of the fears of my day, of the last few hours of that dwarfing drive through the huge mountains. I sat on a bench watching our few clothes tumbling together in the dryer. Then I folded these pieces: oddly his, mine. I kept glancing at the street. Jasper. What was Jasper? On the street whole families walked by, tourists, blithely eating ice cream cones, their ease and familiarity an insult to me, alone here, not even sure of where I was—in what country, on what mountain.

Suppose something happened to that red car? Suppose he was stranded somewhere and couldn't reach me? I couldn't be called here; I couldn't call him. It was ten minutes beyond the time we agreed he'd return. He'd been gone too long. He! Who was "he?" A man I thought I'd fallen in love with for. . . what? five weeks? I felt overwhelmingly stupid. I sat on a bench closer to the door, desolate, the small pile of our folded laundry next to me.

A red car pulled up in front of the place, and he (he!) leaned over to see if he could see me through the windows. I ran out to him, so hugely relieved, so happy to be rescued that I forgot the clothes. I had to go back for them.

He told me there were no rooms to be had—anywhere. "We'll return to that last campsite," he said. "The last one we passed. I'll see if I can't persuade them to find us a spot."

I must have looked near tears.

He patted my leg. "We'll be all right." He was made late because he got gas, but he picked up some sandwiches for us, a bottle of wine. "We'll find something," he said. "It'll be okay."

We drove the twenty miles back down the winding road, dusk approaching, to the last camp site, thick with huge trees, and he parked in front of the "Filled—Sorry" sign. "Wait here," he said, and when he returned shortly after, announced, "They're letting us have a small spot. I told them how small our tent was, our car. It's all right."

I have to say that that moment was one of the happiest in my life. We pitched our little tent in the spot they'd allowed us, amid the dense and sheltering trees, and even with the imminent threat of "Bears: Be Careful," I was happy. We had the sandwiches he bought in Jasper; we had a bottle of wine. It didn't matter what else. We even had a little table near our tent. The air was thick with pine, with mountain air, and we were snug, happy, and had clean clothes.

And each other.

Athabasca Falls. I love the syllables of its name, love the cascades of aqua water splashing and crashing around us. We stand on a bridge, no doubt with other tourists, but I have a sense of us, only us, in the wonderland of pure torrents of water, its soft cymbals of spray, and he and I holding each other, alive and alert to the spectacle of this setting.

Alert also to the wonder of us. Who are we, to have invented this life together in the wilds of Canada? A life that expires, as we know too well, in a few days.

That morning in Jasper, as I returned from the women's shower, I walked past and around him, and he didn't notice. He was sitting on the bench of the picnic table, eyes closed as in a trance, and he started to teeter. I reached out, grabbed him. His eyes opened.

"Were you meditating?" I asked. I barely knew the word.

"Yes."

I nodded, a little confused, and felt excluded. Odd. He was capable of having a private life, of course. I hadn't thought of it.

We drove on then, to Athabasca, to more glaciers and mountains and small towns.

I call home collect, call my kids. John answers, says Susan is at work. "I'll pick you up Wednesday," he says. He means at the Philadelphia airport where I am supposed to land in three days. Three. To what life? I miss them, it's true. I've been gone seven weeks; I've never been away that long. They're young adults; they're managing.

How do I survive this life that I am living? I panic at the thought that I will have to leave him; I feel I can't ever leave him, I love him too much.

I try to get my home into focus in my head. I try, even, to get the seminar folks, those people I just spent six weeks with, into focus. They blur into these mountains and lakes and soon the Strait of Georgia where we will be on a ferry heading to Victoria, a city he insists I should see. "You'll love the Butchart Gardens."

In the car, as we drive toward the dock, I say, "When we get on the ferry, I'm going to look at the map and figure out where some B & B's are."

"What a peach of an idea!" he says. I laugh, as I always do, at his ironic endorsements of my own simplicity of thinking.

Our days in the mountains have involved stops at towns of sleaze bars and exquisite bakery shops, purchases of fine whiskey and cheap wine. The days of wonderment have wound down, and we are on our way to Victoria, a city of quaint charm, before heading to the civility of Seattle, to Portland, his apartment. My airport.

"You're wonderful," he tells me, as he often does. "You're bright, beautiful, have a great body, and you like sex as much as I do."

"And I live 3,000 miles away."

We say nothing for a while and drive on, wondering, each of us.

It's over.

Everything is over: the Portland to Portland jaunt, the Shakespeare Seminar and all those exciting minds and personalities, the summer of romance, the extra week in the wilds of Canada. I want desperately to hold on to this happiness. I want desperately to be rescued from wanting so much.

The situation seems impossible.

After the fairy-tale week of traveling with him, I can't go home. I just can't. I can't leave him; I don't know who it is I will return to—and why would I want to return anywhere since I am so happy here with him? I know I must go home.

We grasp at each other; we are both depressed.

When we arrive in Portland, I make a decision. I call the kids again. "Please don't be upset," I say. "I'll be there for sure *next* Wednesday." I have extended my stay yet another week.

They are disappointed and I feel guilty, but only mildly. I am overjoyed to live with Bruce for seven more days. This joy lasts only five days and then we repeat what we did on the road: we fret the last two days.

9   *Last Days*

So used to making love in the evening, in the morning, when-ever—as I guess all young lovers do in the beginning (although we weren't that young)—we found ourselves faltering.

"You're brooding," I said. "Worse than I am."

"I can't imagine you not being here," he said.

It's what I could not imagine either. My eyes filled once again. We clung.

The next-to-last day—oh, that "last" was ungraspable!—was one of brilliant sunshine, as it had been every day that summer, and we enjoyed the city once again, walking to the Yamhill Market where we ate pita sandwiches and Bruce wanted to buy me earrings. I didn't want him to spend his money and so refused, but I regretted my refusal because it seemed to reinforce the impending rift. At the Blue Grass music festival we ran into people he knew. I found them dull. I found everything and everybody dull next to him; I just wanted him. At that outdoor event with the friends, I perched on a picnic table next to him; he was sitting on its bench. When I smoothed my hand across his broad back, the pain of longing in me was so strong I thought I would actually swoon, that old word from Shakespeare. How could anyone love this deeply, this much, and then walk away? Or, in my case, fly away?

I would have to. I had a job in New Jersey; I had children, who were 19 and 21, I reminded myself, but still needed a parent, and I'd abandoned them for eight weeks. I had a house to attend to, bills to pay, school to report to. I had to—had to, *had to!*—I iterated the phrase like a drum beat—go back to New Jersey.

And Bruce needed a job, a real job. He had family in Portland; Preston, his youngest son, lived there. But he wanted to be with me. It was all impossible.

Then, on that last day, something awful happened. Here it is:

On that final day in Portland—when I absolutely must fly out the next morning—Bruce has a "date," as I see it, with his ex-wife, who is not even "ex" yet. The occasion is Preston's 15th birthday. Bruce is obligated to go to the birthday dinner; he wants to go. Well, yes, that makes sense. I certainly understand. But: it's my last night!

Neither of us can reconcile this situation.

On that evening—when he must attend the party—there's also a concert scheduled at the Willamette waterfront, and so I plan to go to that. I can handle this, I think.

I will buy a sandwich and walk down the Park Blocks in a city that I am now quite familiar with. I will take a blanket to sit on, the one we've taken to the Jazz concerts at the Zoo. All day Bruce has been tense, been quiet. We'd gone to Silver Falls Park, hiked around, not communicating much, the weightiness of the parting, the impending birthday party, making even breathing difficult.

We get home ("home!"—his place, his apartment); we shower, we move around aimlessly; we say little.

He stands near the door. "I have to leave now," he says.

"Yes." I gather my blanket for the concert, fold it over my arm. "I'll be leaving, too, soon. For the concert."

"Right." He looks at me. I look at him. Neither of us moves.

"Well," I say.

He nods.

"I'll buy a sandwich," I say.

"That's a good idea—the place on the corner." We stare at each other, stare at each other's face in pain.

"I wish you'd go," I say.

"Yes. Okay." He doesn't move. His eyebrows are furrowed.

I can't bear the thought of his leaving, although I know he has to. "The situation is far too weighty," I say. "It's been weighing on us all day."

Another pause. "I know. I'll go."

Then abruptly he turns and walks out, and the door closes shut. Just like that! He was there and then he's not. I take a deep breath, lecture myself: *I can do this.* Haven't I done it before? Haven't I coped before? Why is this situation so different?

I pour wine into a thermos, carrying out my "independent" plans. I purchase the sandwich on my way to the riverfront, and stake a small claim on the concert grass, spreading my blanket in a nervous sort of frenzy. What am I doing here? Who am I? What did I think would happen? I've been in love with him for seven weeks, inseparable from him for two, and now I have been put in my place, a place which is "the other." I picture him with his family and friends, some of whom I've met. I picture laughter and hugs. I can barely focus on the music, which is what I claim I came for.

I will return tomorrow to my house in New Jersey. I will be on my own again. I don't want that, either. Aside from seeing the kids again, there's nothing I want back there. I don't know what I want besides him, the thought of which brings in a floodtide of longing again, of jealousy over this evening, our last, his spending it with others.

I half expect him to show up at the concert, to claim me again. Surely he will leave the party early, come get me. But no. When the concert is over, around 9:30, I gather my things and walk back in the dark to his apartment. He is not there.

Who am I? I stand at the corner windows watching the blankness of the night.

The door flies open. "You're here!" he says. "I went to the waterfront looking for you!"

I stare at him. Who is he? What are we doing?

10   *In Flight, August 18*

It was happening as though to someone else.

From the airplane window the mountains jutted through the clouds into the expanse of blue sky, luminescent from up here in the sun. First Mt. Hood (where we'd thrown snowballs), then Mt. St. Helens (whose crater-damage Alan and Jane and I had driven through), and finally the grand Mt. Rainier, surpassing the others in its size and majesty, one I had no history with, but seeming to represent the enormity of the entire Northwest. Each brilliant snowy mountain top appeared as if by a magician's wand, each one piercing me with regret. As the plane flew me beyond them, I could feel my face wince in pain, my insides grow leaden; I gasped in huge, sighing cries of anguish.

"Are you all right?" the man seated next to me asked. I feared turning my wet face to him, feared he'd see my distress and be embarrassed for me. "Yes," I whispered.

I had let go of happiness and felt, at that moment, truly miserable. What sense did it make?

I was going home. "Home." The word itself refused to register; I had to concentrate on it, on images I remembered, to determine its meaning. I was returning home. Re-turn. Turning from weeks of soaring—so I felt—soaring with the heady words of Shakespeare, the constant challenge and company of my seminar fellows, the height of my feelings for the man named Bruce paralleled only by the mountains of Jasper, the rush of emotions like the tumbling waterfalls of the Athabasca. My "world" was then one of blue skies and aqua rivers and green forests and sunshine. And him.

You have to go home, I reminded myself, in a mantra I was trying to parse the meaning of.

Home. Yes, there was the house that I'd lived in for over twenty years—my house, our house, the kids' and mine. I rehearsed its rooms, as in recalling pieces of a dream, rooms I'd painted. I tried remembering the colors, starting with the rose walls of the living and dining rooms. It was a paint color that my friend Barbara's husband, who owned a paint store, mixed after I'd rejected several other possibilities. Ed had called the final product: "Jacquelyn Rose." I painted cream-colored woodwork and doors as its trim. Then the kids' rooms: John's a neutral beige, Susan's white below and wallpapered in pink and green above, a bright green strip dividing the two. Mine—well, mine? I couldn't remember my own bedroom.

I wanted his. I wanted his futon on the floor; I wanted him in motel beds, in sleeping bags in tents. I didn't want my own bed. I couldn't even remember its spread, the color of the walls.

The house's downstairs, a large room which we called the rec room, short I suppose for recreation, I remembered as a pronounced green. Barbara and Ed had given me lots of their old green shag carpeting and I had "carpeted" my rec room with it, painting the woodwork bright green to match, the walls a lighter green. I painted and painted. My house. Was that a home? What was a "home?"

Most important in that place were the children. I was eager to see them again. Even then I wasn't totally sure who they were: John and Susan, 21 and 19, alone for the eight weeks I'd been gone, working away, complaining. Who knew what else? They would be at the airport.

I would land at an airport in Philadelphia and we would drive to that house with its paint colors and in a few weeks I would go to the high school, to the yellow brick building in the next community, where I had also "lived" for sixteen years. Hadn't I been with some of those people, the ones I'd called my colleagues, eight weeks before in another Portland? I could not remember any of them.

I also had to return to Rutgers University, its Camden campus, to complete the final courses for my Master's degree. I'd taught English for seventeen years before I had the opportunity to pursue another degree and relished all that I was doing in my graduate courses. In addition, I had to take "Administration" classes to become a fully-fledged Department Chair. I financed the courses by means of a loan against my retirement. Maybe I could learn to focus again. There was every reason for me to leave Portland, Oregon, and return to Cherry Hill, New Jersey, and be me again.

Me. Who was the me I'd started with? Was it the same me I was returning with? It seemed apt that I was floating in a stratosphere of unreality such as a plane in the clouds, drifting and spaceless, me-less, him-less. Him. Bruce.

"I haven't been that happy in a long time," he said that morning on the futon.

"I can't believe I won't be with you again," I said, my eyes blurring once more.

"Don't think of it," he said. "It's not the end. Things are necessary."

That morning we'd made love again, tears streaming into my ears, before we had coffee. Then the showers and packing and off to a restaurant, the Bijou, where we talked of a possible future, decisions to be made. The first order of business, he said, was a good job. He thought he'd look for one around Portland for at least a while longer. I couldn't see what good that would do. Or, possibly, he could move back East and find a job closer to me. We'd work it out, he assured me, looking forlornly unconvinced himself. I left to get on the plane, and he stood there. Stood there, hands hanging at his sides. Then where did he go? Where was I going?

Cherry Hill, New Jersey

11 *Home Again*

For a few minutes I couldn't get them into focus. They were at the airport, waiting for me: Susan with a dozen roses and bag of trail mix—my favorite snack—and John with his eagerness (really!) to hear about my experiences. They were familiar—and yet not: shorter than I remembered after Bruce's height, their faces sweet and welcoming. My kids, my own, my life.

I'd just gotten off the plane where I'd cried almost the entire way, finally washing my face and powdering it in the bathroom before landing.

That first night back in New Jersey Susan cried with me when I told her of parting from Bruce. John said, "Write your adventures, Mom." I helped myself to cheese and crackers in my once-familiar kitchen as I talked to these young adults, feeling as though I'd been dropped from the moon, grateful that they were there to talk to.

But the house! I didn't know where to begin. All the clothes and books and souvenirs I'd carried back as well as those I'd sent ahead had to be dealt with. Clutter and disorder. I was forced to return to lists: bills, appointments, tuitions, laundry, groceries.

By the next day I was plunged into real life concerns: John had been despondent, wanted someone to talk to. His father thought his philosophy courses were useless and insisted he go into business or something where he could make money. "It's not like he's paying my tuition," John pointed out. "I have the scholarship; I work; you contribute." I winced a bit here because I didn't want John to know what a huge burden it was for me to pay my small share and send him spending money as well. "I don't want to do business," he said, bitterly. "I mean, what's Dad have in mind? He can't even sell insurance himself."

I felt his pain. "You're doing well," I said. "Take what interests you."

He stared out the front window; we were sitting in the living room. "I already dropped the Russian course because he said that was stupid."

"John."

"Yeah, I know. I'm not doing what he says. I just hate listening to it!"

"I know."

Susan was faring far better. She had rearranged her education plans—all on her own!—and had transferred from our local community college to William Paterson State College in northern New Jersey. She intended to drive to Paterson the next day to choose classes, check out the dorms. I was surprised and impressed with her initiative. And I was home again, fretting when they would each return that evening.

My good friend Janet came over and informed me that she'd talked to Doug at the RB, the singles bar we all often went to, and he'd told her he hadn't heard from me for weeks. She said she thought I'd been pretty busy and hadn't written to her much either. Janet and I had often gone out together, checking out "the scene," particularly at the RB Friday socials and she knew Doug from those months before I left. I told her about Bruce and the summer. Were there two men now, she wondered? Should she be amused or appalled? I shook my head, denying that possibility.

Suddenly I was plunged into the once-familiar: my house, my family, my friends. My old life started to impose itself on me once again, and it was as if the summer had vanished. I didn't want it to. Susan, in catching me up about household matters, also told me, by the way, that Doug had called a week before and asked when I would be returning. She'd said she wasn't sure.

Bruce also called to say he'd written to me and missed me more than he could tell me. Yes, I missed him, I said. I did. I missed everything about him. And yet I also thought: *You're 3,000 miles away.* It had all been the most beautiful and memorable experience I had ever had. But it was over. You're gone. And I am here, with my children, and my painted walls, and my old life again.

A week later I sat in the dark, writing. I was in my own backyard on the patio with its weeds sprouting between the bricks, made visible by the light coming through the big window of the rec room, with its dusty corners, its old green fiberglass curtains that Barbara offered, and I accepted. Next to me was the picnic table, fairly intact, and its two benches. I was in the webbed lounge chair, listening to crickets. The night was warm, the air close.

I was waiting for something to happen. John was supposed to be home, and the old anxiety of where the kids were had returned. I did not pay attention to their whereabouts for eight weeks, but I was again anxious. He was 21, and upset about returning to Harvard—maybe frightened, apprehensive—and that concerned me. He talked of needing a break. (He does at some point, take off a semester and returns, still in the class of 1985, but finishing in December of that year.) In any case, at this point we were all now sharing the Tercel, and I needed to make sure the car was available for Susan, who was out at a girlfriend's this evening, who needed a car the next day. I lit a cigarette. I smoked too many cigarettes. I sat.

In the house—cooler because of the air con—I poured a whiskey and water and returned to my chair in the dark

I had told the kids about this special man named Bruce. I had told them in bits and pieces on the phone over the summer, but I hadn't stopped talking about him since I came home a week ago. Just for company, I call women I know, whose names—Debbie, Barbara, Helen, Anne—sound as mechanical as my life seems to me at the moment. Janet, my close friend, is sympathetic.

"Let's go to Long Beach tomorrow," she suggests. "See the Atlantic Ocean for a change." It's a plan. I'll drive with her, in her car, I guess. (When will John get home?)

It doesn't matter what I do. I make cookies. I make dinner. I sit in my chair in the dark.

Bruce and I talk. He really doesn't want to live on the East coast, as he'd done for years before he moved his family to Portland for the good job. "It's too hot and muggy," he says. "And the winters are too brutal. I have vowed never to shovel snow again."

I picture the greens of Reed College, the lushness of Portland and its parks.

"But I'll do it," he says.

I can't begin to picture such a thing. It's so dull here. It's too much. He has no job.

And, if he gets one in Portland, I can't give up my job, my house, my life here and move there.

He calls me. Long distance phone calls are expensive, but he's found some sort of loophole. He sits alone in the dark, too. Tonight, I know, he's going to a friend's house for dinner. "I walked around the Willamette waterfront," he tells me, "where you and I were, and couldn't stand it. I had to leave."

The moon is a sliver over the roof of my house. This is my house, on its well-traveled road, facing a barren field. The grass back here is a mix of odd weeds, but I mowed them down this afternoon and the air smells of grass, which is pleasant enough. If I weren't so lonely.

I hear tires close by—could it be John coming up the drive?— and a car door slam. It is.

I go back into the house through the back door to greet him at the front door.

It's what I do now.

12   *The "Affair"*

When I look back on events, attempting to understand who I was then, one thing puzzles me: Why had I accepted tension in any relationship—perhaps even defined it in that way—and distrusted ease? Bruce was easy. I became enveloped in the ease with which we related, the ease of our similar rhythms.

"Ease" was not a word that I'd apply to Doug. There was much I admired about Doug, but our relationship had seemed to thrive on tension. My creation or his? I felt uneasy initially because he was seven years younger, but I assigned the real tension to him—he seemed to hold all the cards, the male privilege then of initiating phone calls, of deciding what we would do, of being able to foot the bill for it all; he called the shots. I "waited" to see what my next cue would be.

But with Bruce—well—we'd always been equals. Maybe it was the money—the fifty-fifty split that defined the relationship and created in me both the simplicity of being involved with someone else (neither of us "holding the cards") as well as an anxiety that this was too different, maybe not a "true" or genuine alliance. His insights and acceptances were calming. He was easy to be with by day, quiet and easy by night; he never snored, slept peacefully.

Could such a relationship be real? How I always hated the power I felt Doug had—with his possessions, the good job that sent him traveling everywhere. I remembered well the house I grew up in and how worn everything became, how crowded its size, the sacrifice my parents made to give me lessons and opportunity. I was conscious of how, as a single parent, I was forced to let so many things go unfixed, eager to accept the largesse of friends.

Having enough money seemed to define a kind of authority, and I felt uneasy about a man who didn't have it. On the other hand, it was the acceptance of who Bruce was and we were, individually and together, that had made me feel so relaxed and happy. The sum total of Bruce and me was beyond defining in terms of "power."

In any case, a continent now separated us, and what could we possibly do about that? As wrenching as it had been to leave Bruce, I now had a future—or no future—at home, back in New Jersey. How would I survive? Just me and my job at the high school, both kids going away to college?

Janet had relayed that Doug had asked about me not once but twice. He had called the house and actually risked asking my kids about my return as well. Those were big moves for him. And signals to me.

I did not act immediately. I took care of my house, mooned about the loss of Bruce, dealt with the kids—well, enjoyed them, actually. Susan had a friend visiting—also named Susan. John was preparing to return to Cambridge. We talked, went out for simple dinners. I called and visited friends. But I missed Bruce and felt alone night after night. I even resorted, one evening, to dialing Doug's number. The phone rang twice, and I slammed down the receiver. I couldn't risk a call going to his machine. And what if he answered? What would I say?

One afternoon in September I agreed to meet Janet at the RB, our favorite social scene. This was a gesture which would have been fine in itself, but I was aware that Doug could possibly be there too. My hair had been freshly cut that day and I wore a new dress, one of the three I'd bought on sale when I opened a Nordstrom account on a Portland afternoon.

At the RB Janet and I had drinks with some friends of hers. Janet went to the RB often by herself and had a little group she sat with. That day I joined her group, and, although I feigned an engagement with them—pretending to follow what they were saying to each other and smiling on cue—I kept my eye on the entrance door. I'd hoped Doug might walk in. I just wanted to *see* him again, I told myself. See what I left behind. I must have studied that door for a full hour, but Doug did not enter.

Then I saw him *exit*. He had been in the RB all along, somewhere. "It's Doug!" I cried to Janet, almost knocking over our cocktail table in a sudden pursuit. I ran outside and called to his back: "Douglas!"

He'd been walking away, but now turned, regarded me. It was apparent he'd known I was in the bar. "Yes?"

I could see his eyes taking me in. I was aware of my dress, white, full skirted, with its wide patent belt, my high-heeled patent sandals. I was aware of his well-groomed good looks, his dark hair, his tie and jacket. We were a few yards apart, like two mannequins arranged in a department store window.

"How are you?" I said helplessly.

He didn't answer immediately; I waited. "Fine," he finally said. "How are you?" His voice was polite; he hadn't moved. He was going to play the mannered game I'd begun.

"Okay," I said. We stood facing each other on the narrow sidewalk that led from the front door to the parking lot. "I tried to call."

"I wasn't home."

"I know," I said. My arms seem to hang at my sides, and I wasn't sure what to do with them. I'd left my purse in the bar, my sweater.

People passed us, forcing both of us to step temporarily toward the hedges that bordered the sidewalk.

"I didn't expect to see you again," he said when we were repositioned. His eyes narrowed a bit behind his dark-rimmed glasses. "You have been rude."

"Rude. Yes. I guess so." I assumed he meant by not calling for weeks. I wasn't sure. The situation was so awkward I couldn't even apologize. Finally, I just said, "It's good to see you." I felt stupid offering such a stilted line—and yet he had not walked away.

"It's good to see you," he said.

I stood there. No purse, no cigarettes, nothing to do with my hands. Cars hummed by on the distant highway. "I have no props," I said, lifting my hands in a gesture of emptiness.

He reached in his jacket and offered a cigarette; I shook my head.

He studied me a moment, considering, allowing another couple to get past us. Then he said, "Let's go in and have a drink."

That was it: the mistake.

Someone might ask, What were you thinking? Meaning, I think your behavior was totally irrational, or, more to the point, Were you out of your mind? Weren't you in love with someone else? Actually, I asked myself that question at the time and yet I did what I did, knowing what I was doing. I do not redeem my behavior by saying I was wracked with guilt. Guilt was no impediment.

Doug and I went back into the bar from the sidewalk where I'd just pursued him, accosted him, on his exit. There, on those bar stools, drinking the Manhattans he'd ordered which we'd always drunk together, we sat in silence, the scattered voices of those around us amplifying what we were not saying to each other. I wondered: were we really sitting here, the two of us, and not going to say anything more? After ten or fifteen minutes I took a breath and started to talk. I tried to sound natural, as though I were merely catching him up on things. I told him about the Shakespeare I'd studied— not just the four plays of the seminar, which he knew about, but the readings we'd done in the dorm. "I really liked *Merchant*, I said—I got to read Portia, which was fun—but *Coriolanus* just lost me. Did you ever read it?"

He blinked his eyes slowly. "No."

I took a breath and then spoke of how good it was to be with my kids again, although they were soon heading off to school, and I even the mentioned problems I'd had sorting through finding a new dentist. I tried to keep my voice natural. He still said nothing, just stared ahead at the tiered assortment of colored liqueurs flanking the mirror behind the bar. Despite talking to his profile, I was conscious of his physical presence—his good haircut, crisp white shirt, navy blazer—he was always so perfect!—conscious of his listening. Occasionally he glanced at me, his eyes surprisingly tender, then resumed his stiff posture. The place, the RB, gradually buzzed with voices and clinking glasses as it grew more crowded. Smoke hovered over his silence, which I finally joined. I sipped at my drink. We sat, both of us quiet now. Yet I didn't want to leave.

I took a deep breath, pursued a new tack. "I met a man. I had an affair."

Now he turned to me. "Pardon?"

"I had an affair."

He nodded, then stared again at the array of bottles behind the bar.

Imagine my saying that—about what I regarded as the greatest thing I'd ever known, the summer with Bruce, the man who was making plans for us to be together—imagine calling him "an affair." I cringed at my own words. And yet I continued. "I felt guilt and betrayal towards you—although I don't know why! You always held me at bay, but I felt it."

"Hmm," he said. He seemed to be deliberating my sincerity. I was deliberating it myself. *Affair*, I'd said. That word suggested an intrusion into an established relationship. Had Doug and I had one? In Portland I had doubts about any "relationship" I'd left behind, and I'd wondered only vaguely about a "loyalty" to Doug.

"Why did you come back?" The question was sudden.

What did he want me to say? I seized the obvious: "Because I have a job and responsibilities—people I like."

He made a dismissive sound. My answer apparently was not the one he wanted.

"Anyway," I added, "I couldn't make anything up. I couldn't do anything but avoid—avoid all of you. I even stopped writing to Janet and Barbara."

I stopped talking. There was nothing more to say. Another silence.

"I hope I don't hear too much about this," he suddenly said. The line stung me. He was suggesting that he was willing to forget the summer's "interruption." The scene at that moment was like being in a play. I wanted to discover what would happen next.

"Nothing," I said. "End."

"Good." We didn't speak for a few more tense minutes, finishing our drinks. Then he suddenly turned to face me directly and placed his hand on my leg. "Let's go home," he said.

Home! He meant his place. *Home.* He wanted me. He wanted me back in spite of all. All what?

The situation—the conflict, the betrayal—was mine. How could I have been "home" with one man for an entire summer and then, two weeks later, succumb to what had been a steady but tenuous, passionate yet removed, relationship with another?

I know that sitting at the bar that late afternoon with Douglas was one of the most uncomfortable silences I have endured. I felt his pain at the time. Having been hurt badly in the past, I understood the feeling, and yet could not believe that I had caused it. I just sat there with Doug, enduring his silence. I didn't know.

I didn't know that Doug cared enough to be hurt. I didn't know that he cared enough to forgive. I didn't realize that these were qualities he had at all.

What did I think were his "qualities?" He was handsome. I realize that we see beauty in those we care about, but here I'm talking about superficial beauty. I was attracted to his looks—an odd thing for me because for most of those years until I met him, met Bruce, I dismissed good-looking men. I felt inadequate to them. Douglas was handsome and I dared to measure up to him. I took pleasure in the reaction of introducing him to others. "You're dating *him*? Wow."

He thought I was "cute." "You're such a cutie pie!" he would say, confusing me. I'd return to my house and stare at the mirror and think, okay, maybe I'm attractive enough, but "cute?" The word was a diminutive, and I liked that his use of it made him seem the older of the two of us.

He was very bright; that was the biggest draw. I would have been drawn to his mind without his body, his face, his bearing (almost unnaturally stiff). He seemed to know everything: music, politics, geography, Shakespeare. I remember once in the car I felt good that I identified the music on the radio. "The Brandenburg Concerto," I said.

"One of them," he noted, steering past another car on the highway.

"There's more than one?" I was chagrinned.

"Um-hmm." No judgment there, just information.

He was witty, too; he made me laugh. I once told him I often wrote down the funny things he said, and shortly after, having made some remark, he turned to me and asked, "Did you get that, Boswell?"

Surprised, I said, "Have you read any of that? Life of Samuel Johnson?" Again, the modest "Um-hmm." He knew musicians, the history of the Middle East, the geography of, seemingly, the world. He loved Shakespeare.

And then there was the bedroom, where he could perform over and over.

So: what didn't work? What made me suspicious, uncomfortable, wary?

In the past Doug did not commit from one week to the next or to when we would see each other next. He could be moody. I always assumed that he saw me as temporary, as I saw him. He seemed to want me and not want me at the same time. Until I went away to Portland. Until I didn't come back from Portland. Until, frankly, I could have stayed in Portland with Bruce forever if there hadn't been the children, the house, my teaching position, a very solid life in New Jersey. I did over-stay there as it was. And now I had chased after Douglas from inside the RB to the sidewalk, and he hadn't walked away.

His presence—his physical presence—affected me, as it always did. He was similar to Bruce in one way: the moustache, the height, the glasses. Now there was a new similarity. Doug, too, liked me. Maybe even loved me. Why would he forgive? Why would he take me back? Why did he suggest "home," as though it was a place we'd shared? Bruce had, more appropriately at the time, named his apartment as "home," which it had temporarily been for us, until I forced myself to go "home" to my kids and my regular life. What was "home?"

Doug actually turned to me, touched my leg, said, "Let's go home."

"Okay," I said, and slid off my bar stool. I gathered my purse and sweater from where Janet was sitting, shrugging helplessly to her silent and questioning glare, and Doug and I walked to the parking lot. I had to drive my own car. I willfully followed him to his townhouse, now filled with more furniture than before: two sofas instead of one, ample space for them to square off to each other. We both sat on one, sat again in silence, until he jumped up and said he'd make Irish coffees. I stayed seated, wondering who on earth I was in this world.

Who was I that I could succumb so easily, having just two weeks before been numb with love, dizzy with love, for Bruce? Yet I had to admit that I had immediately—when I first met Doug and for all the time thereafter—been attracted to him. Now here he was: his exact physical presence, his comfortable surroundings. I was curious. No, that's not right; it was more than curiosity. It was visceral; I felt the old pull towards him, the desire I'd felt when I first met him. I should have censored that feeling immediately. . . and yet. Why not?

He brought in the drinks and joined me, and we sat next to each other sipping those wonderful concoctions of coffee and whiskey and cream, not talking. We sat. I could not improvise any more excuses; he seemed to be mulling things over.

Suddenly, having made a decision, he relieved both of us of the glass mugs, placing them on a side table, and turned to me to kiss me in a way he'd never kissed me. Before I'd left for Portland I couldn't remember much of our kissing; it seemed we just went to bed. But the way he reached around, bringing me close, the intimacy of our lips touching, confused and enticed me.

I followed him up to his once-familiar bedroom, where I was simultaneously involved and repelled by myself. I thought of Bruce throughout the next hour or so; I reviewed my silent "Portland prayer" of *Please don't take him away from me!*

But Bruce was away—far away—and Doug was right here, making love to me, seeming to care about me, which made things rather crazily removed, unreal.

He kept saying "I missed you, I missed you so much." It seemed easy to guess that he hadn't been with anyone for the eight weeks I'd been gone, the several weeks I'd been home. He kept telling me he was providing a "Welcome home" to me, reminding me, impossibly, amusingly, of the line in the musical *Oklahoma!*, where Will Parker grabs Ado Annie and bends her backward in what he calls an "Oklahoma Hello."

"Welcome home," he said, embracing me, mounting me again. "I missed you."

I did not say what I was thinking; I just went on being the recipient of whatever Doug was doing, thinking, with Rosalind's line from *As You Like It* in my head, "Oh the difference between men and men!" I reminded myself that I once really liked Doug and still liked him. But "love," the word that came so easily to Bruce and me, had never been mentioned.

When I got home that evening from all this sexual activity, I called Bruce in Portland—he was three hours behind my time. He seemed distant and polite. He'd called twice that evening. I volunteered nothing, of course, and when he said "I love you," I responded, without a qualm—because it was true—"I love you, too."

His son Preston was there at the time, sleeping on the couch. Bruce had company for the evening.

And I? What had I had "for the evening?"

Absolutely nothing I could talk about, which Bruce sensed, and I sensed that he sensed, and I had no idea what I was doing or why. Something had to occur to me, I thought; I longed to find out what it was.

13   *The New Doug*

Bruce at his end deals with disappointment.

I at my end deal with deceit.

Bruce had been telling me over the phone about his various efforts to find a job, but recently I'd lost track of what he was doing. I didn't have an answering machine, so I didn't know if the phone rang unless someone was home. Which I was not; for the past four days I was mostly with Doug. Once, just before John left for school, he joined Doug and me for drinks at the RB—an odd combination of men which delighted me. Susan was at college already, then John left for Cambridge, got a ride from a friend.

Now it was just me in the house again, but I was hardly there. I was at the high school from 7:30. to at least 4 each day; I got together with Janet or Barbara or former students; I taught my classes, drove to Rutgers in Camden twice a week, wrote papers for the courses I was taking there, that semester: Hemingway/Fitzgerald and Shakespeare. I was back to running the department that Randy, the principal, had named "Performing Arts," although it consisted only of three full time music teachers, a drama teacher and me. I taught dance as well as English and juggled all the schedules for both classes and music lessons (the school offered them), ordered instruments and supplies, arranged and announced concerts, dealt with four different budgets.

Overriding all these activities was the nagging deceit and conflict: which man am I committing to? Shouldn't I commit to one? Who is most important to me?

It turned out to be whomever I was with at the moment.

One evening Doug and I had a little too much to drink and he was insistent with his questions: What was I doing? Why had I come home? Was I merely playing a game? What was the point of games?

"If you like games," he said, "you realize two can play at them, right?" Maybe he'd assumed that my naming my liaison an "affair" meant the relationship had ended. Now he filled me with fear that he was "catching on" to the fact that it hadn't.

And Bruce's silence! What a weapon, I thought, but only briefly. Bruce wouldn't use "weapons." His silence suggested pain, withdrawal. I didn't want to lose Bruce. I recalled everything he was to me, and I was shattered to think that he would not be there. In spite of his financial insecurity of looking for a good job and my always paying my half of everything when I was with him, he was like a stone pillar I could lean against; he was consistent. Doug, with his position and money, with whom I engaged in abundant and guilty sex, was, in comparison, like a column of plaster. I could lean in the sense of counting on his being who he was for several hours, even days, but I was always afraid that he might crumble, or have a "tantrum," which is the way I described his sudden outbursts of impatience. I treaded carefully with him in spite of the lavish attention he had been paying me. He was with me but didn't seem graspable. Bruce was graspable but distance forbade his being grasped. Doug remained tentative, Bruce, constant.

One day a beautiful poster arrived from Portland. It was titled "Portland Jazz" and pictured a grand piano on a meadow, Mt. Hood in the background. It said, "Summer 1984." I was deeply moved. The summer of 1984 was our summer.

The poster was a poignant and guilty reminder. But my receiving the poster didn't stop me from doing what I was doing. It was now October; it was no longer summer.

The thing was that I was dazzled, when I returned, at the "new" Douglas. "Dazzled" was a good word since I had been wide-eyed

with brightness and wonder at discovering a man as solid and com-
passionate and intelligent and sexy as Bruce, and I had fallen in love
with him. I had been dazzled.

And now, back in New Jersey, here I was with Douglas, and
also dazzled at the new courtship he engaged in, his seeming to
want me. Doug was intelligent and sexy, too, and although I had not
discerned a sense of self or compassion near Bruce's, he had other
things to offer.

He had a comfortable home, a solid job; he was generous. I
delighted in peering at his underwear drawer when he opened it, at
all those colored briefs lined up. I loved looking at the row of smart
loafers he kept near his front door to slip on. I loved all the "accoutrements" he had—the VCR, the big color TV, (I had only black
and white at the time) the enormous record collection and stereo
systems. One of his townhouse bedrooms was his "library," with its
wall-to-wall bookshelves, easy chair and dramatic lamp arching over
it. He had coffee makers and grinders and a bed with built-in lights.
All these were in high contrast to what I could afford in my house
and certainly well beyond anything I grew up with where, like the
D.H. Lawrence story, the walls constantly seem to whisper, "There
must be more money!" Once I mentioned D.H.Lawrence, and the
next time he saw me Doug had a leather-bound copy of *Sons and
Lovers* to give me. Doug took me to good restaurants and paid for
both of us.

Bruce was jobless, lived on the scraps he had taken away from
his marriage—scant furniture, clothes that had seen better days.
Except for my having to share expenses, those shortcomings hadn't
really bothered me. In fact, they'd had the opposite effect on me that
summer: a man had to be solid to exist on his own merits, in his
determination to move on. And, after he met me, moving on meant,

possibly, moving to me. Moving to New Jersey. That was what Bruce had been talking about on the phone, what he wanted to do. I hedged.

Now Douglas was actually courting me—driving us to New Hope to walk around, planning travel to maybe New York, maybe D.C., taking us to the theatre, to the symphony.

But I sensed he, Douglas, might be a mistake I was making. It seemed pleasurable enough to connect with him—the dinners, the sessions in bed—even listening to all he said and thought when, before, he hadn't revealed much to me. We went back to reading Shakespeare together, choosing *Henry V,* checking the history. He read about the battle of Agincourt to me in bed; I listened avidly.

At one point, having a glass of wine one evening, Doug wanted to know about "the other guy." "You had to have been serious, or you wouldn't have stayed so long. And, if it were serious. . . what then?"

Good question. For which I had no answer. "I made a mistake."

Doug frowned. Then he seized on one of the recent play's lines: "So now it's once more into the breach?"

"No. What? *No.*" What did he mean? Was he the "breach?"

He looked thoughtful.

Bruce was silent for a few days—no calls, no letters—and I absolutely panicked. What if I lost him? Which man was the mistake?

14   *The Old Me*

Doug's suggestions were seductive. "I have tickets," he said over the phone. "I have a suitcase you can use if you need one."

I had just charged an overnight bag at Wanamakers which now sat at my feet, within range of my own admiration that I'd purchased such a smart piece of luggage. Bruce and I had traveled half of Canada with our few clothes in the slim space above the Fiat's engine. "I already have a case," I said, feeling worldly.

He'd be there at 8 in the morning. I was skipping school; I'd called in sick. In all my years of teaching, even with the children and their demands, I'd very seldom lied my way into a sick day.

"Or come over now," Doug suddenly urged. "Drive over. We can leave from here."

"Doug! We'll be together all weekend." His desire for me remained a constant surprise. "No, I have things to get ready." At his urging, I agreed, drove to his place.

The trip was an exciting prospect to me. Doug and I were flying to Boston to spend several days and nights together, something we'd never done. He'd arranged the tickets, and I, used to driving the six or seven hours each way to visit Pam or, now John, was thrilled at the idea of flying there. We started the weekend by taking a cab to his airport club for drinks. Cab. Club. These were new words to me. I had never traveled first class and delighted in the wine and food we were served on a flight that was not very long. We checked into a lovely suite at the Marriott, where we spent an hour or so in bed before dinner, then walked to Faneuil Hall, returning to round two at the hotel, and out for drinks at the Landmark.

I thought of Bruce and me encased in the small tent in the wilds of Canada, the pine trees outside, the threat of bears, our meager trappings arrayed next to our sleeping bags. I had been happy, more complete than I'd ever felt. I had loved him. That had been a mere few months ago, and here I was walking around Boston in my heels and new dress and lounging at mahogany bars with Doug. I didn't have to worry about driving and parking, nor the long ride back. I blithely crawled in and out of cabs with him. And it was great fun.

I told myself: *Just don't think.*

That mantra helped. I continued to exist in the physical world of Doug, heady with the new man I'd returned from Portland to, worried, puzzled about the man I left 3,000 miles behind.

Theoretically I was still in love with Bruce. Yet I continued to luxuriate in Doug's command of the situations, his largesse.

At my return several days later, Bruce called. I told him I went to Boston—my good friend Pam lives there. I omitted that Doug was with me at Pam's, that we had dinner with her and her daughter. I told Bruce I saw my son John in Cambridge. In fact, Doug and John played pool at John's club in Cambridge—but of course I didn't say that. I omitted how I got to Boston; let Bruce assume I drove. His voice was deep, reassuring to me. He missed me. He loved me.

And I loved him. Didn't I? I did love him.

And I loved Doug, too.

It was a tough time, particularly since each of these men was alert to odd signs in me. "You're acting—formal," Doug accused. "What's going on?"

Bruce was quiet over the phone, waiting for me to say something.

How long could I carry on like this?

I think that by late October if either man could have filed a complaint against me, he would have. And I would have joined in and filed yet another against myself.

Bruce's would read something to effect of:

She's not involved the way she was last summer; she seems 'removed' somehow. She makes declarations of love, but I can sense that she's forming the words we once used, but . . . she seems evasive. She's hiding something. I think she's involved with that guy Doug again and I don't want to ask. I don't want to know. I want her to extend a real invitation: Yes, please come out and be with me. I want to be with her, have her sign a pledge that she'll never see him again if I come out.

Doug's would read:

I can't get a grasp on what she's about. She's totally mine for hours, particularly in bed. And I've taken her places she likes: the visit with her friend in Boston, meeting up with her son in Cambridge. King Lear in Washington, D.C.—that more-than-weary trip on the train. Then she says something in that Greek restaurant about having been to Greece. I don't like hearing about what she's done without me. We spar and duck and probe with words and I never know where I stand with her. I'd like her to sign something: "I've given up that other guy, the one from the summer, and I'm totally devoted to you now." I don't trust her.

Mine would read:

I'm filing a complaint and need help filling in the blanks. What do I want? Whom do I want? I demand in my complaint that the complaintee make clear what will happen if I choose him.

Doug keeps asking me what's wrong. Even last night, even after a wonderful weekend together, he said, "Is anything wrong?"

"No. Why?"

"I don't know. I just wondered."

I protested that how could anything be wrong—that I'd just told him at lunch how wonderful I thought he was, and he agreed that yes, I had said that. I tried to assure him that I cared about him, that I was grateful for the day, the theatre, the adventure.

"What would you like me to say?" I asked.

"I don't know. You're right. But I see you as distant somehow. Formal."

"You've used that word before! I don't know what to make of you. If I don't know what's going on or haven't experienced it, you see me as naïve. If I have—or mention I've been places—you get angry. As though whatever I had done before took away from the specialness of doing something with you."

"I guess that's what I wonder about," he said.

"What your specialness is?"

His eyebrows furrowed behind his glasses. "Yes. Or—back to the usual: what we're doing."

How could I answer that? What was an answer to "what are we doing?" Once again, I was thrust into our guardedness, the almost cryptic way we communicated. I still feared making demands. I couldn't say, *I fear asking of you something I'm not sure you want to give.* I'm afraid that saying such a thing will ward him off. I couldn't say, *I want us to be serious, don't you? Are you serious?*

Instead, I answered his "What we're doing," as though he'd invited me to a commitment. I drew a breath and said, "My question also! I assumed—"

But he interrupted. "No need now," he said. "I think we're both tired." Thus the conversation was shut down. I wondered why *he* didn't say something serious—a different question such as "Do we have a future together?" or "Does all this mean as much to you as it does to me?"

He didn't, though. I didn't either.

Maybe what I was doing was living through a crucible of sorts: a crucible of two relationships disguised in too much sex and distraction to determine who I was, what I wanted. The problem was that my crucible involved the use of—dare I say, the suffering of—others, whom I claimed I did not want to hurt. It also involved the avoidance of recognizing emotions that kept creeping up about Doug: "fear" "afraid." Of what? Did I dare ask him real questions?

"What are we doing?" he'd asked. What was I doing?

I felt on the brink of disaster and feared falling in the wrong direction. That autumn, during September, October, November, I was also on the brink of exhaustion, running, running, eating, eating, going to bed with Doug at his place and talking to Bruce when I returned home. I'd eat randomly to distract myself from thinking, to give myself energy; I was gaining weight. Between the "men," so to speak, Susan came home from college for a few days and I drove her back; I carried on my high school routine of classes, management, meetings, budgets; I drove to my graduate classes, I wrote papers: *King Lear* (again!), Hemingway's *To Have and Have Not*—as propitious a title as ever there was one.

Around all that I was with Doug, going to bed with him, repeatedly. How? Not even How, but How could I?

His allure was irresistible—not just all we did together, but his physical self. Even sitting next to him in the car, I studied him, longed for him. And yet I also looked forward to Bruce's calls at night. When I was with Doug, the immediacy of him, his voice, his deep laugh,

I wondered who Bruce was; when I read Bruce's letters—the large handwriting that declared love for me, a search for jobs—or when I talked to Bruce, his voice so familiar and reassuring, I wondered who Doug was. I avoided looking at the brink.

Brink of what? Some sort of showdown. A decision that I must make. How long could I go on being duplicitous? And that duplicity, those betrayals, were in full view of my children, who were more than aware of what I was doing. In Susan's case, she would pick me up at Doug's house when she was home and needed the car; in John's case, having drinks with us—even shooting pool with Doug when we were in Cambridge.

I made porkchops, Sacher torte, roast chicken, in some gaps of time I could barely work in, to take to Doug's. I made sauerbraten and spaetzle. I made Waldorf salad. I was always running food around when he wasn't buying us cheesesteaks or pizza or taking us out to dinner. No wonder I was gaining weight. And yet we went on and on. I went on. I was a juggler by day, an acrobat by night, a charlatan on weekends. I felt I couldn't go on living like this, and yet, unwilling to commit anywhere, conscious of the risks involved, I postponed doing anything at all. I even told myself, like a petulant child, that it wasn't my fault that I fell in love with two men at the same time.

And yet it was my fault.

Always restless, seeking, insecure, I was "out there," looking when there was no need to look. Well, that's not a totally accurate analysis. I never really trusted or relaxed in relationships. I'd met Doug at the RB on the heels of the breakup—rejection, really, by Sam—of a relationship that had lasted five years. I was forty-two at the time. As I've said, Doug never seemed to be more than a playmate—not that I used that word. We didn't use words for what we were doing; we didn't analyze, explain. I hadn't admitted how much those hurt feelings from my past lingered with me, and then, after my summer in Portland, I'd played down my very deep involvement with Bruce. The fact that I was available and never asked any questions of him must have confused Doug as well. I never said, "Will we be going out next Saturday, too?" or pretended: "This is so last minute! I'm afraid I'm busy." I always just said yes.

Doug and I were more than compatible in the bedroom, a big pull for both of us. Intellectually, too, I think. I was in awe of his intelligence and told him so several times. Once he said to me, "Cool it, Sport. Obviously, after a year, I want to be with you."

He often called me that—"Sport"—like Jay Gatsby, creating an amused distance between us. So ours did not seem to be a serious relationship. I felt that any moment he would say, "Hey, Sport, let's not do this anymore." If he actually had said that phrase, I would have responded with "'This?' Whatever 'this' is."

When I traveled to Portland for the Shakespeare summer, Doug had, I recalled, been more attentive than usual, almost clinging. He was going to visit me in Portland, or so he said. He probably was waiting for me to confirm such a plan before he showed up, and I didn't do that. Instead, I fell in love with Bruce so completely I stopped calling Doug and he stopped calling me. Who cared? Until I got home eight weeks later when Bruce and Oregon and Canada took on the aspect of a mirage.

And Doug was there. Doug was not only there but had been hurt by my absence. He was more than eager to "court" me—that's the only word I can think of. His prior indifference turned into genuine reaching out, making plans. His attention was disturbing and wonderful and I didn't know whether to trust it. Doug didn't know whether to trust me. Bruce, long distance now, tried to cling to the trust he once had and to pretend that I was still committed to him, although he knew better.

I'd even told Bruce that I saw Doug occasionally. Which was a bald lie. I saw Doug constantly. In this new life with Doug, we called each other all the time, another anomaly. In the time past, I had to wait for Doug to initiate things. Now I could drive over to his place, even as we both were weary with jobs, and listen to Chopin or Tchaikovsky with him. I could take my books for grad school or English papers to grade. He would look up as we sat on his sofas having a drink. "Do you want to study?" he asked, eyeing my books about Hemingway, a twinkle in his eye, "or mess around?"

"I think I want to take a bath—if I may—and then mess around."

"Well, you can't," he'd said. "You have to study."

That was a joke.

Afterward, we would listen to more music before I'd leave for home. At the door I would say, "It was a lovely evening."

He'd say he'd see me Friday—two days away.

"My God, Doug," I said one evening when I arrived at his place, this time carrying a casserole and book about Fitzgerald I'd brought. "This is the fourth evening in a row we have seen each other!" That number had been unheard of in the past. Twice in a week would have been crowding him.

"The fifth," he said, kissing my cheek. "But who's counting?"

15   *Torn*

One weekend Doug drove us to Cape May and suggested the ferry. I felt outside myself, remembering vividly the ferry from Vancouver to Victoria a few months before where I had been so much in love with Bruce I'd grown weak in the legs just watching him stand at the deck railing. Doug put his arm around my waist and kissed the top of my head. We stared at the Chesapeake Bay, at the beauty of the world, together. That day. Doug was now definitely on the winning side of the competition for me. The idea of "competition" was such a foolish one that I blush even now to write that word.

Half of me felt more than competent. I was managing my dance and literature classes, running the department; I had friends; I was in touch with my children all the time, I reported to the dentist. The other half of me felt unworthy: I wondered what either man saw in me, particularly this one, Doug, who saw me a great deal. I looked in my own mirror and cringed. My face looked strained—my eyes tight, my forehead furrowed.

One evening, when Doug had just returned from a trip and had a slight cold, I tried to cancel our date, but he insisted. After the cheeseburgers, which he made for us, he wanted me to stay there with him and watch *Civilisation*. We had watched a number of episodes—which we both loved—on the VHS and TV he had at the end of his bed. This arrangement was impressive to me since I thought only organizations, like my high school, had a VHS player. It was the concluding segment of *Civilisation*—and, reading from the case, he said, "This one features Tolstoy—you'll like that," and I agreed. But after that episode, I told him I was going home—he didn't even feel well.

"Stay," he said. "Don't you want to snuggle?"

I demurred, saying it was Sunday night and I had school in the morning. He pulled me to him and said he would make coffee for me in the morning. What was I to make of these gestures, except the fact that he wanted me, even needed me?

At the same time I had such fun with Bruce on the phone, mostly on weekday evenings when he called. We talked—or he now talked—about my coming out to Portland for Christmas. This was his idea and beyond anything I could logically think about. We could share the price of an airline ticket, he said. I had a break from school then, right? So, why not come to Portland? I said, always hedging an issue, that I would think about it.

I did think about it, but only during the interims when I was not with Doug. I had such a good time—almost—with Doug. I felt he cared—but there was something missing, and I couldn't think what it was. It didn't feel solid; it had never felt solid but, compared to the way he had distanced himself before my absence of the summer, this new Doug felt more—accessible. I laughed at my choice of words. Should a romantic companion be described in terms of "accessibility?"

In addition to my emotional doubts, I was insecure financially. My car needed repairs, the roof needed to be patched where there was a leak on Susan's ceiling, John needed dues, Susan needed clothes, we all needed books. Those needs all fell on me.

And I was, as the song goes, torn between two lovers.

Tension

16   *Ringing Phones*

But then there was a shift, precipitated by a sound.

Doug was at my house, oddly on a weekday evening. It was around 11 p.m. and we were sitting on my sofa when the phone rang. I knew it was Bruce.

I didn't answer.

Doug stared steadily at me as we listened to the ringing. At that time phones rang until someone picked up—or the caller quit.

"I'm not going to answer that," I said, as the phone rang on, too many jarring times.

"That's probably a good idea," he said, his eyes narrowing. The ringing finally stopped; the implication did not.

Doug had suspected several times that I had not severed ties with "the summer." Still, he had not let me go. Now, with that ringing and unanswered phone, he was suspicious, as Bruce no doubt was at his end. *Where is she at 11:00 her time on a school night?*

Bruce never did ask me that question; it was not the sort of thing he did. A characteristic I early learned of his was a policy of not objecting, not judging, not questioning, and thereby—somehow—causing me to realize myself the full implications of what I was going.

As far as Doug was concerned, I later realized that the unanswered phone was a turning point in his attitude toward me and our relationship. That evening I tried to push the event aside.

Then it happened again. A week later, a Friday I think it was, Doug and I were in my bed, an unusual fact in itself since we were mostly at his house. I assumed it was Bruce calling from Oregon—again!—and again the phone rang and rang. This second occurrence precipitated a heart-to-heart talk with Doug. He accused me of having acted "superficial" around him, and he'd wondered why. Well, I admitted to its being a good question, one which I shot right back at him since he was never forthcoming either.

We talked, each of us accusing the other of evasiveness and admitting that we cared, with the final admission, the words spoken for the first time by either of us. "I love you," he told me, the first time he ever said such a thing. I was taken aback, but readily returned the phrase. "I love you," I said. I meant it. We cuddled, clung, slept.

A few days after that romantic declaration he became what I saw as the typical hot-cold Douglas. It was the Tuesday before Thanksgiving, and I was upset because my car had to go into the shop for repairs. Doug volunteered his sports car for me to use (he also had a company car), which I thought was generous of him. However, when he found out I wanted to drive to Paterson in North Jersey to get Susan, he protested. He didn't realize I wanted to "go that far." I understood, I said. Maybe my car would be ready after all; it wasn't. My friend Janet said she would drive us north to get Susan on Wednesday, which she did. Doug's car stayed in my driveway, and he actually called to make sure things were all right, assuring me over the phone, "I love you, you know."

But either that feeling didn't last, or he gave serious thought to those unanswered phone calls. In any case, he must have mulled over the incidents sufficiently to lead to the culminating incident the next day, Thanksgiving.

At first there was only the day itself, Thanksgiving, innocuous and predictable. Susan was now home from college and her friend Susan was visiting, and Doug joined us, too. I baked pies, roasted a turkey, and the Susans and Doug and I had a good dinner. We played Trivial Pursuit afterward and were almost imitating a family.

Almost.

Everything with Doug was that way—almost but not quite— and I couldn't put my finger on what was missing. I sensed a distinct tension but dismissed it. Hadn't he just declared to me how he felt?

That evening, Thanksgiving, with the girls at my house, he invited me back to his house. I said I should stay home; I had another Shakespeare essay to work on. "Bring your typewriter, your books," he urged. Okay. I asked if he wanted a turkey leg to take. "Yes," he said. "I'll make soup." He wanted the extra pumpkin pie as well. He loved pumpkin pie. "Oh, and pack a bag," he told me.

When we got to his house in two cars (both his) and I carried all this stuff in, he banged around viciously, slamming magazines, pushing chairs, and finally sank onto one of his sofas in exasperation, arms outstretched along the back, one leg crossed over the other knee, and said, "I have a question."

I was taking books out of a canvas satchel. "Yes?"

"Are you planning to stay for the entire weekend? Don't you think it's presumptuous of you?"

I froze in mid-gesture, humiliated, angry. *What?* I was standing at the dining room table, holding a book, not knowing what to do. I wanted to leave. I couldn't, though, because I had no transportation. I didn't even try to reason with him, remind him of his own invitation, which surely he remembered. I was too stunned, too outraged. Silent, seething, I sat at the table, my back to him, pretending to work. He read in the living room. We stayed in those places the remainder of that evening. Eventually we went to his bed, on our separate sides; eventually I must have slept.

In the morning, he more than tried to make up for things, I could tell. He fussed over bringing breakfast, making love, suggesting his big desk for me to work at. Later, he took me to the mechanic's garage to retrieve my own car. I drove home; he called, cheerful once again, making dinner arrangements for Saturday.

We pretended nothing had happened. The day, the issue, was temporarily smoothed over. Doubt lingered.

Bruce wrote. He composed letters of longing in his big scrawling handwriting, several a week. At first, I eagerly opened these reassurances of his love, of his efforts to plan a future for us. Later, I put the letters aside, my guilt prohibiting my even opening them.

Bruce called. I urged him to not call. I'm not sure what "excuse" I gave him: something about my being too shallow to deserve his attention, not worthy, some phony stance he saw through. He must have been assured of my love during the summer, as I was of his. It was all-encompassing for both of us, no mistakes there.

Bruce was confused. He said, "I know you're seeing Douglas. You never gave me any indication that Douglas, when you talked about him, meant anything to you. What are you telling me?"

That was then, I wanted to say. Now things are different. But I didn't say that. I wondered if I felt it.

Bruce again urged me to come to Portland for Christmas. "If you came out, we'd have so much fun," he said. The idea of him and Portland excited me, made my breaths grow shorter. I couldn't imagine, really, capturing even for a week the excitement of last summer, or, more accurately, I *could* imagine it and realized that in order for me to even consider flying to Portland, I would have to say goodbye to Doug. Again. And for good. I couldn't think about doing such a thing.

"How do you feel about Christmas?" Doug asked in early December. "I got you a present a while back." Oh God! That I would have the power to hurt him. I didn't want to hurt him. I didn't want to lose him. I wasn't sure what he was asking me.

I did want to go to Bruce. I wanted to see if that ease, those rhythms, would happen again or whether they were just the result of the headiness of the summer and Oregon and Shakespeare and novelty. But I couldn't test the waters that way.

I stopped in a travel agency to check prices. I had agreed with Bruce to split the cost of an airline ticket to Portland. I would purchase it; he would send me his share. A ticket didn't mean anything I told myself. It was like buying insurance. Insurance? I asked myself. Against. . . what? Doug's mood swings, his possible rejection of me? I bought the ticket.

Then, a question occurred to me: What happens when a good person gets involved with a good person and, at the same time, with another good person? I answered: She turns into a not-good person. I felt horrible at the possibility of hurting Doug. How could I possibly tell him I would be going to Portland during my Christmas break?

The things Doug said on the phone a few evenings after Thanksgiving haunted me: "Are we imagining something that's not there?" he had asked me. And: "Why are we superficial?" And: "Do you ever think of your future?" These questions stunned me; I thought they were only mine, of him. Besides, I had no idea what he meant by "your future." The fact that I'd always taught high school and possibly might never go beyond doing that? Or, that I would soon be without children at home? Or did his question relate to him? He didn't elucidate further. He left it hanging: "your" future. Mine, not his, not—hard to even consider—*ours*. Yet, I didn't really answer adequately, nor demand answers of him. To the first question, I voiced a confirmed denial: of course, "something" was there— we'd sustained that "something" for quite a long while. I should have asked what "superficial" meant. Or, volleyed it back to him: was I superficial more so than he? Had I asked the last question of him, about a future, he would have answered, I'm sure, in terms of his job promotions, thus proving (although I wouldn't point this out) the "superficiality" of our involvement.

The day after that conversation, I pounded away at my typewriter, composing a draft of a Fitzgerald paper. I was using a line from Yeats' poem "Among School Children" and trying to establish that the question "How can we know the dancer from the dance?" was applicable to *Tender is the Night*, which, I was claiming, had little merit as a novel without the distinct and fascinating biographies of Scott and Zelda. I kept pausing in my thinking, haunted by the questions of the night before, as well as the possible application of that poetic line to myself, to Doug and me. Were we each a dancer in something that was not a mutual dance?

What about with Bruce? Pursuing that odd metaphor in my head, I could see that he and I moved together, smoothly, as though we had been choreographed and rehearsed. But where was that going?

I was devastated at the thought that I would lose Doug. Aside from the interruption of "summer," I'd been with Doug over a year, and I'd remained thrilled with him in many ways, in awe. I was also insecure, frightened, embarrassed by my duplicity. It was awful. I wanted him. I wanted him to want me. I drove to Doug's place at 4:15 the afternoon after that conversation, abandoning my Fitzgerald paper. My excuse was to get the casserole dish I'd left there. Doug was sitting, morosely, on a sofa. I sat, tentatively, at the other end. He had been brooding; he had obviously been mulling over those unanswered phone calls. He was clearly angry. "I can't trust you," he said. "I can't spend sleepless nights wondering where you are." He saw no point in continuing. There was no trust.

I knew he was right.

I should have bowed out gracefully. I should have accepted his accurate assessment of me and walked back into the sunshine, telling myself I could use that airline ticket to Portland; Doug had made a decision for me, one I was incapable of making on my own. I should have walked away.

But I didn't move. I couldn't bear to. My own weak question to him was, why, after he knew I was involved with someone else all summer, did he take me back, say he loved me?

"Because I do love you," he said. "I just can't live with this; I refuse to be a used man."

I sat there looking at him. Finally, I meekly said, "Oh, Douglas, I love you, too." It was not a lie. It was my own anguish at the thought of losing him, the truth of my anguish. Was that the same as love? I felt at that moment, a wash of relief—as well as that tiny prick of . . . what? a loose nerve, a slim shadow of fear, which I attributed to my great fear of not having Doug.

After a few minutes—a seeming eternity—of our sitting at either end of that sofa, he said, "Come here." He held me against him like a child and I cried. "I'm sorry!" I said. "I'm really not a shallow shit."

He embraced me. "Well, if you are, you're my favorite shallow shit," he said, kissing the top of my head.

We watched a movie. We ordered a pizza. We cuddled. We could not sleep. We drank and smoked. "I know why I can't sleep," I said. "I'm scared of loving you. And there's nothing I can do. Words."

"I love you," he said. "And I don't know what to do about it."

So there we were again. There. But "there" was not clear. We never did seem to talk about "it." A possible future together? What the relationship itself meant to either of us?

After our strange conversation and staying up half the night, Doug and I attempted a sort of reconciliation in the morning over coffee and—finally—making love. He suggested maybe we saw too much of each other. I must have looked perplexed but said nothing. His backing away, in a sense, of having me around so much startled me. At the same time, he assured me that, although he didn't know where he'd be traveling that week, I could get in touch with his secretary to reach him. I was guessing that he was, by his declaration, in a way "protecting" himself. Still, when I got home, I couldn't concentrate; I felt desperate. I had the airline ticket to see Bruce, which I wanted to do, but I would have to cancel it. I couldn't hurt Doug anymore. I had to make a decision one way or the other.

I called Bruce and I told him the trip was off, that he and I were "off." I was too involved here, I said, to be fair to him, Bruce. He said my reasons, my behavior, made no sense. I stopped trying to explain what I really couldn't explain.

"You chose him," he filled in for me.

"Yes." I was sitting on my bed, smoothing a bedspread that had not been touched, taking deep breaths.

"Why? What went wrong? I thought we had a future."

My response was the usual self-denigration: I was contemptible, I was unworthy. Words! I was good with words.

"I wish you hadn't planned for Christmas," he said. "Why did you?"

I was leaden inside with humiliation, sinking into myself. How did I dare to hurt someone the way I was hurting this gentle man?

"I love you," Bruce said at the end of the call.

John called from Cambridge, and I bemoaned my plight to him. He assured me that he knew I would act with integrity. "He'll get over it," he said, but I was not sure which "he" John meant, and I absolutely winced at the word "integrity."

The phone rang again, and I was afraid it was Bruce and that I'd have to face again my own cruelty. But it was Doug. "Hi, Cutie," he said, throwing me off altogether. He asked if I had just tried to reach him. I had not, but I was flattered he was checking. I wanted to announce, "I'm free, Douglas! I've done it. I've broken away from 'summer!'" I couldn't, though: it would be an admission that all this time I had been stringing along that "summer" person. Instead, I invited Doug to dinner on Wednesday before I remembered that we had plans for Saturday and so backed off, trying to respect his theory that seeing too much of each other made us too demanding, or whatever his point was. He agreed that we would wait until Saturday. I felt we'd regressed to the come-close, stay-away "original Doug" and felt disappointed, confused.

The week moved on; I had a tremendous amount of work—with the graduate papers and my department obligations and classes and dealing with house and kids long distance.

I had a dream one night: *There is a train and a hallway and I arrive where Bruce is, outdoors somewhere. We need a room; I remind him he must pay for half. There are lots of people, a cocktail party, and my plane is leaving and I have to get on it. I remember with horror that*

Doug doesn't know I'm in Portland and, even if it's a writing confer-
ence, he will know I saw Bruce.

Suddenly I am high on a building, falling from ledge to ledge. I
land on people—oddly students from class—and Bruce watches.

The implication was obvious: the confusion, the "landing" on
innocent people, represented by "students," hurting them. The day
was Thursday; Doug was still away on business, I had canceled Bruce
and committed to Doug, and I had to wait until Saturday to see him.
That was it. I guess I had chosen. But I didn't know how I could grow
used to living with my choice.

17   *Riddles*

Question: Why should the admission of mutual love be painful?

Answer: There was no answer. I kept trying to find it.

I felt I was boring away at whatever Doug and I admitted to. Boring, as in drilling, although perhaps Doug had second thoughts and now found me dull, didn't love me at all. We never stopped talking. Talking was the incessant digging, probing, questioning. It frustrated him; it frustrated me. We groped for firm footing.

"I don't know what to do about you," he said, over dinner that Saturday night.

"What do you mean?"

"What I said. I don't know." He stared at me levelly across the table.

The evening faltered. Lovemaking was tepidly initiated (by me) and not followed through. Later, as we were watching TV in his bed, he grabbed me and kissed me all over.

Then he fell back on his pillows. "Sorry it's been such a rotten weekend for you."

"Rotten isn't the word I'd assign it."

"Sorry it's been such a not-rotten weekend," he said.

After a silence, a cigarette, he said, "You know I care about you." I noticed the shift from "love" to "care."

Later, when I was leaving, he said, "I'm sorry I made you feel bad."

I spent the week on my Fitzgerald paper, fretting that it would not be an "A," that it would affect my A average. I talked to Susan, I talked to John. I thought: I love my kids. I love Douglas. I love—but

I cannot add—Bruce. I thought, What about Bruce? After my call canceling Christmas with him, there had been no letters. I felt I was out in a field of vulnerability by myself now.

Sitting in the Fitzgerald class I composed, in the notebook I was presumably taking notes from a professor in, a story about tight-rope walkers. I thought that the analogy fit my situation, the anxiety I'd caused. Because I save so much, I still have a copy of it and will reproduce it here. The "byline" referenced Doug's suggestion of the way I could sign my Shakespeare singles ad: "Just call yourself 'J,'" he'd said. "Just J.—Period."

The Tale of Two Tightrope Walkers

By Jay Period, Mental Analogist

Once upon a time a man and woman were walking along a tightrope. He seemed firm and sure while she had tricky moments when her balance wavered, but, since he didn't turn around, he didn't notice. Besides, the rope was low and she didn't worry.

So she jumped off. The ground seemed solid, although she missed the wire and wanted to get back on. He helped her up, the rope now being a little higher, and they walked on. This time she had rigged a prop that could reach the ground and was able to be as sure as he. Sometimes, now, he even glanced over his shoulder and smiled, knowing she was there. Then he noticed.

"Oho!" he said. "What have we here?"

She blushed and looked uncomfortable.

"It's not the way it's <u>done</u>," he said. "You're either on or off. Let's not be dishonest about it."

She saw his point, let go the prop, sought her poise.

"Oh, why don't you just get off!" he said. "How do I know what you'll rig up next? Sky hooks. Invisible threads."

They tottered.

"No, I'll be okay," she said. "I'll be behind you again. Go ahead."

"Ahead! I can't think ahead. All this awareness has been rather unsettling. My equilibrium, for instance."

"Hold on to me," she suggested.

"Worse and worse," he said. "I don't want to fall. And I certainly don't want to be responsible for what happens to you up here. I just don't know what to do about you."

The rope is higher than ever. And they stand there, balancing, wondering.

The End

I typed it up (thus the carbon I kept) and sent it to Doug. It's dated 12-10-84.

When I went over to his place a few days later, he was holding up the typed story, furious. He waved it at me. "This is insulting!" he said. "Are you blaming all your problems on *me*?"

Now we talked talked talked again. We were circumspect, admitted to nothing. We ordered a pizza and had drinks. We went to bed but did nothing. I said I would leave, he walked me to the door. Feeling desperate, confused, I told him I loved him. He said, "Yeah, well I like you a lot, too." I declined the verbs: *love, care, like.*

When he called a few days later, he asked what I'd like to do with the evening. Go to Philadelphia—or come to his place? He just had a new bar delivered. "A wassail bar," he said, "for the holidays."

I thought: more furniture.

"How about a two-person orgy?" he suggested. "You were always good at orgies."

He was his playful self again. When I got there he fussed over dinner for me. He also unabashedly admired his new bar, told me his new car was arriving the next day. He was obviously making clear that he had a life beyond me. I didn't know where I fit, who I was.

"You chose him," Bruce had said.

Doug's and my relationship shifted in ways I didn't understand. And yet I did. After his lusty and vigorous pursuit of me for three months, after the declarations and admissions of jealousy, Doug grew haughty and distant. That arrogance was always mollified, though, by a sudden burst of affection, creating an atmosphere that had me constantly on edge.

One evening we were sitting in his living room, the fire crackling, the room pleasant with wood burning and music playing—a scene nice enough except for the fact that he had presented me with choices for the evening: Philadelphia or his place—what did I want to do? When I said let's go to Philly, he said he had logs and wanted to use them; we'd stay at his place. Okay. A song came on the radio and I commented that it was "silly." He rose from his end of the sofa and dialed up the radio's volume, almost blasting us out of the room. I stared at him. He turned it back down.

I made some comment about wanting to talk to him, to understand why on earth he was making me feel so insignificant.

He asked me if I felt the weekend needed an anxiety attack?

"No," I said. "I started in a good mood. But I need to know that I am *here*."

He assured me that I had "much to offer," infuriating me all the more. I said I wasn't talking about my sense of worth.

"Oh yes you were," he said. "You just said you had no significance. Well, I'm sorry. I can't give that to you."

"I'm not talking about that. I meant no significance to you."

He countered with "Well, I think each person ought to be able to take care of himself. Or did you want me to take care of you?"

I was aghast. How did we get here? I pushed on, determined to save myself and us. I said it was a need to share; I needed the sharing.

His eyebrows frowned. "Let's not confuse need and appreciation."

Suddenly I saw: he had no needs. He wanted to be appreciated. He'd announced his upcoming trip to the Caribbean, on business, as well as his travel to other exotic places, and maybe I hadn't reacted. I hadn't cared sufficiently about the lovely bar he had acquired in his living room. I was too engaged with Hemingway and Fitzgerald and writing papers, of my high school classes and running my department. Was that it? Did he have to assert his own importance?

But, two days later, before he traveled, he was apologetic and all over me again; he was gentle, caring, assured me he loved me. "I love you," he said. "You know that." Actually, I wanted to say, I'm not so sure. Later in the week he even called me from Puerto Rico.

I remained wary. I had given up Bruce, whose consistency and gentleness served as painful contrasts to what I had "chosen." The word itself was laughable. I felt that Doug was encased in an armor of sorts and I merely hammered away at it until he let me in, and when he let me in I felt good. But that was not relaxing, that was not love. That was existing by means of analogies: walking a tightrope, pounding at armor. What had I done? What was I doing?

Our sex life—Doug's and mine—became more frequent, almost frenzied in its efforts and variety—exhausting, too. And yet I became increasingly detached in it. Why? Because—I didn't say this, although he asked me what was wrong, sensing something—it had become a "sex life" and not love-making. I missed the simplicity of bed with Bruce and wondered if I imagined such a thing. Why not with Doug? His big bed?

At home I got out Bruce's letters and read them all at once. I clutched them on my lap. Really? He cared that much. He cared, still. He was doing all he could to get a good job. Please come, he had said. I miss you so much.

Please come.

18   *The Ticket*

"You've been a guest for a year now," Douglas observed, pouring us wine at his new bar.

I smiled and silently parsed that remark. Had he never had a relationship that spanned a year? Did he want to remind me of his steadfastness? Yet it's not the word "year" that registered. What registered and rankled was "guest."

Rankled, and yet was apt. I wondered if my summer in Portland had been a mirage. If Bruce had been a mirage. Possibly one reason I felt ill at ease with Doug is exactly what he had named, maybe inadvertently. I doubted anything with him was inadvertent.

I had been a guest.

It was a week before Christmas and Doug's latest trip coincided with my final exams at Rutgers, my shopping for the kids' Christmas, my making cookies. I ate far too many cookies; I was generally unhappy and nervous.

Doug called me from somewhere in the Caribbean and I felt it was just to boast about where he was, but I was happy to hear from him. I wondered again about dismissing Bruce; I wondered what Bruce felt. I marveled that there was a time—a month ago?—when I was pulled between two strong attractions. Now I was seemingly thrust between two losses: Doug's recent guardedness and Bruce's silent distance.

Or was I?

I called Bruce. "Hi. It's me." I fidgeted with paper Christmas ribbons strewn on my dresser top. My heart, thumping uncomfortably, drowned out their rustle.

"Hi, Honey," he said.

Honey. I dropped the ribbons, sank onto my bed. We talked as though there had not been a hiatus. Somewhere in our conversation Bruce mentioned our being "buddies and lovers." The phrase both stabbed and reassured. What were Doug and I? Lately we hadn't even been lovers. We'd been distant servicers of each other's needs.

I told Bruce about the holiday concert at school that I emceed. As Department Chair, I had to step out onto the stage with a mic and introduce the acts, the featured musicians and singers. I told Bruce our school Show Choir actually performed "Birdland"—did he remember how the Manhattan Transfer had sung "Birdland" last summer when we went to their concert? I told him that one of the few Black students in our school sang the tenor solo from Handel's *Messiah*—at my urging and against the music teachers' protests that the student audience wouldn't tolerate such a thing, but how the student body was totally subdued at the beauty of the boy's voice and gave him a standing ovation. I told Bruce that former students came up afterward and said hello, and how good it was for me to see them. "I felt loved," I concluded. "Loved and useful."

"You are loved," he reassured me. He laughed lightly. "And I can put you to good use."

I concentrated on Christmas, on the kids' gifts. Doug was still away, and my graduate courses, too, were actually coming to an end. Susan called when she finished her last exam and after school I drove the hour and a half to Paterson to get her. She was surprisingly organized about packing up, but the traffic was dense on the way home and we were exhausted. I had to wait up for John to call. He was getting a ride from Cambridge to somewhere near Philadelphia, and I needed to go and get him. When the phone rang at 10, I jumped on it. It was Doug; he was home and was weary. "I thought it might be John," I said, and I heard a hesitation, a silence on Doug's part. I asked him to join us for dinner the next night and he said, "Yes, that sounds good." But his voice was clipped. It occurred to me that he thought I was waiting for another call.

But I wasn't waiting. "Waiting" was what Bruce had been doing. I'd already talked to Bruce when he phoned the previous afternoon. "I miss you," he told me. "But I'll wait," he also told me. For what, I thought? For me to determine what I wanted? And what did that depend on? Seeing what Doug might do next?

Was that what I wanted?

It's suddenly three days before Christmas and there is much to do. Around the gifts and the baking and the cards and the flutter of wrappings, I manage to entertain my friends, asking their advice: what would they do if they were me? I ask, as though their opinions would sway me one way or another.

I admit to my friend Barbara that I have actually completed payment on my airline ticket to Portland. She is aghast. "You have the ticket? Going there would be flighty," she says, then laughs briefly, self-consciously, at the pun. "But you'd risk everything you have here. Wait it out." Janet, with whom I'm shopping downtown in Philadelphia, says, "Really? Just go to Portland? It sounds romantic—running off to Bruce. But I like Douglas, too."

Yes, I know. That's my problem.

In any case, Doug comes over on the 22nd, having returned from the Caribbean, and he and I and John and Susan have drinks and dinner. Doug loosens up, quipping about the food on the island, the odd behavior of several people on the plane, amusing us all. We laugh a lot. The kids then head to their father's down the shore, taking my car, and I go with Doug to his place. Sounds simple enough, and yet it is not.

As we are driving over, I am chatting about our faculty lunch buffet, the way the women go straight to the dessert table, and Doug says sharply, "Do me a favor and stop talking."

I stop, silenced as though struck.

"Okay," he says after a few minutes. "There was a police car behind."

I guess there is a connection but don't know what to say. We pull into his driveway, and I am still "silenced."

He turns to me, ignition off, and asks, "What's the matter?"

"You told me to shut up," I say.

"Do you want to go back home?" The question is so unexpected and irrelevant that I am stunned even further. When I catch my breath I say, "Oh, Douglas, what is wrong?"

"Let's go in and talk about it," he says. But we don't. We practice the solace of ritual: he lights a fire, we cuddle, then move to his bedroom, watch a movie on his big TV and, in the morning, he offers the loan of his car (one of them) because he has "lots of things to do" and doesn't want to take the time to drive me home.

So I drive myself home in his car. My children return and are caught up in holiday events—calling friends, going shopping, chatting to me. Doug has said nothing of Christmas since that rather idle question early in the month. Nor has he mentioned New Year's. He has said nothing of anything. I haven't, either. I fear initiating anything while I am wavering about staying here versus going to Portland and hoping Doug will take some sort of initiative. At the same time, I am relieved that he hasn't. I wonder if I would trust myself to refuse him? Or, again, commit to the hope that this time it would work between us? I also wonder if he wonders why I don't bring up the holidays either, or whether—disturbing in another way—he's relieved I haven't.

I still have the airline ticket to Portland, round trip; it is ticketed for December 25, and it is now December 23. As of two weeks ago, Bruce thinks I canceled the ticket, although on the phone he is kind, still loving. To get on a plane, though, to fly to Portland, to even announce I'm flying to Portland, seems so horribly risky. *Do I dare, do I dare.* I repeat the Prufrock lines of T.S.Eliot. Portland in winter? Was I in love with sunshine, with novelty? Suppose Bruce is a horrible let-down? What have I risked for what?

Do I dare disturb the universe.

My universe.

That same day of December 23 our arrangement is for me to return to Doug's place (with his car) and together we're to go to Janet's annual Christmas party. She always invites a number of people from the high school and few other friends. Doug knows Janet well from the RB and has met Barbara and Ed and Bill and some of my colleagues on occasion. When I ring his doorbell at 6 o'clock, he doesn't answer at first, alarming me. I ring a second time, then a third, and he opens the door wrapped in his robe. "Sorry!" he says. "I fell asleep."

His indifference is impossible to miss.

Earlier that day I'd received two gifts—George Winston records and a book of poems from Bruce—Christmas gifts that affected me with their thoughtful simplicity. I think of them while I wait for Doug to get ready.

Janet's townhouse has a cathedral ceiling in the living room, a feature she takes advantage of at Christmas, erecting a ten-foot natural tree and decorating it in silver balls and colored lights. She's prepared several hors d'oeuvres, which are arrayed with chips and dips at a long table covered with a silver cloth. Red candles are placed strategically around the room, along with aromatic pinecones, creating a festive atmosphere. The party is in full swing when we enter. Bill, a fellow teacher, is closest to the door and greets me with a hug, turning to Doug. "We met at the faculty party, I think," he says, extending his hand. "I'm Bill."

"Doug," I say, gesturing.

"I can introduce myself," Doug says, shooting me a dark look. I laugh. "Yes. Of course."

Bill tells us Barbara and Ed are here, too, but I want to greet Janet first. She's a Christmas hostess, wearing a long plaid skirt, and is delighted to see us. Doug relaxes around Janet; she's familiar. She leads us to the "bar," a card table in a corner of the room, where Barbara and Ed are standing. They too hug me in greeting and Ed extends his hand, which Doug shakes; Barbara smiles a lot. I wonder whether I can circulate around the room, say hello and mingle with others, and hate that I have to decide whether I can leave Doug here with Barbara without seeming to abandon him or take him with me, as though dragging him around. I accept the drink he hands me and ask him.

"I'll stay put here, I think," he says. "Go ahead. Do your thing."

My thing. I resent the words, but I do move throughout the room, saying hello, admiring dress-up outfits, asking about plans—the usual holiday banter. I keep an eye on Doug, still hovering near the bar, watching the scene with no particular interest on his face. Barbara and Ed are elsewhere now, but I find them.

"Help me here," I say to her. "I think Doug feels a bit out of place. Go with me."

She and Ed and I work our way through the crowd, Bill joining us as well as Janet again. We have hors d'oeuvres, mix another drink. Lisa and Thomas—from school—arrive late and Janet rushes to greet them, escorting them, too, to our little group.

Doug, who has been relatively quiet, but civil enough, to my relief, raises his glass and says, unexpectedly, "Let's toast Janet and this fine party." Of course we all do. Then, even more unexpectedly, Doug announces, "I'm having a party myself next week. I've acquired this new bar—a wassail bar, I call it—and I am having a party with it."

Those standing around exclaim, oh, what a good idea. How big is a wassail bar?

I am truly puzzled. Doug doesn't mention a date, doesn't even say they'll be invited. I smile with the others and pretend to go along with it, but I don't believe him. Both Janet and Barbara shoot me a look: *Do you know about this? Is it true?* I try to shrug a response: *I don't know.* The matter is not pursued, and Janet urges more food and drinks. Doug mixes another one for himself; I demur.

After the party he and I return to his place for coffee, which he claims he needs. I try to help him by retrieving the whipped cream he likes in his coffee, but my reach to the refrigerator is ill-timed. He suddenly turns around with two hot cups and, averting me, sloshes some of the contents onto the floor. I reach for paper towels immediately.

"My God, look what you've done!" he says, dismayed out of proportion. "Why were you in my way? Couldn't you see what I was doing?"

I mop up the spill with paper towels, and standing, without thinking, I say, "I want to go home."

He looks stricken, but his response is clipped, "Yes, that's a good idea," and he gets his overcoat. In the car he says he's sorry, he's been traveling too much. He'd forgotten it was the holidays.

Forgotten.

"I just wanted to get home and relax, take a break from it all."

"You have it," I say, not even hesitating. "Your break. I don't want to see you anymore. You pull me down. I don't know what it is. I love lots of things about you, but I can't do anything for you."

He is silent, staring at the dark windshield.

"Do you want that box?" I ask.

"What box?"

"The one in my living room." He'd hauled a big box, partially wrapped, to my house two weeks before and set it in one corner of the living room.

"It's yours."

In the driveway he leans to kiss me, and I pull away. "I'm sorry," I say. Again, I wonder why I feel the need to apologize.

"Well, it's too late to talk about it all now," he says.

I get out of his car and enter my house. I hear him drive away. The kids are not home. I sit alone staring at my artificial tree, one the kids and I "screw" together year after year and adorn with all the ornaments of their childhood. The evening at Janet's comes back, her big tree, the congenial people, the spill in Doug's kitchen. After half an hour I pick up the phone and dial Doug's number, so unwilling to let go, or maybe seeking some sort of words about it all—everything just falling apart.

When he answers, he tells me he's feeling "put upon." He apologizes for "ruining" my evening, but I hear great relief in his voice that I called. Again, he suggests we can talk about it. We leave it at that.

The airline ticket is for December 25. It's under my dresser scarf. But I can't leave my kids on Christmas Day, as my friend K.E. tells me. I can't stay. I can't go. I need to call Bruce. The kids come in and talk about their evenings before going to their respective bedrooms, but I'm up half the night, thinking, agonizing. I fear everything: staying, going.

I call Bruce in the morning, December 24. I tell him I still have my ticket—for the next day. Maybe I'll use it? He has made plans, and I feel foolish. But he assures me that the plans can be changed. He seems nervous.

No one trusts me. No wonder.

When I broach the kids with this bizarre plan of mine, John is reassuring. "Don't worry about me," he says. "Doug doesn't have a heart. He has a good mind."

Susan says, "I think it's great you're going."

It is Christmas Eve day and I have told my children—ages 21 ½ and 20 and both home from college—that I am going to fly to Portland on Christmas morning; I am going to use the ticket I purchased a month ago. John is keenly logical; Susan likes the romance.

I've also told them I am writing a letter to Doug, breaking things off with him permanently. Neither is disturbed or surprised by this gesture.

Although I am. And I keep trying to figure out why. Doug has been rude and uncaring for weeks—and yet, confusingly, he keeps wanting me around. I have wavered, kept both men on a string. Bruce has tolerated the arrangement—he's 3,000 miles away in Portland—and has maintained some sort of faith about us that I have clung to, even in my humiliation, having been so involved with Doug.

Doug suspects I am still "involved" with Bruce although he has sought no explanation or commitment from me and, in fact, has done the exact opposite: he has put me at arm's length. I interpret his contradictory behavior as his way of not getting hurt by me again, his saving his pride against being, again, what he himself labeled as a "used" man.

Where is my courage? It is further dampened by money. The ticket—which I originally claimed to have canceled—was to have been paid in half by Bruce. But when I told Bruce that I was involved with Doug and was not coming out, Bruce spent his share. He has no money. Doug has money.

I make a decision.

I write the break-up letter. It's the day before Christmas. I begin with "*I'm jumping off again. And staying off.*" I tell Doug that his recent behavior towards me suggests he wants out; "*I mourn the passage of the happy times and think if I just hang on it will all come back again.*" I name all the things I liked about him, loved about him. I say he's been giving me little signs of affection which I interpret to be his way of being a nice guy, but "*there are no big signs.*" I suggest that he seems afraid of commitment—at least to me—and I apologize for having "failed" him. It is a very difficult letter for me to write. I end with the sentiment that there are things about him I will always love and remember and "*I'm sorry.*"

When I finish it, I wonder what to do with it. If I want him to read it the next day, I'll have to drive it to his house, his mailbox. I can't risk being seen doing such a thing. If I go to the post office, he won't get the letter until the day after Christmas. What will happen Christmas day? I suspect he will not get in touch anyway after my dismissal the night before.

I drive to the post office, drive home.

I can barely breathe.

And so, with that one fear "down," so to speak, I concentrate on my next fears: the fear of traveling to Portland, the fear of who I will be when I return from Portland. Again.

New Old Doubts

19   *Christmas, 1984*

I was leaving my children on Christmas Day. I was flying off to Portland to meet a man I loved last summer. I felt insane thinking about such behavior.

When I'd finally reached Bruce—it was surprising to me that it took several calls to him before he answered—to tell him that I never canceled the ticket, he was embarrassed that he'd spent his reimbursement and couldn't get more money together—yet. "We'll have fun," he reassured me and perhaps himself in his sudden confusion.

I was a nervous wreck about being with him again. Suppose we disappointed each other? Suppose I was let down, having perhaps built up in my mind an exaggerated memory of our once closeness? Or suppose he looked at me and asked himself why he'd been insistent, or how he would manage to live with me for a week? There were other misgivings. I would barely be able to pitch in for my share of expenses this time. Christmas and my kids had depleted me pretty thoroughly. I even calculated what I could "get" from returning the presents I bought for Doug. $80. That would help, later.

"I feel shy," I told Bruce, surprising myself.

"Yes," he said. "Well, so do I. We'll work on it."

It was Christmas Eve, and I had finally gathered the courage to break off with Douglas and return to. . . well, that was the issue, wasn't it? What was I returning to?

A summer romance, now in the winter.

That Christmas Eve, sitting alone, I asked myself: what was it I wanted? I wanted to feel secure somewhere. The children were not children, I knew, and yet, it was difficult to reconcile that I wasn't really "Santa" anymore. I had loved that role when they were young. I'd loved stashing the gifts and toys in my upper closet or the back of the garage, retrieving and wrapping and arranging everything under the tree.

This evening under the tree, its white lights glowing and blinking, our decorated boxes are arranged strategically, leaning against one another as though for a stage set. The cookies on the plate are arranged, too, one with a half-moon "bite" missing, a bite I deliberately took earlier. Originally, the bite was proof that Santa had come and now. . . what was it? A gesture I clung to, perhaps just to feel I was providing some sort of tradition, that I was needed. It seemed rather stupid and contradictory to play "Santa" for "children" who were no longer children and yet rely on those same "children" to be adults for an entire summer and now for Christmas day itself.

John was asleep upstairs after we'd spent an evening together making hamburgers, talking about Nietzsche as well as about Sharon, the girl he was dating, and watching part of an Andy Williams Christmas program on TV. Susan was still out with friends. I fretted: I was going to leave my children for Christmas week. Then, they would be gone—back to colleges—and I, having broken up with Doug, would be returning from Portland, perhaps totally dismayed by the fact that Bruce was not at all the way I remembered him, and now I would be alone.

I analyzed that fear. I was 43 years old and had an interesting job and students I loved and, I recalled, I had a number of friends who greeted me warmly at Janet's party two nights before. I recalled as well that Doug studied me and my interactions while he'd stood to one side.

At 1:30 a.m. I was drinking wine when Susan pulled into the driveway. "Hi, Mom," she greeted. "You still up?" She was totally sober. She didn't care about drinking and on that account I didn't need to worry. She sat down next to me on the sofa and took my hand in hers. She was happy I was going; she'd been taken by my stories when I returned from Portland and liked the idea of another chapter. Besides, her emotional life was not tied to me but to a guy named Rich. She told me about her evening with friends, their dancing in Darlene's basement, how they laughed. She rose to go to bed, assuring me, "We'll get up early and do presents before we take you to the airport." Then she leaned in for a goodnight kiss before heading upstairs. "Good night, Mom. Don't stay up too much longer—it's late."

I was no longer the secret Santa who rushed to closets after kids were in bed. It had been the three of us as adults more or less for years, often going separate ways after opening gifts, often their driving to their father's house, a duty they felt they had to meet. Was I a duty, too? John's calmly going to bed with a "See you in the morning, Mom," and now Susan's taking charge of that morning rather suggested that they were pleased that they were not duty-bound to me.

Whether they were pleased or not, I had determined a course of action for myself, right or wrong. It felt more right than wrong, but now I would know for sure. I poured another half-glass of wine before I turned off the tree lights and put myself to bed.

In the morning I enacted a typical but abbreviated Christmas morning scene, rushing downstairs to put LPs of Christmas carols on the Hi-Fi, making eggs and toast and juice for us. We opened the packages under the tree and exclaimed over choices; we ate cookies from the Santa plate. It was a quiet and valiant affair—and then we were all off to the airport. I wore my black suit and red sweater and high black boots and saw several other women in suits. "I wonder where they're going," I mused.

"Probably off to meet a lover in some distant exotic city," John answered. "On Christmas Day."

His tone was amused. The kids really didn't seem to mind at all. We said goodbye at the gate, and they waved, an audience of two, as I walked off to board the plane. I found my seat by the window and peered out, hoping to wave again, but I couldn't see them from where I was.

The plane was delayed, causing me to fret my connection. But the delay was short, and we took off into the sky. I of course remembered the flight away from Portland in August where I cried the entire time at leaving Bruce. Now here I was in my good black suit, staring at clouds and mountains and landscapes in the broad daylight of December 25. At 6 p.m. the plane would land, and I would see. What would I see? I was not sure, but I thought I would know when I saw *him*.

I attempted to write in the journal I carried, to analyze what got me here on a flight to Portland, by way, annoyingly today, of Denver. I attempted to figure out what caused me to write that horrible letter to Doug (as I wondered how and even if he would be reacting to it, tried to picture him reading it—tomorrow, it would be) at the same time wondering what he would do with the two round-trip tickets he said, at one point, he had for us to go to Europe. His flight miles. Or so he said.

I really thought he loved me. And I loved him, or thought I did, or why would I have been with him the better part of a year? What would he be doing with this day? Did he have any expectations? Had he been waiting for a Christmas dinner invitation? Why did I feel so guilty about rejecting him? In any case, I had burned those bridges.

I wondered what John and Susan were doing. I left "dinners" for them in the fridge, but I thought Susan would go to her friend Darlene's and John to his friend Steve's. Far from being bothered by my sudden and literal flight, they'd cheered me on, their adventure-some mother. I saw myself as the irresponsible mother.

From the plane—the beautiful day it was in the sky—the Rocky Mountains came into view, the Snake River, the Grand Tetons.

Oh God, what would we do, Bruce and I? Greet each other? Assess each other? Wait for luggage? His place? Do what? Dinner with his friends? Portland in rain?

The pilot announced it was 39 degrees under clear skies in Portland. I turned my watch back to 3 o'clock.

Oh god, oh god, oh god—the plane was landing!

20   *Us Again*

Twenty-four hours later, on December 26, I asked myself where I had been all this time; I asked myself how I got so lost. I asked that of him, too, I think, that first night, through my tears.

At the airport he was waiting at the exit aisle as I got off the plane. He wore a suit and tie, held a long-stemmed lavender rose. He was super thin, but beautiful. As soon as he hugged me, I felt I was home, that I belonged somewhere again. How could that possibly be? We kissed and fondled our way to luggage pick-up. I felt a little unkempt from the flight and awkward and strange and, impossibly, *real.*

The wonder of it! The touching each other, the realness of him. The sensations were totally mystifying to me. In the parking lot we had to push the Fiat out of its space since, he told me, "reverse" no longer worked. I remembered the Fiat's problems when we were in Glacier Park in Montana—and we laughed about the car's idiosyncrasies. Once we got the car pointed in the right direction, the windows steamed up. The rose lay dramatically across the dash, and I stared at him, his angular profile. How had I forgotten?

We returned to his apartment. He'd arranged a little Christmas tree, real and strung with colored lights, on the wide corner sill where the windows met. I could see the lights of the Park Blocks beyond. We were just setting down my suitcase in his bedroom when his mother called. His phone was there, in the bedroom, and we had a good time in silent amusement as he talked to his mother, who was in Boston, and undressed me and himself simultaneously, before he said goodbye and we fell onto his futon. I was startled to remember, to experience, what it was to make love—to relate to someone physically so completely. What we did felt so genuine that I was struck by the "imitations" I had recently experienced with Doug, the machinations of sexual performance that hadn't satisfied.

We showered and re-dressed and drove to his friends' house. Ken was a planner in Portland—in the department where Bruce once worked, and Carrie, his wife, knew Bruce well, too. They were delighted to have Bruce bring a guest for Christmas. They'd heard so much about me, they said. I loved their house—one of those slope-roofed Portland houses that have front porches, and I genuinely raved about her green and white décor. The house smelled warmly of pine and roast beef and chocolate. I felt I'd landed from a cold planet into the warmth of their setting. Bruce, next to me at the table, lightly touched my leg. I was with him again. All guilt was gone.

The days were happy and unsettling. His presence was reassuring to me—the loving way he regarded me, a way I had not been regarded since last summer. He treated me as a gift. We showered together; we made love, drank, walked, talked, and everything felt genuine. What loomed, however, was the money situation. He had little; I brought little because I, too, had little money. I wanted him with me, but I agonized over inviting him to move in with me in New Jersey because I could not, I thought, absorb him.

He was hurt by my fears. Two days after Christmas we were sitting on his sofa, staring at the lights on his little Christmas tree, which were reflected in the windows flanking it. He said, "You know, I will not be a financial drain." His voice was soft, hurt. "I will find a job, help you fix things around the house." I was embarrassed that he felt he had to say this, but indeed he did. The next day he said to me, "I'm at the lowest I've ever been in my life and you find something to love. How could it change if my situation can only improve?"

I considered this, too. I considered so much about him as we reestablished our bearings that week, driving to the coast as we did in the summer, watching the clouds come and go, stopping to sample cheeses at a dairy, always eating too many samples, like teenagers, as we did when we went for the free hors d'oeuvres at a local bar. We scraped by.

And yet, as in the summer, if I could erase those doubts, I was happier than I had been in a long while—since that summer. I could be me; I could say what I was thinking, and he listened and responded. He was consistent.

I saw him with his boys. The second day after I arrived, Scott, who was 21 and very handsome, came by to see his dad. I was in the shower just then and had to scoot across the hall to the bedroom wearing only a scant towel. Dressed, I joined the men in the living room and Scott, restless to connect with a girl he knew, went to the bedroom—where the phone was—to give her a call. She was busy or not available, and he was disappointed as he returned. He studied his dad, me. Later, when I entered that bedroom, I saw what Scott had seen: the rumpled sheets on the futon, the washcloth on the floor, my underwear. Later I laughed, embarrassed about it, with Bruce. I said, "Scott must have been thinking, 'I'm good looking and 21 and I'll be alone tonight and Dad knows exactly what he'll be doing.'"

We laughed. "Poor old Dad!"

Two days later Preston, 15, came over for the day and evening. I saw how he idolized his dad, imitated Bruce's gestures, inflections. I saw Bruce as a father and was jealous my children didn't grow up with such a man.

But, as good a time as I was having, as solid as I felt in Bruce's physical presence, I remained haunted over money. I felt the $400 I spent on the airline ticket could have gone to Susan's tuition, paid the dentist, repaired the roof, unclogged the sewer—all of those responsibilities that consume me. Bruce figured that he could take a few jobs—whatever he could get in New Jersey—pay half of everything, but, despite his earnestness, I remained tentative. I obsessed over the situation, and I was back to where I always seemed to land: not knowing what to do, what to decide.

Then, when I called the kids, Susan announced she was going to have a New Year's Party and spent her $50 (bonus gifts from me) on decorations. John asked to borrow $100. As I was talking to them, the cap on my tooth fell into my mouth, a marble that swirled around, tragically. Bruce and I had to find an available dentist. I had to pay $15 of the $45 left to me to have the cap cemented back in place.

Portland in late December was gray, and my life hovered around gray as well—the mix caused by the light of being with Bruce, loving and being loved, and the dark of my fear of making us permanent, meaning having him move to New Jersey with me, in my house. It was all wonderful to walk and talk around Portland, but I was troubled: could we be a couple? Could I really invite him to move to New Jersey with me, in my house? I wavered. I wanted him—then rejected the possibility—continuously.

Sometimes, when I saw him sitting in his red chair, for instance, I felt weak with love, with adoration. I thought of how compatible we were and how much fun it would be to cook for him, to tour around Philadelphia and do things with him. I considered what John and Susan would think; I assured myself they'd accept him, see how accepting he is. Then I retreated into my own insecurity, almost anger. I thought: I cannot absorb him, it's too much.

I was also aware that he would have to give up Preston, who was very close to his Dad and needed him in Portland; he'd have to give up his car, his apartment, his friends, and so on, to be with me.

Some of those friends invited us to dinner and I wore my black velvet pants and cream-colored blouse, and Bruce loved the way I looked, making me feel even more special. I had to arrive empty-handed for a dinner, but—oh, it was this little stuff!—I knew he couldn't buy wine and I couldn't part with any more money, and so we just went. I felt I had to be even more animated, the desirable guest, but all I could think is that these people were our age—in their 40's, and look what they had: this house, all these possessions, together.

I assessed Bruce again, looked at him. Loved him. But this relationship could not be permanent. Doug's couldn't be either. Doug made lots of money and was bright and witty, but emotionally not available, even draining. Bruce was also bright and witty and emotionally very much there, but, I fear, would be financially draining. In Portland Bruce was working from 3 a.m. to 7 a.m. delivering newspapers to distributors, a job that kept him in spending money— he left the apartment while I slept. While I admired the fact that he was willing to assume any inconvenience to make a few dollars, the lack of a real salary upset me.

Maybe, I thought, I should give up men. Just give them both up, all up. Or, more to the point, decide what was ultimately important to me. What sort of security was I in search of? What was it that satisfied most? What was I looking for beyond what I had "found" here, with him, that made me so complete? What could possibly be beyond being happy?

Bruce was always eager for adventure. One morning, as he returned from his deliveries, he said, "It's going to be a beautiful day. Let's drive to Mt. Hood. The snow will be beautiful."

It was New Year's Eve Day. The roads were somewhat slick, but the scenery was magnificent, as though the mountain had adorned itself for Christmas: the many pine trees laden with thick snow, the tall silver trees hovering over the road, the clear blue sky, the clear cold air. We parked the car and walked along that road, among snow-drifts twice my height, and I felt like a child in a fairy tale. And I was with my prince as well.

Or was I? We had coffee in one ski lodge where we watched skiers trampling across the boards and out onto lifts, and we returned to the car to repeat the same routine higher up the mountain, between snowdrifts even higher. We drank spiced wine and ordered grilled sandwiches. Skiers again thumped in and out, and I fought against the sensation that I was missing something. I'd learned to ski at the Montreal Lodge where I'd gone with Sam several times; I'd been part of that "set." Now I was not doing, but watching. Did it matter?

Then I stared at this man on the bar stool next to me. I loved the way he traced his cigarette filter around his lips when he was thinking. I loved the high cheekbones of his face, the cleft in his chin, his long legs. I loved everything about him.

I smoothed my hand down his back. I would be leaving the next day, returning to my house, my kids, my classes, my shows. The colored lights around the lodge bounced off the icy white snow outside the windows and I wanted to rush out and kiss the snow, kiss the man, package this happiness. How could I leave him? How could I ask him to move out to New Jersey, move in with me?

"Let's consider the factors," I said at that Jazz Quarry, the scene of our first meal together that afternoon we met in June. It was now New Year's Eve.

"All right," he said.

He knew what I meant. We'd been over these "factors" so many times.

"I love you. You love me." (He nodded.) "I like it here. I have a job back there. You could more easily find a job back there." He nodded again; I was reciting a litany we had both memorized. "If it doesn't work out, then what?"

He didn't admit that possibility but, if it made me feel better, he was open to contingency. He would return to Portland. We put the decision on hold for a few weeks. We tried to relax, listened to the jazz, held hands.

That was the week's end—when I had to get back home—and I still didn't have an answer. He didn't want to apply for good local jobs if he was going to leave; I understood that. I had pressing duties to attend to: I needed to work on the script of the musical *Oliver!*; I needed to make up to my kids, whom I missed, for abandoning them during their Christmas vacation at home. I needed to assess what it was I wanted. There was so very much I feel inadequate to do.

The week, the year, came to an end. It was now 1985.

What would not seem to come to an end was my journey from Portland to Philadelphia.

My flight on the 1st of January was canceled, and I was rescheduled for the next day, a day where Bruce tried to get out of his early morning paper-delivery but could not, so we had to start for the airport before the sun came up. We were distraught. He had to leave, and

I had to sit and wait. The plane (the first leg of the trip) was further delayed. But finally, hours later, I boarded and was served breakfast.

It's odd to think, in the 2020's as I write this, that air travel was once so comfortable. The seats were spacious; meals were served on plates with silverware; we could even smoke, a concept which is now preposterous to consider. I was not as torn apart on this return trip as I was when I left Portland in August, perhaps because Bruce and I really were considering getting together.

The money, though! At a change of planes in Denver, I felt I needed yet another cup of coffee. A woman collecting for a local hospital or some good cause asked me for a donation, and I had to deny her. "I had two dollars," I said in my defense, "and I just bought a cup of coffee with it." I probably didn't look like someone who was traveling across the country with $2, and in fact, it was not even true. I actually had five, so I still had $3 left.

Susan and her friend Darlene picked me up at the airport and I rode home with the girls and snacked with them until they left together. John returned from where he had been and was upset—about a girl, about returning to Harvard. He toyed with the idea of another semester off—he was entering the first half of his senior year; it was a risky suggestion. I suggested his girl come here for a day or two, but that option was not likely. He and I sat and talked about decisions, making both of us feel a little better.

I sorted through my life as well—I was 43 years old and wondering how many "starts" I intended to initiate, starts that ended up being ends, forcing me to start again. I was mourning a rejection from a previous relationship when I met Doug, whom I saw as a sort of temporary replacement, until I came to really care for him. Still, I did not regret the "Dear John" letter I sent to him before Portland.

That, too, was over. Had been over. And now Bruce. He "came to an end" with summer's end. Must he come to another end with the year's end? In spite of my relationships with men, I had lived alone in this house—just me and John and Susan—for nine years. Could I really have someone else move in? I thought maybe yes. Then wavered again.

Bruce and I talked on the phone. We missed each other. When I was chopping celery or stirring cookie batter, I imagined making meals for him. I studied my closet and thought, I can shift my things to one side; it's a big closet. Then again, that arrangement seemed so permanent, so—invasive.

John decided he would return to school after all, and Susan would leave for college, too. The house would then be just Bruce and me—but I wondered: How would they feel about returning to a house with a man living in it with me? How would Bruce get along with my children? My friends? How would he adjust to my always being at school, at rehearsals? How would it work?

But I wouldn't know unless I tried it.

What had I got to lose except another chunk of my life?

In the meantime, before they left for school, John and Susan proved great distractions for the first weeks of the new year. Their college semesters started later than my high school one. Susan dashed around in my car—took off with friends—and always had me waiting on the sofa for her to get home. John alternately discussed Leibnitz and lamented dealing with his father to the point where he shut down, shut himself in his room and I had to wait until he recovered, helpless to do anything.

I must insert a footnote about the kids' relationship with their father. I left him when they were around nursery school age because

I was supporting us anyway and always, seemingly, alone. They were solely *my* responsibility. I didn't think about it at the time, but, although he had been absent a good deal, he was still their father, and when I left the man, I had also removed the children from their father. Thus, I said nothing negative about him, letting the kids form their own judgments. Those judgments ultimately concurred with my own, but they were both loyal, as children are to a parent, even though each complained about him to me. The good thing was that he married again, to a woman with four children, and John and Susan had a "family" to visit.

Most of the time his way to support the kids was to offer shallow advice. He had presented each with a credit card and no means of paying the bills they ran up. He hadn't volunteered that part. Or: he advised them about how to place bets at a racetrack or explained at length how one could get "an entire education reading the Want-Ads," or insisted they get in touch with distant relatives they didn't even know because "family is important." He lectured on responsibility but reneged on his own. I felt bad for them. He had always been highly critical of my behavior, never having recovered from the ultimate rejection by a wife who one day packed up most of the furniture, took the children, and moved to an apartment. He made it clear early on he wasn't, in his words, "taking the kids" to give me time to "fuck around." So, there really was never any visiting schedule he adhered to. He remained as unreliable as a part-time parent as he'd been as a husband, often standing them up even when he'd promised them a visit. I marveled at a father who "took" the kids every other weekend, or some such arrangement. Never happened. Support was erratic and mostly missing until the courts brought him in, surprisingly to me, because I hadn't initiated the action. I paid for nursery schools, then hired sitters until John and Susan were adolescents. Now they could drive on their own to him, or not. They tried to be loyal.

In those early weeks of the new year I was also supremely busy at school, working on the show choir, on my classes, beginning rehearsals for *Oliver!*; I entertained my friends, too, and seemed always to be cooking or eating or drinking. Bruce and I talked each evening, missing each other, but I could not say with full conviction: *Come, please come.* The words remained trapped in my throat.

And yet. What was the "and yet?" I was, except for those adult children, alone, and, when they left, I would be "it" in the house. I took the train to Philadelphia by myself, attended a parade by myself. I showed up at the RB to meet Janet by myself, hoping Doug would not be there and he wasn't. Who were there were several men who mingled with us, perhaps even flirted, but they made me lecture myself: *You're going to let Bruce slip away from fear, and wade through the likes of these men: perfectly nice and perfectly boring? For how long? You cannot return to Doug after dismissing him so abruptly, and now you are rejecting the man you are really in love with because you're worried about money?*

Won't he earn money? my own voice answered. *Hasn't he in the past—his past? He raised those three fine sons, didn't he? He was a real father, unlike my kids' father, or the vain single Doug who had only himself to think of.*

I questioned my values. I was beginning to see that what was important was not what I thought was important. Perhaps I had been looking at all the wrong things, all the external things like salary and position, and thinking that's what I wanted. Why couldn't I recognize and accept the "trueness" of what was in front of me, of what had made me happy? What was the risk in finding out? The kids encouraged me to "Go for it, Mom."

John left—Susan took him to the airport—leaving the vacuum he always did. Then I drove Susan to William Paterson, giving her money for her dorm—money I'd set aside for John's fees, wondering how I would make it all up. Back home I stared at my closet, my bed. My house.

Finally, on one of my evening calls with Bruce, I said, "I want to give it a try."

Bruce was working those two jobs in Portland and would begin—he was excited—to untangle himself from them; he would sell his Fiat, make arrangements about his apartment lease.

"It sounds like so much to do!" I said. "Doesn't all that make you want to quit?"

"Yes," he said. "I just want to quit it all and go."

"No—I mean, give up on having to deal with all that and just stay put."

There was a brief silence. Then he said, "That never occurred to me at all. No."

There! I had done it. Done something—put wheels in motion. I let the kids know. I told myself that Bruce and I survived happily in his small apartment, in his little Fiat, in a tent. Surely we could exist in all this space. I was going to give it a try.

21   *Forward and Reverse*

I cleaned my cupboards and sorted the drawers in my kitchen. I washed its gingham curtains. I cleared half my closet, making room. I dug out paint and re-coated the five doors of the upper hallway: to John's room, Susan's room, the closet, the bathroom. My room.

Our room?

"It's an adventure," Bruce told me that evening on the phone. He sold his Fiat, quit his jobs.

Were we both insane?

My former neighbor Paul, with whom I had a brief and exciting affair before he moved away, called me from time to time—as he did in Portland in my studio that afternoon when Bruce was sitting there. Then he wanted me to join him in Aruba, a word that gave me pleasure to say, although I wasn't sure where the place was. Now, although he was aware that I was not visiting him in Florida, he had become a sort of guardian, which was good. I was grateful for his attention, aware that I was going to sever that connection, too. I told him my plans, feeling a pang at letting even him go.

I reviewed my life to date, actually digging out old photos, wondering in general where time went. I sorted through pictures of me and men I'd dated in various settings, or I just fingered odd souvenirs of dinners, of dancing, remembering. I had spent so much time seeking, trying, searching. There were many good times I'd had, it seemed, freedom and opportunity. I recalled, also, evasiveness, insecurity, tension. A new search. I had souvenirs of New York and Boston and D.C. from jaunts with Doug, photos of Sam and me in various travels, and the photos of Bruce and me in Oregon, in Canada. I thought, *Will I be tied down now?* And I asked myself what the value was in being "untied." I fretted that I severed Doug

so suddenly and assuaged that guilt by reminding myself of his prig-
gish and inconsistent behavior. Well, he hadn't trusted me. With
good reason.

"It's an adventure," Bruce said.

Was it? Or was it a lack of opportunity hereafter? One Sunday
I painted a table that I found in the garage and placed it next to "his"
side of the bed. His. I would need a lamp there, too, wouldn't I? Time
was closing in. I settled into one side of the sofa and read through
half of the *Oliver!* script again, then got up, found cashews to eat. I
choreographed a scene from *Oliver!* I was restless.

So restless I actually called Doug. I did. I dialed his number.

He was civil. He always was. He said, "I figured it was something you wanted to do all along."

"Maybe," I hedged. "I felt I was banging my head against the
wall with you."

"I was tired," he said.

Why did I care what he thought? I did. I said, "Remember
when you asked me at the end of summer why I came home
from Portland?"

"Yes."

"Well, it was also because of you," I said. This was only partly
true—Doug's still being here was just a hope then. "I missed you,
sought you out, felt things were unresolved. But things are rather
confused now. I'm not sure what I'm doing."

There was a half-beat of silence. "You're moving to Portland?"
he asked.

"No. Portland is moving here."

I heard the exhalation. "Ha! Now I know why I fell short. I wasn't crazy enough for you."

I hedged. I sputtered. I didn't know what I was doing. I added, "I just wanted you to know I thought you were great, that I loved you."

"I still love you," he said.

His voice was so plaintive, so genuine, my guilt at hurting him on Christmas day swept over me, made me gasp—almost pant—with the suddenness and sadness of that admission. After a silence—I had to recover my breathing—I said, "I'd like to come over."

"Hmm. I'd like to see you, too," he said, his voice steady again. "But I don't see any point."

"You're right," I said. "I just hated to drop it. I guess I did drop it."

"You certainly did."

I was sitting on the edge of my bed staring at my troubled reflection in the dresser mirror. He hadn't hung up. I didn't know what to say next.

"If you want to come over, you can," I heard him say. "I'll make some coffee."

It was 7 p.m. on Sunday, and I was expecting Bruce to move in with me in a week or so. I had finally committed to that decision. "Okay," I said.

Why oh why did I anguish over Doug, over the way I'd treated him—when he'd treated me so rudely, so abruptly? I heard real sorrow in his voice, that's why, and what I felt, too, was a great sorrow that we had spent such an intimate year together (except for the summer's interruption with Bruce) to no avail, that it had just—well, fallen away. But how could my going over to his place change any of that, change anything?

I think what intensified my—my what?—my insecurity over giving up Doug and committing to Bruce—was my fear that both men would be so annoyed with me, tired of me, that I would have no one. No one is what my friend Janet had at the moment, and I'd spent the evening before visiting her sadness. Her sadness was at least not my doing; Doug's was.

I drove over to his place.

He nodded a brief greeting as he opened his door and gestured to his kitchen, where he headed. There he found a can of coffee, opened it. He again apologized for being rude the days before Christmas. "I was just tired." He set down the coffee can, leaned back against the counter. "I had been traveling so much." He glanced at me, looked down, said no more.

I apologized, too. I remained standing in the entranceway to the kitchen. I apologized for my letter, written Christmas Eve. I said, "After you told me to leave that night, I thought: What's the point? What am I doing? If *he* doesn't care, why on earth am I hanging on?" I removed myself from my guilt by referring to Doug in third person although he was right in front of me. "I did go to Portland," I said.

He looked away but didn't move. He was suffering over the loss of me. I could see that. In finding what was important to me, I had hurt others, like Doug. Especially Doug; I had really cared about him. I leaned my face into my arm, which was braced against the doorframe. I didn't want to stay—I was obviously hurting him again—but I didn't want to leave him either.

I turned to look at him, standing there in his trim jeans, his cashmere sweater, his bare feet. I felt compelled to reassure him of something, even though I had rejected him. What a ridiculous position I had put us in now. I was so uncomfortable. As was he. I told him there were reminders of him everywhere in my life. "I can at least return the TV you gave me." It was his Christmas present, the box that had been set inside my front door, to my annoyance at the time.

"If you don't want it, dump it in the garbage," he said, no doubt weary of this prolonged and pointless encounter.

Why had I even shown up? Maybe I hadn't wanted him to think I had acted lightly, but this visit made things worse. "Oh, I want it. It just makes me feel guilty." The word "guilty" did not begin to cover what I felt. It was a stupid word.

"Well, now you have everything," he countered, bitterly. "A color TV and a roommate. Unemployed."

We stared at each other. But then, suddenly he walked over and reached his arms around me and pulled me against him; I allowed myself to be embraced. "I guess I was being cautious," he said, his voice over my head.

"Cautious?" I echoed into his shoulder, then pulled away, studying that face I had loved. "You were being cautious? What good is caution?"

He said it didn't matter now. "You exited and got involved in complete and irreversible circumstances." Then his eyes filled with tears. I backed up a few steps, not wanting him to be embarrassed, and retreated to the hall where I sat on the stairs. The silence was sad, heavy. After a few minutes I returned to the kitchen. He was facing the counter now, his back to me. I walked over to him, embraced him that way, the side of my face against his back.

"I have to go," I mumbled, and he turned around, put his arms around me.

It was a full minute before I could pull away. I picked up my coat, which I had flung on his once-familiar desk, and he walked me to the door. Neither of us spoke.

And I left, for the final time. I never tried to see Doug again. Or he, me.

22 *Arrival*

The following day I got tangled in contact paper, its huge adhesive sheets wrinkling against the front of my refrigerator. I thought I'd cover the refrigerator's rust with a cheery strawberry print, but the undertaking had met almost immediately with defeat and frustration. I knew I had to do something about the sticky paper—lift it off, put it back, fight against its adhering to itself—give up—whatever—but I couldn't think.

Bruce let me know he would be arriving Saturday—in a week. It was definite, "done." That was that. I had the flight number now, the time. He told me that that afternoon he was going to drive to Salem, Oregon, taking Scott, middle son, with him to get Bruce, Jr., and bring his oldest son back to Portland so they could all be together. Bruce and his three sons. He was giving up his sons to be with me.

Me.

And I was tangled in far more than contact paper, upset beyond what I could possibly have imagined over the scene I initiated with Doug. Irreversible? Doug's word. Maybe. I loved talking to Bruce, being with him, but I feared. . . what? The responsibilities, the finances, would all be too much, too lopsided. I stared at the mess I was making. I tried to pull away one sheet of that sticky paper to maybe start over, but it adhered to itself in huge wrinkles, glommed onto my arm. I abandoned the project temporarily; I saw it as too symbolic, like Lady Macbeth's "What's done cannot be undone," like my decision.

Janet volunteered to come over and help, and together we moved the refrigerator away from the wall and re-stuck the contact paper. The strawberry refrigerator was now blatantly predominant in the kitchen—with its yellow walls and green table, white chairs. "It's original," Janet observed. Its craziness seemed too emblematic of what I was doing with my life.

Barbara had me over for dinner the following evening—she was another good friend who had followed all my romantic machinations. Now I was worrying about how Bruce would fit into my friendships, how my friends would switch allegiance (if they had any) from Doug to Bruce. I lamented to Barbara, "Will I feel crowded in my house? I really worry about that."

"Well, Doug has all that space, doesn't he?" she reflected. "Maybe you could ask Doug if Bruce can stay with him for a while—while you work things out." We laughed.

I saw the absurdity, particularly of the way I must have looked to my friends. I looked that way to myself. And yet. When Bruce called, he was loving and reassuring, and I felt better. He was eager. I was frightened.

I had been in love with two men for a long time. It was time to settle, if I could, with one. I returned to my list of things to do for the house to Get Ready and hoped that Bruce was not disappointed in me, in my house, that I was not disappointed in having a roommate, that he would find a job, that it would work out—the list went on.

And Saturday was almost here.

On that day, January 26, 1985, his arrival was delayed two hours, a fact that those of us waiting for planes could not discover until we were at the airport and read it on the monitors. My nerves! I walked the corridors, took Tums, sat down, got up, checked the boards again. I worried about the shrimp dinner I'd half prepared at home, worried that somehow this situation would be the end of "me," forgetting that the "me" had analyzed these odds over and over and decided to take the risk. In the airport, waiting around, I was beset, once again, with doubts, almost paralyzed in the realization that there was no turning back now. I told myself I would remind Bruce of the informal agreement we'd made over the phone: we'd give living together a chance for six months and then reconsider. I was already reconsidering.

Then I watched, heart pounding, passengers streaming up the exit ramp into the airport waiting area, and finally he strode into view—his tall, lanky frame dressed in a suit—as he searched me out, his face falling into a smile of relief. And he was carrying, of all things, daffodils. We embraced, and in that embrace my fears fell away. I felt I too had arrived.

The weather was freezing, literally zero degrees that day, and the roads were rimmed with dirty snow, but he responded to it all as though I had beckoned him to some wonderland. I took him "home," my house that is, sort of touring him around. It was a split level—a cheaply made house on a busy road—but roomy enough, and he admired my colors, the whole place; he even loved my strawberry refrigerator. He was a happy man. What a difference.

His boxes (eight of them, to my prior concern) were in the rec room, but he unpacked his suitcases in John's room since John wouldn't be home from college until Spring. Susan, would, though, the following weekend, and already I wondered how she would like him, accept this man moving into our house, although of course both kids had heard so much about Bruce. That evening I finished my shrimp dinner, as I'd planned, and we had wine and made love, something that we did so easily, so without tension.

Sunday morning we woke up to more lovemaking, and I was aware, again, of how easy he was to sleep with, and, in the still-frigid weather, we headed into Philadelphia. He had mentioned an Alice Neel show he saw in Portland, and I exclaimed that I'd just read about her—her show was at the University of Penn museum—so we headed there. Later we walked along South Street, stopping in an Old Town bar for drinks. We were so happy. Bruce loved cities and wanted to see more of this one, even freezing Philadelphia in scrappy snow, frozen into dirty banks of ice so high that we had to park next to them.

The week went on and I couldn't believe how much fun I was having, how eager I was to get home from school to him. I feared the feeling would not last. And I also wondered what my friends would think of him: a tall, rangy man, loud of laugh, who was unemployed. I felt defensive, protective, about him. The lyrics from a song in "Cabaret" ran through my head: *If you could see him through my eyes.*

There was no need to worry; quite the opposite happened. Janet came over one evening and, although she'd lamented to me just last week, "I fear losing you!" she was instantly part of us, becoming a familiar third at our table in weeks to come. Barbara and Ed came over for dinner the following Saturday, and we four chatted and relaxed as though we'd always been two couples getting together. I recalled the tensions I often felt with Doug and was grateful they had been replaced by Bruce's easiness to be with.

Janet, however, at first meeting Bruce, said to me privately, her voice tentative, "Do you know who he reminds me of?"

I waited, anticipating what she would say.

"Doug," she said.

The comment made me uncomfortable. "Maybe it's the height. The moustache."

"Maybe," she said. "But something else, too."

I'm not sure how I felt about this remark, although I told myself maybe that was why decision-making had once been so difficult for me. No one else says such a thing. Beyond those externals— they both wore glasses too, for that matter—the difference in men was pronounced.

We overcame the minor hurdle of incorporating Bruce into my friendships; then we faced my joining his family. His mother, who lived north of Boston, had a birthday in early February and we decided to surprise her with Bruce's physical presence, fearing, at the same time, provoking a heart attack with such a gesture. We arranged the surprise through Bruce's brother Bob, who lived in North Reading with his partner whom I'll call Jim (because of name duplications); we would be staying with them. I phoned my good friend Pam Painter, as well, and let her know I'd be in Boston.

Since we had just the one car, my tinny Toyota Tercel, it was what we drove north through the snow and ice, mostly in the dark since we couldn't start out that Friday until after my day at school. The weather was so frigid that the insides of the car windows were covered with a layer of frost that we had to scrape with our fingernails to peek through.

Bob and Jim, gracious and witty men, welcomed us, late as we were to arrive, to a beautiful guest room in their suburban home. Everything in the room matched: the bedspread to the cornices and drapes, to the pillows and sheets and rugs. I was struck by what a couple without children can afford and can do. Bruce's mother was large of stature and rather commanding of presence but was so happy to see her son again that I, who had brought him to her, was also welcome.

On Saturday afternoon Bruce and I drove into Boston because he wanted a hot fudge sundae at Bailey's—a favorite place of his childhood—and I wanted to see my friend Pam. I felt I kept putting Bruce through litmus tests. Pam was married to a wonderful older man, an editor well known in literary circles, and I, Pam's close friend, was showing up at their Back Bay house with yet another man. I had been there with Doug just four or five months before, with Sam the year before that, and now here I was again, with Bruce.

Pam was always effervescent and welcoming, and Robie more than accepting, yet I was tense as we sat around their formal living room with cocktails. I was worrying about Bruce's silence until I realized he was totally engaged with what Robie had been saying, and while the men had a conversation, Pam and I managed a little tete-a-tete of our own. "You're well out of the Douglas-thing," she told me. "And Robie didn't like Doug at all."

The pronouncement made me uncomfortable and relieved at the same time. I wanted to ask why, what had they seen that I was unable to see at the time, but I let it go. I valued their opinions, but that relationship was the past and I would keep it that way.

Bruce and I walked the Boston Commons in snow and returned to celebrate his mother's birthday at an elegant restaurant Bob and Jim were treating us all to. I was grateful for their generosity and their inclusion, as well as the chance of knowing even better this man I had begun to live with. I was touched by Bruce's tastes—his observation of particular pearls in a store window, his insistence on good boots, his references to books, his ability to hold his own with Robie. We were heartened, both of us, by family and friendship.

One dark Monday, a week later, I drove us over fresh snow and ice to a distant town so Bruce could check out a Lancia, an Italian car

I had never heard of. He was thrilled that he found an ad for such a rare car. It was used, of course, but in good shape, with leather interiors. He and the owner bargain a bit, but the money Bruce had left from selling his Fiat wasn't enough. That time. The man called back in a few days and accepted Bruce's offer, and Bruce acquired a big brown Lancia—a car that would fascinate John when he saw it months later.

Still: there was the matter of a real job, one in a planning department. Bruce had resorted to his make-shift way of earning quick money: picking up bundles of newspapers to cart to news-stands early in the mornings.

23   *Oliver! and More*

Meanwhile, my job—teaching high school—consumes my days. In addition to my English and Dance classes and running the department, I am laboring over the musical *Oliver!*. I have a month to straighten out the crowd scenes. Rehearsals leave me stymied about how to manage so many kids on stage at once, frustrated with students who might or might not show up with any consistency. The show is scheduled for March, and it's already February, and I haven't yet accomplished all the blocking or choreography. I want to cry in frustration.

My leads in the cast are good. Since the high school is attached to a junior high school, we have enlisted ten 7th and 8th graders to be the orphans in the Workhouse. The eighth grader playing the lead, Oliver, is a charmer, his soprano voice high and clear. No problems there. (The fact that he is the son of the burly, loud history teacher is an added piquancy.) The orphans, in other scenes, become Fagin's singing and dancing ragamuffins. And thank god for Torie, who is playing Fagin.

Torie, a senior, was a hit as the Mayor's wife in last year's *The Music Man*. She was brilliant in my English class. One day, prior to tryouts, she stopped me in the hall. "How open-minded are you?" she asked.

I laughed. "I don't know. I try to be."

"I want to play Fagin," she said.

I stared at her. She was pale-complexioned, about my size, fair of hair. Fagin, in the script, is the corrupt old Jewish guy who sends kids out to steal.

"Can I try out?" she asked. I agreed, of course.

She was brilliant again. She could walk in a crouch, talk and sing in a husky low voice. The boys adored her. So: Fagin and the boys were set. Ultimately, in makeup—beard and all—no one knew Tory was female. "Nancy," too, had a great soprano voice. I had to work at "Bill Sykes," her character's tough evil partner, because the boy was gay and had to be a heavy. The high school was small. It's not as though we had endless talent to choose from. But those kids were reliable, eager to perform. It was a large cast, filled in with various degrees of talent, plus all the "townspeople," called upon to react to situation. Then there were the sets.

Every scene required, in addition to new characters, new settings. We had to represent the orphanage, the rich man's house, the street, the tavern, Fagin's den, a bridge for Nancy to jump off (a bridge!) and—early on—the Sowerberrys' undertaking establishment where Oliver had to hide in a coffin. We needed a coffin.

Bruce, my full-time partner now, said he could build me a coffin.

So: on a Sunday afternoon he came to one of these chaotic rehearsals—where the junior high boys when they weren't on stage ran through the aisles; where my colleague Hazel, the choral director, often countered my choreographic ideas because "the singers need to see the conductor;" where the rehearsal pianist said, "I have to go home early today," where the many students who made up the townspeople fooled around with each other and stopped long enough to ask, "Where do I go again?"

Into this chaos, Bruce appeared, through ice and snow, and sawed away backstage at plywood he'd ordered, and built and painted a black coffin that Oliver could hide in.

Who knew?

But my job continues to overwhelm. I must drive over to rehearsals each evening. Bruce gets up before dawn and has taken on another paper-delivery job while he applies for real jobs.

Still, I am happy. We are happy. "I wish I were where I was five years go," he tells me one evening in late February. "Not the person I was—or where I lived—but what I had."

Yes, me too, I think.

One Friday evening we plan to go to Philly to see a colleague's wife in a small opera and are invited to meet up ahead at the RB with others from the music department, including my friend Janet.

As I walk in the door of that familiar bar and restaurant, I immediately see Doug. He is positioned at a small table, somewhat elevated from the bar, facing the door. For a moment the room goes totally out of focus. I should have known. It *was* the RB, but I assumed (maybe?) that he had moved on. He sees me, too, and, after an intense second, averts his eyes.

"Doug's here," I say to Bruce, who is next to me.

"Do you want to leave?"

"No, let's just go to the other end—Janet's over there. Others will join us."

But I have seen myself through Doug's eyes (shallow); I see Bruce, now at the hors d'oeuvres table, through Doug's eyes. Bruce is wearing a suit tonight, tall and composed as he always is, and helping himself to free food (unemployed): that's what I think Doug is thinking.

"So what?" Janet asks, when I confide this thought to her later.

As the evening goes on—the performance in the city, the friends—I forget this scene. I hadn't looked around the RB again until we were leaving, and Doug was no longer there.

It doesn't matter. What matters to me is Bruce.

I can't spend enough time with him and love the way he has become such a big part of my life. We make love every day, sincerely. I have this thought about him and sex: that he is not the best lover I have had but he is the only lover—the only person who ever made love to me, felt sex the way one can feel love or pain. Not an activity, or a ritualistic need, but the expression of feeling.

I never stray again.

With his second part-time job, Bruce, too, is exhausted from petty responsibilities that yield little. Support for his son Preston gets first priority, which I understand, having endured neglected support for my two children for years. I want Preston to be supported. Still: there's that dent in the finances. Bruce has gone to interviews for "good" jobs, but they have so far yielded nothing. He assiduously studies want ads, pecks out his resumes on his electric typewriter, now set up almost permanently on the dining room table.

We are both troubled. Tired. And have endless energy for each other.

Together we have more fun and more enjoyment than I've ever experienced with anyone. He is appreciative of all I do, whatever I cook, is eager to be out and about always. We go to museums, jazz performances, the St. Patrick's Day parade, movies. Susan comes home for a weekend and we play Trivial Pursuit with her and a friend and Janet until after midnight. Every minute is taken up.

One Sunday afternoon Bruce's almost-ex-wife Sharon calls. She tells me she wants to talk to Bruce about money. He's late with money.

I summon Bruce to the phone and watch him wince and listen. I make dinner, tight-lipped and tense, realizing that whatever he intended to give me from his pay will instead go to Sharon/Preston. He returns to the kitchen, shrugs: "I have to do it," he says. Susan is in the next room vacuuming, dusting, alert to any possible tension. She loves Bruce, much to my delight, and doesn't want anything to go awry.

"But I'll work it out," he assures me.

I nod in agreement. He's abandoned his son in Portland. My friends love him, have accepted him. My kids love him. I love him. "I know," I say.

Nothing like this has ever been commonplace to me. "This" equals being a couple who gets along, who share intellect and energy and sex and the rhythms of life.

I had no "mutual" life with the kids' father, whom I initially loved, but who was so totally irresponsible that, as I've said, I was forced to break up that marriage to survive. I had to work, teaching high school, hiring a full-time baby-sitter, turning over my paycheck to him. He was seldom around. I was always lonely. When I got up the courage to leave, the kids were 3 ½ and 5 years old and had always been my sole responsibility anyway.

After the divorce, I married a reliable man, a fellow teacher, who was conscientious and caring. He came with grandparents for my kids, cousins, family, and, although superficially we looked like a unit, sex was almost non-existent and tension plentiful in so many ways. He was obviously gay and fighting against it, but no one talked about it. For the next few years I was miserable until I made plans to move out once again, as difficult as that was with the kids now 11 ½ and 13 years old But he, considerate, said no, that I needed to stay in the house to let the kids continue in the same school system; he would go, and he did.

These were difficult episodes in my and my kids' lives. They were adolescents by then, and I dated several men over several years before I met Sam. Sam and I had a good partnership, I thought, at least for a few years, even though he and I stayed in our own houses. Each of those alliances—two marriages, commitment to Sam— lasted around five years.

Sam's impact was the strongest, on all of us. Our lives over- lapped only a few days of the week, but consistently. We did so much together, and he often included John or Susan—on his boat, or ski- ing, or at his shore house. We'd have pizza together on Sunday nights at my place. He was enormously helpful to me, fixing things around my house, advising and even employing John. I thought all that was working out, but Sam broke up with me, wanting to explore more. He fell out of love. I was crushed, almost annihilated, by that rejection.

Then there was Doug. I think of the hours and hours I sat around with Doug, reading, being together—true—but sitting. The hours in his bed. Of course, there had been several lovely jaunts out of town, and dinners in good restaurants, but he was so often tired from travel, and I'd subdued my energy to his. Besides, I had been preoccupied with all I had to manage at school, the productions, my own graduate courses at Rutgers.

But the likes of Bruce! He consistently surprises and delights me.

We drive on an April weekend to New Hampshire. It's his birthday. We do this by way of stopping again at his mother's and brother's in North Reading and Amherst, Massachusetts.

"Oh, how wonderful this feels!" his mother says, hugging him.

We drive to Portsmouth, to visit Liz, who had been my college roommate. "He's so easy with himself," Liz says. "I mean not only with his size, but easy in himself." I realize that this quality has been what most attracted me from the beginning—Bruce's sense of self. Doug had used the word "self-dom," but about me. He thought I didn't have enough "self-dom," that I undervalued myself. And maybe I did, with him.

I consider some of the adaptations I made to the men I was in love with. Or perhaps thought I was in love with. How would I know? Sam said I had a case of penis envy, an idea that enraged me, although I probably felt some of that with him. He made it clear that as a man he had privileges—privileges that extended from earning power to position in the world to sexual freedoms. Maybe I assigned those same "values" to Doug since he too earned far more money, had more privilege than I did. Both of those men called the shots, so to speak, and both they and I assumed that that was the natural order of things. But, looking back, I think my own behaviors—studying, teaching, putting on shows, managing my family, and so on—challenged those men, forcing us to compete, them to complain, and me to be, perpetually, uneasy.

Bruce, even from a family of sons and having nothing but sons himself, had no such attitude about the roles of the sexes. His good friends from the Portland planning agency, where he'd once been employed, were both men and women. His sense of self was not defined by power. He liked and accepted everything I did. He allowed me to be me.

With Bruce's firm sense of "self-dom," my own emerged. Perhaps this was what I had always wanted: the freedom to be me. I thought of the old Marlo Thomas song on a record I bought the kids years before: "Free to be you and me." What did I originally think "free" meant? Wearing your hair the way you wanted to? Pursuing an activity you liked?

Now I began to realize that freedom came with acceptance, with ease, above all with non-judgment. With Bruce I did not feel judged. I did not have to wait upon a man's "moods." Bruce never had any artifice, and thus I did not either. That was the freedom.

It was new and—well, freeing—and I hoped it would be enough.

24 *Intrusions*

Once the show *Oliver!* reaches the performances, the tensions of getting it together are replaced by the anxiety of worrying how each show will go; I must arrive early to attend to props and kids and costumes and makeup. It's not until the show's third and last night that I become part of the audience, at that point giving up altogether anything I can do. I enjoy sitting in the audience with Bruce and Susan, who is around that weekend and goes with us. I enjoy seeing former students who attend the performances and want to talk to me afterward; I enjoy getting together for drinks with Janet or Barbara or friends after the shows. That part is fun; exhilarating and rewarding.

What is not rewarding are the repercussions. Randy, the principal, summons me into his office and berates me for giving in to Vince's demands for professional players to augment the school orchestra. Vince is the strings teacher, the orchestra director, a man who was totally suspicious of my taking over the chair position, annoyed with the principal for putting me, a mere English teacher, in charge of him, Vince, a musician. I'd worked with Vince on several musicals, but now, remembering his resistance to me, I tried to yield to his requests. Besides, his demands made perfect sense to me: if we wanted the sound of an orchestra, he had to have the instrumental parts covered, at least minimally, right? In several cases we did not have student musicians who could play, say, the complicated violin part, or serve as an accomplished drummer. Vince knew musicians to fill those roles, and I said go ahead, hire them for the musical. I'd gotten permission ahead of time, but now Randy says he didn't realize how much they would cost.

The budget, he reminds me. Yes, I know. What on earth is the choice here?

Even after the musical is over, I have day-to-day pressures. I need a new routine for the dancers in the elementary dance class. I can't find the time to create one since every moment at school is committed to some project—my English papers and lessons, the bulletin board in the lobby, the department meetings and supply orders, conferences with students, with staff.

I rush from teaching a new step of the number "All That Jazz" to my advanced dance class on the school stage (where the dance classes take place), to changing my clothes in my little office, then hurrying to a classroom to talk about the themes in *Jude the Obscure* in my honors English class. Those roles are fun. Then I must make calls about new equipment and meet with Dennis, the band director, during his prep period about the field trip for student musicians to the Philadelphia Orchestra rehearsal, the forms, the permission slips, the buses. There is the after-school meeting with the music teachers and their scheduling demands for the next semester, before I finally drive home to fix dinner. I love the students in the dance classes, adore the students in my English class, get tense facing the music teachers, and, paradoxically, am bored sitting through the Department Chair Meetings, a group I longed to be a part of. I wait to be summoned, which I am regularly, to the principal's office to be lectured on the budgets. I even entertain the vain notion that since I often have to report to Randy's office in my dance tights and leotard, maybe he just wants to see me.

Randy arranges yet another meeting for us, this time to approach the superintendent to enlarge my department. As we walk from one building to another to get to that meeting, Randy takes the opportunity to ask why I had to hire a rehearsal piano accompanist for the musical. Wasn't there a student who could play? I try arguing the complications of the music score and the time commitment, but he's convinced I'm splurging for no reason. He even suggests that we probably didn't need music to rehearse a musical.

I lose sleep that night, composing a letter that I will write apologizing to the principal, vowing to try harder. I fret with Hazel, the vocal teacher, over the lack of spirit in her concert choir and what to do about it. Randy likes my letter of apology, but waxes on about management and obedience. I get pains in my stomach, which make matters worse.

I debate quitting the chair position. I'd always love teaching and still do: my English class, my dance classes. I like the fact that I have a leadership position, but I guess I hadn't realized how much it would entail, how personalities would get so involved, how the "job description" seemed to have no boundaries.

Maybe Randy hadn't taken seriously my own background in music, didn't consider that I'd go to bat for the music teachers when the previous chair had been passive, timid, returned moneys in his budgets that he never spent. I hate confronting the constant tensions, even the pettiness, hate dealing with my headaches and stomach aches. One day there is a minor crisis with Hazel over buses to transport the junior high chorus to a local mall for a spring concert; that afternoon through the auditorium lobby windows I watch their departure, leaning my head against the window in relief that they are finally leaving, out of my hair—so to speak—for a while. I devote my afternoon prep period to cutting out letters to put together a new display for the glassed-in lobby bulletin board. A teacher passes by and points out that I'm making a bit of a mess with those clippings: do I plan to clean that up? I almost cry.

But beyond all this, each day I come home to him. Him! There's never been anyone like Bruce, his endless energy, his love for me, my love for him. My non-rehearsal evenings are totally his, as are the complete weekends, the mornings and nights—even afternoons, when we have a chance—in bed. I remain thoroughly in love with him and just deal with the school situation because I must. It's what earns me a paycheck.

One Sunday afternoon we drive to Brandywine Park and lie in the grass, me in my new sweater with the embroidered cherries and he stretched out beside me, leaning on an elbow, reading the brochure of the battle maneuvers. I feel that someone could take our photo as an example of compatibility, ease. We stop in a Revolutionary-vintage saloon for drinks and snacks and head home, and the following Sunday, another gorgeous day, drive to Atlantic City and walk the entire boardwalk, in and out of casinos, collecting the free parking and free food coupons and eating hotdogs and cookies, like kids. We drive to the charming town of New Hope another day, and sidetrack to a place called Peddler's Village to watch square dancing and eat chocolate-covered strawberries.

I fight against intruding images: the rolls of quarters Sam would hand to me so readily in a casino, or the dinner Doug insist we have in New Hope or elsewhere. But Doug is over, in the past. Sam is in the past. Those tensions are in the past. Why do they intrude?

I am here in the now and I am in love and happy and why do I analyze it? Because it seems too simple, too easy? Because we keep waiting for Something—like a real job—to happen?

Then Bruce does get an interview for a real job, meaning a planning job, minor but in his field. The opportunity excites us both. We celebrate its possibilities with Big Macs, and a few days later he is told he has been hired. Life is moving on—his, anyway. My own, at school, is weighted by rehearsals and concerts and meetings and budgets and field trips and confrontations and classes and faculty and buses and bulletin boards: but at the end of each of my days, he is there.

I consider purchasing a new sofa, maybe even two. My old ones are quite worn. "Maybe by fall," I say. I turn to him, suddenly, remembering my haughtiness in January of telling him we'd give it six months. "Fall," I repeat. "You will be around this fall?"

"And the fall after that and the fall after that," he says. "Do you want me around?"

Do I want? I want and I want and my wants are fulfilled. Who knew life could be like this?

Suddenly we are given a full a weekend in New York City, paid for by the recent job Bruce has acquired. I am grateful, but the trip does not reassure me. The hotel room might have been "free," but beyond that we are on our own. Sam had several times presented me with a Christmas present that amounted to sets of theater tickets and a "weekend in New York City." That meant he'd purchased those tickets, acquired the hotel, took me to meals—twice at the World Trade Center—made the arrangements. Bruce and I are a bit at bay on this trip, wondering where to eat, where to park the car, what we can afford to do.

"Have you seen Grand Central?" Bruce asks me, and, on our way there, I recognize the plush hotel Doug and I once stayed at. "We can walk around," Bruce suggests. "Look at its remodeling, its ceiling."

On this trip Bruce and I take paper bags of wine and snacks to our room at the St. Regis. We find cheap restaurants to eat at, delis, diners; determine which day the Modern Art Museum is free. We cannot stop for drinks at the Algonquin, which I long to do; they'd be too much money. In rebellion, I charge tickets for *Sunday in the Park with George*, aware that they are the first show tickets *I* have ever paid for.

I remind myself, as well, of the general uneasiness and often dissatisfaction I felt with those other men, and remind myself that this man, Bruce, in his sense of self and acceptance, his reliability, is worth so much more. What worth am I measuring? I dislike myself for even thinking these things.

Bruce suddenly says to me, "Sometimes, even when you're with me, when you're present, I feel that you're absent, that you're not over Sam—or Doug. I feel I'm competing."

Oh, my God! I deny that, deny the truth.

He is trying. He is following through on everything he promised: keeping his end of the bargain, finding a job. He loves me. I love him.

And, I tell myself, tell my inner voices: *just shut up.*

One day, in late Spring, I phone to tell Bruce that Janet and I are having a drink together right after school and that I'll be home a little later. I feel freed, really, from the fact that I do not have after school rehearsals or any evening duties at the school, nor any place I have to be.

I feel good, settled in a way. Bruce and I just celebrated our "four-month anniversary" of living together the weekend before.

It's a Thursday afternoon, and I've agreed to meet Janet, whom I'd spent so much time with before Bruce. As it turns out, our "date" cannot have been much fun for her—the old RB, an easy middle ground for us, is fairly deserted on an early weekday afternoon, and I'm sure she tires of hearing how happy I am.

When I return home around 5:30, Bruce looks anxious. "You're home," he says. I sense tension in his voice.

"I was boring Janet, I think." I flop my handbag on the living room desk. "And the place was pretty much empty. No snacks, no music." I kiss him on the cheek in greeting.

"Oh," he says. He looks upset.

I laugh. "What? Were you picturing me surrounded by men—by—"

"It's not men," he says, interrupting. "It's Douglas. I can't stand being so jealous."

What? He totally surprises me with this comment. The idea also makes me nervous, even as I find it mildly flattering. I begin dinner preparations, pretending to be indifferent, but tuned in to what he is saying.

"That day you and I went to the RB—to meet your friends," he blurts. "And you saw him—"

I nod. I remember.

"I saw your face then. His face too—before he looked away. That was a look of love."

I feel my eyes widen at this observation; fortunately, I'm not facing Bruce.

"And I knew then," he continues, his voice tense, "that whatever was there, whatever happened, wasn't entirely over."

I can't think how Bruce could be right—or wrong, for that matter. I look at him, shake my head in denial, dismissal.

"I just don't want you to see him," he concludes sadly, as though he is miserable with himself for feeling this way and admitting it.

I feel sad, too, because he is always perceptive.

"I'm not," I say, but it isn't enough.

We get through the evening and later struggle with lovemaking a bit before we both relax again. It's been a minor crisis. He's right that he hadn't known how deeply I had been involved.

He's also right that "whatever" would never be entirely "over;" but it was done, finished.

The Summer of 1985

25 *"Home"*

In late May Susan returns from college for the summer and gets a job at a pizza place. I'm troubled by the weight she's gained, and I say things like "College food must really be good," or "Will the pizza place allow you to have all the pizza you want?" These remarks accomplish nothing and cause more embarrassment to all of us: her because she's helpless, me because I am so judgmental, Bruce because he's forced to witness us.

Preston, now almost sixteen, arrives in early July for a two-week stay. He is tall and awkward and finds me lacking at every turn. "Yuk!' he says about the corn on the cob I'm making. "I can't stand that!" Bruce forewarned me that Preston lives pretty much on Oreos and classic Cokes, which I've supplied. "I'll never have a cheap car like this!" he says of my old Tercel. Preston is forced to ride in the back when we drive to his grandmother's house, Bruce's mother's, or, more precisely, the house of Bob and Jim, outside Boston. He takes his skateboard with him, spinning the wheels when he's just sitting with it.

Around his grandmother Preston likes corn on the cob; he loves it. We have a cookout in Bob and Jim's backyard. Preston's cousins Jerry and Sarah, the teenage children of Bruce's older brother who died a few years before, are there, and he has people his age to be occupied with.

Sitting in a lawn chair, I pull the standing Bruce down onto my lap.

"What are you doing?" his mother exclaims. She looks to others for corroboration of the un-ladylike action she's witnessed.

"I like holding him," I say in my defense, my defiance, really. Bruce is large, but I love having my legs smashed against the lawn chair's webbing by his long thighs. I love leaning the side of my face against his broad back. It's been six months, and I still can't get enough of him.

"Well," she says. But she is not disapproving. We laugh.

That summer, the summer of 1985, I apply to take another Shakespeare Seminar, this one offered through New Jersey Humanities Council and held at Rutgers, Camden, where I have been going to grad school. The seminar deals with Shakespeare's history plays studied in the chronological order of their kings, and, although it offers less than a third of the money that the NEH did the previous year at Reed College, and although Camden, New Jersey, is a far cry from Portland, Oregon, the project—Shakespeare again—excites me. Of course I miss those vast green lawns and classic buildings of Reed, but I like the classroom here, too. Rutgers University in Camden actually carved out a great expanse of campus in the city's slum area. One enters a different world—landscaping, classroom buildings, a theater, library, law school, all bordered by brick streets and crumbling old houses.

I report to the campus three hours a day, five days a week, for four weeks. I love it. The seminar is conducted by both a history professor and an English professor and includes a number of guest lecturers and films. What is missing for me is the enthusiasm of the participants. There are again fifteen of us, but only half are Shakespeare devotees. The others? Teachers who signed up for the money, I assume. As a group they are an unexciting contrast to the fascinating individuals of the Reed group. But I am happy enough with the seminar in the afternoons and Bruce to come home to.

I missed one Monday's session, the weekend we took Preston to Boston, but I met John at Harvard that weekend (John stayed in Cambridge with a summer job at the university) and attended a seminar with him on Joyce's *Ulysses*. My cup runneth over, so to speak, with stimulation.

Preston's criticism in those weeks, though, have worn me down. I brace myself for his negative response to everything I do and try not to mind; Susan and my bickering must wear on Bruce. When Preston leaves, John returns for several weeks and things pick up a bit, although I wonder whether Bruce is jealous of the camaraderie John and I have. Of course, he is not; he gets along with John just fine and both kids really like having Bruce there in the house.

However, during that summer, the summer of 1985, the suburbs, where I've been living all my adult life, begin to wear on me. I remember how much fun it was to live in the middle of Portland, to walk out the door into the city. Here, either alone or with others, I spend so much time driving back and forth, not just to the high school, or now to Camden every day for the seminar, but frequently across the bridge to Philadelphia, where the museums and theaters and entertainments are. I think that maybe, since the kids are finishing college, Bruce and I might consider moving to the city, getting a modern condo. I'd still have my New Jersey position, and perhaps he'd be promoted in his new job. It would be a slightly longer commute across the bridge each day, but we could do it.

I run the idea by Bruce.

"Philadelphia?" he says. "You want to move to Philadelphia?" He stares at me briefly, as though assessing if I mean it. Then he says, "If you want to live in a city, why don't we consider a really beautiful city? What about San Francisco?"

I'm a bit aghast. "What? I've never even been to San Francisco. I'm not even sure where it is."

He smiles. "It's in California." Well, I knew that much.

He'd visited the city once. He tells me I would love it. Seized with sudden enthusiasm, he suggests we can at least look at San Francisco, take a vacation there. "Why not this summer?' he says.

This is all a bit sudden, but I'm open to the idea. A vacation. We'll take a vacation for a few weeks in August. Why not? We pool our slim resources (my "pay" has been the money from the Shakespeare seminar at Rutgers) and plan another "budget trip"—this time to California. This trip will be a replication, in a way, of our trip around Canada the year before. School doesn't start for me until after Labor Day; he can ask for a two-week leave from his part-time position. We pack suitcases, not just with clothes, but with his old tent, our mismatched sleeping bags, and my coffee maker. We purchase stand-by airfares, which were possible then. Our biggest anticipated expense will be renting a car.

Maybe it's the anticipation of going to the West Coast again that causes me to turn to him one morning, alarmed. "I had a terrible dream," I tell him. "I dreamt that you went home."

"Home!" He scoffs. "Home is where you are, Honey."

Home is where we are. As we approach the trip to San Francisco at the end of summer, 1985, I have no idea that the idea of "home" will, in a year, shift so radically.

26   *Gone and Back Again*

Before we travel that late August, I must meet with Randy, my principal. For the three years I have been "acting chair" of the "Performing Arts" department that he put into place, he has been encouraging innovations, praising my efforts. At the same time, he has scolded me for draining my budgets and wants to get all the issues straight before the new school year, a year when he has, at the same time, added the two art teachers and renamed the department "Performing *and* Fine Arts." His metaphors for my culpability are cruel: "The school board is out for your blood," he says. "Maybe your skin, too." The extreme addition was perhaps because I didn't react enough to the first phrase. In fact, I do not react because I don't know what to say. Do I say, "I'll be good"—like a contrite child? In a way that is what I do. I apologize. I also suspect he exaggerates in order to seem heroic to me, one who is blocking my interference, to borrow a phrase from another department.

I assure him I will be more diligent with bookkeeping and spending when the fall semester begins.

With that unpleasant obligation behind me, I welcome the few weeks left of summer and our sudden escape to California. The vacation is also a searching, an experiment. Bruce really thinks that we could consider moving to San Francisco. Philadelphia, is, as I also realize, an extension of my old life and not a move worth uprooting for. Portland, which I'd loved the previous summer, is out because Bruce doesn't want the proximity of his ex-wife or the rains; I don't want them either. But San Francisco? Well, I've agreed to check it out. It's just a vacation, right, a look around?

The implications of an "experiment," however, have not been lost on Susan. She fears I will like the West Coast—as indeed I'd liked it the previous summer when I extended the six-week seminar to eight weeks and delayed coming home. She fears I will leave the East Coast for good, give up our home here.

"I have two more years of college," she reminds me. "You wouldn't really move there if you liked it, would you? I mean, I'm working a hard job, too. I'm trying."

Of course, I am aware that her summer job involves long shifts. And she is aware that my school responsibilities of late have pretty much exhausted me. But, even mildly annoyed that she equated her ringing up pizza orders with my managing all I do at school, I understand her anxiety, the one over "home." When I say something very simple, such as, "I went home early Tuesday," or she says something equally simple: "I left my sweater at home," the word "home" pierces me. Would I ever really give up our home of twenty years? How can I even think of such a thing? Well, I will not, I vow. I will go with this man I love so much to visit San Francisco and the Bay Area, as he calls it, and come home. It's my home and I will come back to it, even though, frankly, I am tired of the school, both its sameness and its tensions. I'm weary of the sameness of the flat suburbs, too.

Here is the scene one evening: John calls from Cambridge, humiliated by something that happened at his Delphic Club. He is despondent. I feel his pain as though it were my own. I feel, I feel. I want to offer him the refuge of home—that piercing word again. That evening Susan and I play Scrabble—surrounded by our furniture and the familiarity of all things. Bruce sits in a chair, reading, and smiles at me, and I feel—what?—a shiver, a quaking, a fever, all through me. I love him. I'll go anywhere with him.

But then I look at her as she contemplates the tiles of letters, look at her shiny hair. I am almost crying—over John's pain, over losing her, over giving up all this—no, I cannot, *I cannot*. I will not. I'm not going anywhere.

Our San Francisco tickets are paid for. "It's just for two weeks," I suddenly say to her, and she looks up across the Scrabble board, having lost the context, but understands, and nods.

How can I even consider risking my own job and salary to put myself into Bruce's once tenuous situation, just because I have the idea that my present environment is getting stifling, limiting? Wouldn't I be confining myself all the more?

"It's just a vacation," I tell Susan.

Our flight lands in Oakland, California, on August 15, 1985, a full year after we'd returned to his apartment in Portland from our adventuresome sojourn in Canada. Now a new issue becomes not just a possibility of the two of us being together, but of where we would ultimately live. We were—or at least he was—on a West Coast mission to judge the possibilities of moving there, living there. In Oakland we acquired a car to rent, a motel room for the night some-where near the Coliseum and drove into San Francisco. In 1985 one could do that easily—there was little traffic, and the Bay Bridge was near at hand. Already the sweep of San Francisco Bay had me star-ing, almost gaping. People lived here?

I was charmed by the San Francisco houses, perched in rows on hillsides, their shutters and gables and brightly painted colors, and wished the kids were with me. Susan would love these houses, wouldn't she? I wished John could see the expanse of Bay, of scen-ery. I felt selfish touring the country once again on my own, without them. I pronounced the houses in the Marina District "cute"—with their stucco exteriors and tiled steps curving to a door and seem-ingly smaller than my New Jersey house. I wondered if I could adjust to smaller living. What a joke that turned out to be. This was San Francisco; the Marina houses were worth four or five times that of my New Jersey house.

I was enchanted with San Francisco and the entire Bay Area, no doubt about that. Who wouldn't be? It was clean and bright and colorful and cool—cool! After the muggy 95-degree weather we'd left in New Jersey, I felt I was traveling around in perpetual air conditioning, a Disneyworld sort of setting. There was so much to see. After breakfast we drove through Oakland to the UC Berkeley campus. Then we crossed the San Rafael bridge and the Golden Gate (so gorgeous! so easily done—far fewer cars in 1985) into San Francisco and picnicked on the Marina Green with sandwiches we bought walking the streets: Bay, Chestnut, Divisidero.

We drove to the seaside town of Pacifica, stopping for chocolate ice cream cones, walked along the ocean side there, then headed back up to Golden Gate Park and the Japanese Tea Garden and walked amid flowers and lakes. The following day we drove up to Napa and the wineries (the songs of "The Most Happy Fella" going through my head) and took the arduous, curving road to the coast to Mendocino, stopping in the woods to make love. We were having such a good time. We would spend the third evening in the Oakland motel, but we wanted to go beyond the city—so many destinations on Bruce's itinerary—and our budget forced us to camp if we wanted to explore.

We drove down the Pacific coast to stunning Monterey and, along the 17-mile drive to the more stunning Carmel, finally crossing over to San Luis Obispo to some obscure campground. We were heartened again the next day, heading to Santa Barbara, visiting Solvang on the way and getting totally sticky with a bakery confection we bought for breakfast, which we ate sitting at the curb. We were like children. Everything was blazingly, dazzlingly, beautiful: the ocean, the palm trees, the coastal rocks, the bright blue sky, the clear air. We camped around Big Sur.

On our way back to the city we had to resort to a KOA campground in Gilroy, where the air reeked of garlic. (A waiter in an Italian restaurant, when we asked, was surprised: "Gilroy *is* the garlic capital of the world," he said, as though we should know this.) Returning to San Francisco once again, we toured Alcatraz and stayed—gratefully—in a motel before setting off for Lake Tahoe and Yosemite Park, more and more wonders of nature. We did so much driving in one day that it was very dark by the time we got to a campsite on the other side of Yosemite. We had to try to erect a tent by flashlight; a nearby camper helpfully held a lantern for us.

Finally, it was time for us to go home. What did I think of San Francisco, this area?

The Bay Area seemed to a combination of the excitement of New York City, the light of Athens, the greenness of Portland. This was an amusement park, I thought, and not a place to live, not really, and yet people were walking the streets of the city as though the setting was ordinary. I discovered that property values were beyond what I ever considered anyone would pay for anything. Rentals, too, were drastically high. These we checked in newspaper want ads as a sort of amusement.

I'd managed to call John, talk to Susan, at least. The children were fine—Susan was still working and had a friend staying with her; John was still in Cambridge. Bruce, whom I'd known for a year and yet forever, was with me here, having a good time, but my life of physical comfort—the one I could manage—was back in New Jersey.

I concluded that the Bay Area was fun for a vacation, but there was nowhere for us to live.

San Francisco? Impossible. I needed to go home.

And yet, when we returned to New Jersey, it seemed flatter, duller than I remembered, much, much hotter—grass more desiccated, air stickier. I wondered how I—we—would ever recover the money we had spent. And now I faced a new school year with both relief that I had a job and dread that I had to do it.

On the first day back at the high school I found out that Dennis, the band director—my favorite person in the department— was leaving. He'd sought out a better-paying job at another district school. I considered that he had had the nerve to do what I was only vaguely considering doing, and I felt both jealous of his move and bereft of him. He made me wonder: could I ever "transfer?" In my case it would be across country—to nothing. Could I do that? More immediately, I wondered how I would manage to run the department without Dennis's competence, his humor, his acceptance of all I do. Who would be hired in his stead?

His exodus nudged me to think about the possibility of leaving, too.

John returned at the end of August for a few weeks and was happy to be home. "I like this place," he announced, surprising even himself with the discovery. He had recently had to try to get an apartment in Cambridge that he could afford, cramped with roommates. But what he said was not what I wanted to hear.

Bruce and I were now discussing a move, not to Philadelphia close by as I'd originally suggested, or to Portland, where we'd "lived" before, but actually to California. The thought was enticing in several ways. There was the thrill of a possible new job, the temptation to just pack up and escape my school responsibilities and constant tensions. Wouldn't that be something to announce? There was also the temptation of a new and beautiful place to live. The climate and beauty of San Francisco was compelling.

As I ran from stage to classroom, from meeting to meeting, I imagined myself making such an announcement to the staff: *I am leaving.* I'd be astounding everyone with my sudden verve—or nerve—the fact that I could consider doing any such thing. I had been at the school seventeen years, part of it as an institution, almost.

At the same time, I now regarded everything I had in my present life with love: my simple home, my familiar stage and classroom and office, my salary, my friends. John really liked having Bruce around. Susan had gone back to college, secure in a home to return to.

But I! Throughout the fall of 1985 I agonized over location the way I once agonized over men. *I will leave! No, I can't, I can't.*

I did not want to take another $300 supervisory course, though, which was required to maintain my department chair status. I balked at preparing myself to do what I did not want to continue doing. Resigned to continuing the status quo, I signed up for a course on Supervision at Glassboro College, along with my friend Barbara, who was the English chair. I was disappointed in myself. But this was our home, I reiterated. To emphasize that idea, on the drive with John to Newark, where he could get a plane back to Boston, he randomly remarked, "I've come to realize my mom's an intellectual. Sometimes you out-Harvard Harvard. I come home to that." Home! A place both children assumed they could return to.

Now it was just Bruce and me in that "home," and I realized the decision was not just mine, but also his. It had been so long since I had been a couple (if I ever truly was) that I didn't always remember to think in terms of "we," of "us." Bruce came to New Jersey for me; now he wanted "us," together, to make a new home in San Francisco. I believed in him; I just didn't believe in me. I didn't believe that I was capable of so extreme a change.

27   *December Reflections*

One Saturday in mid-December, that same year of 1985, Bruce and I drive from Cherry Hill to New York City again, this time just for the day. Rockefeller Square is cold and Christmas-y and, unfortunately, also conjures images of Doug, here to haunt me like an old ghost. But they are also here to remind me once again of how close I came to not using my ticket a year ago to suddenly fly to Portland, to Bruce. It's a year later, and I am only too aware of how close I came to losing Bruce. I wavered. I dithered. I hung around Doug's townhouse as though something would happen that would justify my "choosing" him, Doug, at the time.

I'm overwhelmed with relief, with gratitude, that Bruce is standing next to me.

He and I watch the skaters, find hot chocolate inside, walk the Manhattan streets, hand in hand. He says to me, "It'll be a good Christmas. Although it will be hard to beat last Christmas. You were the best gift I ever had."

We have a family Christmas, at least in the morning when we eat the "Santa" chocolate chip cookies (set out the night before, as usual) while we open gifts, before our breakfast of bacon and scrambled eggs, English muffins. Bruce has phone calls to make to his sons and his mother, then, as usual, we all take off again, John and Susan to their friends' or maybe their dad's, Bruce and I to see a Kurosawa movie in Philly. "You're going to a movie on Christmas?" his mother says, a bit aghast. We are amused. I of course also talk on the phone to my own mother who is hoping that I will continue to work things out well this time (after my failed marriages and relationships, which she had a hard time understanding), with this new partner . When

Bruce and I are alone, he gives me an antique ring, suggesting we could maybe think about marrying. I still wear the ring.

A few weeks later, on January 26, 1986, we celebrate the anniversary of a whole year of living together. All of my then-fears have been totally unrealized. When I think about all that useless trepidation, that horrible, haunting hesitation about Bruce moving in with me, I consider that I might now be on the brink of making such a close-call decision again.

This new one has become enormous. The decision involves actually leaving New Jersey to live in San Francisco. Bruce wants to give the idea serious consideration, and I agree. I agree *to give consideration to* such a move. I do consider it.

The allure of that beautiful place—its weather, its ocean and hills, the city itself—is strong. The acting out of that allure seems far too enormous, though, the risks too high, the physicality of it too insurmountable. Nevertheless, I do at least try to weigh the pros and cons.

And I weigh them all the time. I think that maybe a year's insecurity or apprehension would be a good counterbalance to almost twenty years entrenchment in the same job. But I argue against myself as well, noting that one year is not like another at the school and never has been. I've taught so many different courses over the years, and now my position is creative and different from anything that it had been before. I argue (to myself) the fact that the building is the same dull place, and I'm dealing with the same people. Sometimes I even cringe as I pull into the parking lot, the same assigned slot, enter the same door. My rebuttal becomes, So what? You'd risk everything because you're tired of the parking lot?

I bring in my responsibility as a mother. Haven't I done enough with that job? At what point am I finished? I hear that answer, too: *never, really.* And besides, do I think that I've succeeded so well that I can dust off my hands and just walk away? Besides, I don't *want* to walk away from my children. I don't want that at all.

I argue the settings. Philadelphia is drab, the whole area has limitations; it's flat, dull—although I've managed to have a good time living next to it. Then I remember Portland and its greenness; I remember San Francisco Bay, the hills. I was so free in Portland! Was it just the seminar? Or was that happy sensation a taste of freedom that could actually be mine in San Francisco? I loved it, true, but we struggled to finance even a two-week vacation there.

I drive to school, to my dance routines, my English papers, the bulletin board in the lobby; I stay for rehearsal and tell myself: I won't think about it! Not yet! But it's all I think about.

January, when I'd first agreed to "consider," has become February and then March, and I continue to agonize: to stay or to go? My stomach hurts all the time, a lingering indigestion. I make doctor appointments: what's wrong with me?

It turns out there's nothing wrong with me physically.

What's going to become the gravest of anguish to me is my inability to summon the courage it will take to leave a life and a job, both of which I find confining, to take a risk at trying something else, somewhere else. Somewhere foreign and expensive, like California.

I debate and debate. I am again reminded of the other major decision I made, the one that was enormous at the time: between Doug and Bruce. Would staying in New Jersey be like choosing Doug, which, in that case, would have been an uncomfortable super-ficial status quo? (That's assuming it lasted.) Or, would going to San

Francisco be like taking the Christmas-day plane to Portland to Bruce, to the chance of real love?

I am breathless with the close call of not having Bruce at all.

Maybe he's right: maybe together we can do anything. At 44 years of age, I have never before had this sense of "togetherness," wholeness, and am not sure how to proceed with it

Everything I do seems to go into the caldron of making a decision. When Bruce and I travel to Washington, D.C. for a long weekend, a bonus for his new position, and we enjoy the National Galleries and a big reception and even are able to get together with friends of mine from the past—I think, Yes, this life has much to offer me right here. No need to leave it.

Then I return to school and am so depressed over all I cannot control that I want to run, run, run. The show—*Anything Goes*—is awful; the show's "producer," that is, a teacher who has newly assumed the position, doesn't understand the responsibilities that go with the title. We need the set, which is not built. How much can I nag the man? And the kids in the chorus! Some push forward, wanting to be in the front row; few follow directions at all. The tap dancers—sixteen of them—never all report at the same time, and I can't imagine what the routine will look like when they are all there. Some haven't even been there to learn the steps. I ask about the costumes— the ones I designed and bought the fabric for. Various people are sewing these outfits and I have no sense of the progress. "I think my mother's working on it," is the closest I get to an answer.

In addition to my classes, I'm now managing the "Fine" as well as "Performing" Arts Department—the principal folded in the art teachers with the music teachers after all. This addition has caused me more accounts to draw on, to balance. I am reprimanded in new directions: now I'm behind in my observations, a responsibility that involves sitting in on a teacher's class for a full class period and writing up an evaluation. Those observations are one of the time-consuming duties of the job, and my days are too filled already.

With the musical I need to arrange two assemblies (high school, grade schools), put together programs, write-ups, photos. "I can't I can't I can't" becomes the rhythmic mantra of my heels in the hallways. At these times I think I have to leave, I have to get out of here. Move to San Francisco. Move anywhere—escape!

Of course, I also ask myself why I feel this way now—why didn't the setting, the job, bother me in the recent previous years? I think the answer was that I was preoccupied with completing my master's degree, and my children were constant, self-sufficient, and there. I was also focused so much on Doug, or Sam before him, on what they felt, what I felt, where I "fit." Now, there was a sense of completion of one phase of my life: I had the degree; the kids were moving on, too, or would be, soon. I had the great partnership with Bruce, and my entire focus was now on the job, on the setting. I began to question a life without taking chances. Would I regret it? Why not take this chance?

Then I am pulled back once again. John, having completed his studies at Harvard, comes home for a while; Susan returns for a weekend and is helpful, even cleaning our refrigerator before John drives her back to college, which he volunteers to do. When I hear John move about the kitchen, open a cabinet for a glass, turn on the faucet, hit the buzzer for the microwave, I think: this is their home. I can't walk out on their home; *I can't.*

By March of 1986, Bruce and I had almost switched places. He now had an excellent job, and it was only I who was unhappy with mine. Bruce had been promoted to City Manager of the small and charming town in New Jersey where he first worked as a minor planner. In the planner position his admirable achievement had been the concept and the building of a fountain in the town square. Now he had his own office, a fine salary, and a company car—a brand new Chevrolet sedan. Every reason to stay.

And yet, in spite of this security, by the time *Anything Goes* was performed, and I'd taught sixteen dancers to tap dance—as well as choreographed and directed the entire musical—by that time, Bruce and I were leaning heavily in the direction of leaving, of moving to San Francisco.

Anything Goes, which would become one of the highlights of my limited high school musical career, thoroughly exhausted me. For every rehearsal I tapped furiously along with all those tap dancers I was teaching; I finished some of their costumes, sewed satin on the top hats myself. The dancing, I must admit, I loved. I wanted to be one of those dancers, just tapping away, and not be responsible for the whole show, the whole production. Bruce helped to paint the sets, helped make the flat plywood "life-preservers" that introduced all the major characters with their names, one by one, in the show's beginning. I was buoyed up and near collapse with *Anything Goes*—tacked on, as it was, to the other responsibilities of my English class, my two dance classes, running the now-enlarged department—and I was easily brought to question whether there wasn't a simpler way to live or make a living.

On the other hand, I considered the security of my job: my tenure was solid. I'd completed my master's degree and required supervisory courses and could now command the full salary of a "Chair." In addition, Bruce had the great new position. Why would I—we—give all this up?

On the other hand (one more hand here), didn't I yearn for the challenge, yearn for adventure? Wasn't I capable of being a person who dared to do something different? I remember envying my friend K.E. when she moved with her new husband to Germany— across the ocean, yet! I thought of my parents, particularly my Dad, who would have loved to have done something different, but they remained cramped in that little house because they had no opportunities or money to do anything else. I *could* do something different, couldn't I? Wouldn't they—the people I left behind at the school—all be surprised? The drama coach in me, I have to admit, anticipated a reaction from my friends, my colleagues—my *audience*—pictured them agog. I scripted in my head their reactions: *She's leaving? Seriously? She's a staple in our school! How can she leave? Who will replace her? What nerve! What courage.*

There was also the voice that said, *Sounds pretty stupid and risky, if you ask me. And with this new guy? Yet another man? Good lord.*

About the musical Randy, the principal, calls me "the miracle worker." He's never seen the likes of all those tap dancers on stage, the full chorus choreographed (finally!) behind and around the dancers. He is overwhelmed. At the same time he slaps my wrists (figuratively) and reminds me that the school board members are unhappy with paying for—once again—the few outside musicians hired to augment the school orchestra. Must I push all my budgets to their limits? I thought that was what the money was there for, I offer meekly. He stares at me a second and acquiesces somewhat. "Yes, those budgets. But you went beyond—Okay—you got approval, but it still was *beyond*." I can't do anything except agree. Since he has me there, he interjects, irrelevantly, Have I done the requisite observations of all the teachers this semester? Am I working on them? And what about the parents—did I answer Mrs. Brown's request to give her son another extension in my honors English class? He doesn't want her calling *him* again. But: great show, don't know how you did it.

I take deep breaths: am I "doing" it? Can I go on?

I consider the reasons why I must go on. For one thing, Bruce and I have a rich life together right here: We do and have done everything—plays, museums, gardens in the Philadelphia and Bucks County areas, weekends in New York, in Washington, and, occasionally, in Boston, where his mother and brother and my friend all live. And the families have folded in: Preston would be visiting us for a month in the summer; John, having finished his studies, has moved back home temporarily; Susan often comes home on weekends. Surely these are good enough reasons to stay here. Yet I want to escape; I yearn for a change.

John Milton's line occurs to me: "The mind is its own place and in itself can make a hell of heaven, a heaven of hell." I wonder: which will be the heaven, which the hell? To stay or to go?

That Spring we decide. We will go. I ask myself, how will I know if I do not try? How can I exist with the "What If" or "If Only" premises for the rest of my life?

I set up a compromise of sorts. I agree that, with my own "insurance policies" in place, *I will try for one year.* I will give San Francisco a one-year trial. I will apply to my district office for a year's leave of absence; my contract allows that option and guarantees a job if I return within a year. I would not resume my current leadership position, but I would be given a teaching schedule. Bruce will simply have to give notice and that will be final, a situation I see as a real loss. My own further "insurance" is to rent my house on a one-year lease. Thus, I will have the security of a job and a place to live if this lark to San Francisco does not work out.

"It'll work out, Honey," Bruce says. "You saw the city. We'll live right there, walk around in the evenings. We'll figure out a way to manage. It'll be an adventure." I concede: I'll risk a one year "adventure."

That means we will have to prepare my house to be rented. When I survey the contents of that house—the accumulation of over twenty years in one place—I find it impossible to think about ever emptying it. Each room suggests its own inventory: the end tables in both the living room and rec room have stored photo albums, souvenirs, school report cards, picture frames, knick-knacks. The dresser drawers in each of our rooms are filled to overflowing. There is my sewing area at one side of the rec room—with its drawers of patterns and sewing accessories, the laundry room, which also has a closet of shelves holding extra canned goods, tools, rags. The bookcases in the rec room filled with books. I haven't even considered the bedroom closets—clothes, clothes, clothes—or the big storage areas above them, the garage with its paints, tools, old sporting equipment and its loft holding the big fake Christmas tree. Files, desks with drawers. Dishes, linens. I get a headache just thinking about it all.

The final day on which I absolutely must put in a request for a leave of absence, the deadline for doing such a thing, is a day I seem to function under water. It is the last day of March, and I wade through some sort of atmosphere, some thickened substance that isn't the air I generally breathe. That day I robotically visit the superintendent's office, fill in blanks on papers to be submitted to the school board. Eighteen years I have been at that school. I have the sense of watching myself, of not even being there. But I am there, and I do it. I go through those motions. I of course tell Randy, my principal, who is now flummoxed. "How to replace all you do?" he wonders aloud. I shrug. I don't know.

I am breathless and elated at the same time. The principal's dismay, now his seeming admiration of me—that part is over with. Of course, I have the school's semester to finish, and I feel compelled to keep up with it all, to do my best, to make them really miss me.

But the house? How can I possibly empty its contents? How can I walk away from its memories? The kids grew up here. I look around the place in defeat and confusion. How can that possibly be done?

What an apt last musical: *Anything Goes*. *Everything goes*; it has to.

We begin.

In the last weeks and days of May Bruce and I work hard getting the house into shape for potential renters. The more we work, the more appealing the place becomes to me to remain in.

I paint the kitchen. He paints the ceilings of the dining room and living room, renting a ladder which, at one point, he falls off of. Is that a sign? He laughs; he's all right. In following days we both tackle the rec room, getting rid of crumbling books, packing the others, touching up the bookshelves and woodwork, replacing the old drapes. My house looks so cheery I am becoming homesick for the home that I live in.

Susan comes and goes. When she's there I fight with her over her weight, over her messy room; when she's not there, I miss her deeply and almost cry with longing and regret that I am abandoning her. John has approved of Bruce's and my Great Trek Westward, but Susan burst into tears: "You're leaving our home? Our house? Me?"

I deliver lines I've rehearsed in my head trying to convince myself: "But you'll be graduating next year." "You'll have your own car." I'm giving her the old reliable Tercel since I've recently purchased a new Ford Escort. "You'd be wanting to move anyway after college." She's given no signs of this, but I say it anyway. She is silent, hurt.

"I took just one year's leave of absence," I tell her. "You'll be able to visit us in California. It'll be an adventure for you, too."

She nods, wipes her eyes. "I know," she says, recovering a bit. "I am really so glad you met Bruce," she tells me. I think she is now trying to ease the hurt I feel hurting her. "I am. It's just that—" She doesn't finish. We sit there. I feel suddenly so weary that it's all I can do to reach out and take her hand.

She's touched on another misgiving, one that I have felt without really putting into words. The kids—both of them—love Bruce unequivocally. Prior to Bruce's living with us, for years my life had been divided between them and the men I was involved with—men I kept elsewhere except for occasional dinners or special events. My loyalties and affections had always been pulled in two directions, and of course the kids were aware of my running in and out all the time. Now, though, for a year and half, I have stayed home. I have Bruce. They have Bruce.

And I was breaking up again, this time with my own children. That's what it felt like.

The next-to-last day of school, June 19, was overwrought with emotion. Even then the principal was lecturing me on the excessive field trips of the music department. The music teachers, however, were more than grateful for my work in promoting concerts and travel, including a band tour, a chorus trip—the Philadelphia orchestra matinees. The Art teachers, understandably suspicious of me at first, have ultimately been happy and don't want me to leave.

I think of my standing at the mic on stage one more time for that last concert and mourn that I've given that up, that very small taste of "show biz," of introducing myself, introducing the programs, the performing groups.

On the final day of school I have to relinquish my office—it's a cluttered triangle of a room off the auditorium lobby, but mine!—I must turn over my keys. I feel I am turning over my creativity, my power, my very sense of who I am and who I have been. The music and art and drama teachers take me to lunch, and it's wonderful to have all those people surrounding me, thanking me for all I've done. "You've been great," they tell me. "You're so supportive; you listen." I am surprised, really, that I am appreciated, even admired. I had been insecure, trying hard, feeling anyone else could probably have done this better. I recall a conversation I had at a picnic on Memorial Day at Barbara and Ed's house. They had a wonderful backyard pool. A colleague, Don, whom I'd always thought a great deal of, wondered why I wasn't swimming. He and I were still sitting at the picnic table, and he'd gestured toward Bruce, who was in the pool with others.

"Well, I might wade in," I said, looking in the direction of Bruce, relieved he was having such a good time. "I'm not much of a swimmer. I hate getting my hair wet, getting so wet, plunging in."

Don laughed. "And yet you plunge in other ways."

"Meaning?"

When he didn't answer, I justified his implication. "It seems radical, I guess, giving up my job. And suddenly I see—it's giving up all of you."

He watched me for a half-minute. "The school will miss you."

I sort of laughed. "Are you kidding?" I thought of the principal always criticizing the budgets or commenting on my not being present at every performance. "I feel I can't keep up there anyway."

"You do everything," he said, real admiration in his eyes. "You have been amazing."

I didn't know what to say. Don stood and, before he walked away saying he was going to get more lemonade, he saluted me!

And now, at the last luncheon with all my department members, I feel again both astounded and uncomfortable, as though I am not worthy of their praise. But the affection from the teachers seems to be genuine and I feel my eyes getting wet. I blink rapidly, focusing on the chocolate cake they'd ordered, although all I can think is they care, they have all cared.

Bruce, ever sensitive, buys me a gift, too: a glass box and a pair of earrings, in recognition of my years at the school, of my bravery (I think) in leaving it.

Later, I attend the graduation ceremonies and, afterward, the principal's house party. Randy exhibits real regret and fondness for me, embracing me, declaring how much he will miss me. What a strange relationship we have had. But it's over.

Everything is over. I am not sure what to do with myself. I return to my house with its welcoming fresh paint colors, and in the next days force myself to start packing, to accomplish something. But what? I feel I can't talk, can't really function. I seem to have lost my energy. I'm wondering exactly what I have done and how to live with what I have done.

Shakespeare phrases haunt me, as they always have. I wanted my decision to go to San Francisco to be the equivalent of Miranda's exclamation in *The Tempest*: "O brave new world!" I wanted to think Oh brave new me!

Instead, I heard the taunting of Puck in *Midsummer Night's Dream*: "O what fools these mortals be!" I wondered.

The Summer
of 1986

29   *The Chaos of July*

With summer come days of preparation and sadness and fear and—worst of all, as I see it, during weeks in hot July—of being crowded in that house I want to cling to. I'm leaving it, leaving the family, although now it turns out that not only will Bruce and I be leaving; John will be leaving, too.

One day John borrowed the car to drive to Washington, D.C. for an interview to teach at a private school in Oahu and was subsequently awarded the position. He's scheduled to leave for Honolulu in late July. He is excited, but he, too, is suffering his own anxiety about going so far away.

I try to stay calm, try to concentrate on enjoying our relative solitude and status quo for a while. I water my geraniums. I admire my rooms of pink and cream and melon and green and blue, the air con now fixed and humming coolly against the outside heat. The windows are all clean. I get a temporary job for a month or so in Camden, something to earn a few extra dollars, to enable me to get away from the house, escape myself and the people arriving soon.

We are then besieged with company—family—crowding me, stifling me, I feel. I try to be fair. Bruce tolerates my kids; I must his. Those are the rules.

First Scott arrives with a motorcycling buddy. Just after they get there, right off their bikes, they sit, still wearing their motorcycle gear, on my new chintz sofas, and I want to scream. Bruce says nothing, and I am loathe to scold the men when they just got there. Bruce is delighted to see Scott, of course. Scott, middle son, is the adventurer.

They—Scott and his friend—have traveled across country on those motorcycles, an impressive feat if one didn't have to accommodate them in my newly-cleaned, air-conditioned house and watch them do laundry and sprawl all over, sleep in the living room, park their gear around the place. They are big men.

In addition, I brace myself for the several-week visit of Preston, Bruce's youngest son, who arrives soon. He is almost seventeen, and I remember him as sweet and guileless at times, but demanding and selfish at others. I understand. His father left the city where he lives, Portland; his father abandoned him to move to New Jersey with me. He has been hurt, and his retaliation has been criticism of me: my food, my house, my car. I've prepared for his visit with Oreos and Classic Coke and Cheezits, which I have to keep buying. John yields his room to Preston and shifts himself to the rec room. My tensions are overwhelming.

Susan arrives with her friend for a few days—but she has twin beds; they're both in her room.

On a typical day, during that time: I drive to dreary Camden, to my summer temp job, reporting to a metal desk and an electric typewriter where I enter statistics on individuals in various stages of coma. This office is attached to a trauma center. The statistical entries need to be done, but their implications are startling to me. I witness families clinging to a slight shift of temperature, to any shift of a decimal. Once I ventured, with the greatest of fear, into the hallway to view sealed off rooms, bodies in crib-like beds. Only once. I found it necessary to stay in the office with my inexplicably cheerful boss and not think too much about what the numbers mean, or don't mean. After six hours of entering coma statistics, and other typing, I drive home.

On the beat-up lawn next to my driveway two huge motor-cycles sit like animals of prey. I leave my car in the driveway since the garage itself is partly blocked with an assortment of boxes and furniture set up for our forthcoming "garage sale" and also by the Chevy sedan, Bruce's company car that he doesn't yet have to return. He is home early because of Scott and Pres. The air is a thick, humid 97 degrees.

I enter the house to the whirr of the air conditioning system, which I've had repaired twice; now all I hear is dollars chilling the air, churning away, and the laughter of men coming from the lower level, the rec room. My living room now features duffle bags and sleep-ing bags, helmets and motorcycle jackets, boots in a careless array. It reeks of leathers and—disturbingly—of oil and of used boots.

I call "I'm home!" but no one hears. Upstairs, I open Susan's door to unmade beds piled with half her clothes closet, cereal dishes on the desk, dresser drawers gaping open. A bra hangs out from one, a tee shirt from another. I close the door.

I check John's room. Preston's suitcase is open on the floor, empty Coke bottles are arrayed on John's desk, a pile of cookie crumbs are crushed into the throw rug. His three days' worth of laundry sits in a heap in front of John's closet which actually houses coats and gear that have to be packed or stored.

My room—now my and Bruce's room—is an oasis in all this. I enter its cool calm and change my skirt and blouse and heels into shorts and sleeveless shirt and sandals. I go back down to the kitchen.

"Honey?" Bruce calls. "Did we hear you come home?"

"I'm going out again," I call back. He starts up the seven steps to welcome me. Seeing him, I am struck by why I am in this situation—he always generates a gush of love, even when I am annoyed—and a moment of civility prevails. I join him downstairs, say hello.

This area is John's temporary bedroom, but John isn't here. Scott's long legs stretch leisurely out from the sofa; his friend Roy is sprawled in parallel fashion at the other end. Preston sits at a chair near what I use as a worktable, on top of which now are piles of John's clothes and books. On an adjacent chair is his bedding, dumped haphazardly and temporarily. The sofa converts to a bed, but I don't think John bothers with its mechanisms, just sleeps on the cushions. Preston is beating his skateboard idly against the floor: thump, thump, thump!

I hear the washer shift its gears in the adjacent laundry room, the dryer humming.

"It's so hot here!" Preston wails. "I can't even skate. There's no place to skate anyway. Just that dumb road out there. Sidewalks." He slams the board a few more times but the carpet—which I laid a year ago (donated by Barbara and Ed) dulls its slams a little.

"I'm going to the store," I announce. "Hamburgers all right this evening?"

"It's too hot!" Preston says. "I don't want to eat outside."

Others say they're fine.

Preston reminds me to get more Classic Coke. Bruce shoots an anxious look from me to him. "You could say 'please,'" he says.

"Can you turn up the air?" Preston says. "Oh, and Cheezits, too."

I ask where John is and they tell me that Greta, his girlfriend this summer, picked him up and they went to the library. He'll be back before dinner. I turn to go.

Bruce follows me up to the kitchen. "Thanks, Honey." He puts his arms around me. "I know it's hard. Thank you."

"It's okay," I say, a bit guilt-ridden since he has been living with my children for over a year—at least off and on, when they're home, which they both are this summer, our last in this house.

Preston is suddenly in the room, too. "Could you get me more Knox gelatin?" He needs it to spike his hair. I nod. When Preston takes the local train into Philadelphia's South Street, which he likes to do, he fashions himself as a punk. I watched him the first time he borrowed my small vacuum cleaner and sucked strands of his gelatin-ed hair into spikes. Bruce, to my amazement, has made no comment, either on the preparations or their finished result, and Preston returns early from these forays, a sort of "wanna-be" punk.

Bruce now walks me to my car. I ask about Susan. Bruce says she'll be back later—so the guys said.

"God, her room!"

"Relax, honey," Bruce says. "Take it easy. We'll work it out."

"It is so goddam hot!" I say, getting into my stuffy car. I almost back into Greta's car, which stops. John emerges with a big bag, waves to her. He approaches my window. "I had Greta stop at Cowtail bar," he says. "I bought a bunch of ice cream. I've got to get it inside, Mom."

"How much?" I ask. I know I'll have to reimburse him; he doesn't have extra money. He's leaving in a week.

He winces. "Eighteen dollars?"

"On ice cream! Are you kidding?"

"Mom. Be kind. They're only here for a few days. Think of Bruce." Then, holding up the bag anxiously, he darts to the front door.

At Stop 'n Shop I have to cash a check in order to pay for all I am buying, which should last us all until tomorrow when I do this again. I know in two days Scott and Roy will be back on their motorcycles and we'll just have Preston, sitting on top of my throw cushions, banging the refrigerator door, cramming his Oreos. For two more weeks.

Those two weeks are ones I want to cling to. Aren't they my last? I know John will leave for Honolulu, Susan will return to college, and Bruce and I? Will we really drive to San Francisco? I just can't imagine.

Scott and his friend pack up their gear and zoom off. Their absence does not give me the chance of being with John, my intellectual refuge, who now broods, who is upset at sending boxes of his things to Honolulu (where none of us has ever been); he is now silent. Besides, he and I are never alone, and I become increasingly depressed—at never being by myself, at losing John, at the fear of the unknown beyond this month, this place.

Making matters worse is Preston, who seems to be leaping too often up and down the seven steps each way in that split-level house. And yet, at times, he sits next to me and wants to work the crossword puzzle I'm doing; he can be gentle and civil. Susan cries over losing her brother, cries over losing me, her home.

John postpones leaving for another week. He and Preston, strangely, sort of hit it off; Preston calms down. John, I think, likes the idea of a borrowed younger brother or is just being helpful. I am grateful. Nevertheless, I wake in the middle of the night, pour an extra glass of wine, brood that it's my only time alone, resent the fact that, in order to escape the chaos of that dwindling household, I have to type in dreary Camden all day. What will become of me, of us?

I go through drawers and closets and storage areas; I pack boxes and clean and cook. I find a friend who will take the cat. "I'll get her back when I return," I say. "I can't imagine staying in San Francisco." Susan is not allowed a cat in her dorm.

I can return to the school, I tell myself. That's my protection. I can ask the renters to leave, and I can come back here: a year's lease is my protection. Where I will get the money to live on without a salary is another issue.

Then he leaves first. John.

He's arranged a flight to Honolulu, or, more accurately, Iolani School has. *Honolulu.* The word is exotic. Bruce and I are preparing for California, in itself seemingly the end of the world, but my son is going even farther.

I wanted change and I wanted things to stay as they were. Of course, the latter was impossible: time marches on, as they say, regardless.

On his last night in the house, I take John out to dinner, just the two of us. We sit opposite one another in a booth and have wine with our grilled chicken, an intimate dinner in a restaurant that we've never had before. It's hard for me to accept that he is going so far away (as am I!) so I try to talk positively about Honolulu and the great opportunity he has earned, that he deserves.

"Waikiki looks so beautiful," I say.

He agrees. "You have Bruce," he says. I look up, surprised. "I've always been jealous of the two of you. Your best efforts go to Bruce."

I am shocked, chagrinned. "I'm sorry," I say.

He shrugs. "You need to go easier on him, Mom, about Preston. I wish I'd had such a father."

I am pained again.

"But I am grateful that he's been here, that you have him. I love him, too."

Candid, sensitive John. I've leaned on him since he was thirteen. He's been supplanted. Yes, yes, I have Bruce, seemingly. I look at John, at handsome, intelligent John, and he blurs before me. How can I go on smiling around such dissolution of my life? How can I?

After a moment, we recover our bearings, search out the ordinary. "You'll be teaching tenth grade English?" I say. "And those kids are so bright, right? A private school? I think you'll love it." He agrees, although neither of us is convinced. He's not sure about living arrangements, although the headmaster has said John can stay with him for a week or so.

When we get home, Susan is in tears. "I can't believe he's going!" she cries, flinging herself onto a sofa. Her friend Susan stays to comfort her.

Later that night we have a funny little party for John: Bruce and I and Preston and Greta and the Susans. I cannot make eye contact with John; I fear my face will contort with the pain of his leaving. When I do manage to look his way, I see, with some relief, that his eyes are on Greta.

I leave them all and go upstairs, by myself, and sit on the bed and cry. Life has to change. This is all good, isn't it? John is 23 and has a good job in a beautiful place waiting for him. I have a wonderful man with me. I am breaking up my home, though; I am abandoning my daughter.

But John—John!—the person I've been closest to since the day he was born—is leaving me. I can't take it. I have to take it.

I drive him to the airport the next day. He will fly from Philadelphia to Honolulu. And I somehow get myself home where Susan and I pack boxes together, the physical activity almost detaching us from the implication. I take her out to lunch, at the mall. What do we talk about? We both feel totally bereft. I am, in a short time, going to make her more bereft. Bruce consoles me; Preston, missing John, stays out later than usual that evening, although he really never strays.

John has left little gifts for each of us, hidden around the house, which we find and show each other: a book of poems for Bruce, a little flashlight for Preston, colored pens for Susan, a new notebook for me. I wander the rec room, where John had been "living" since Preston took over his room for the month, feeling his presence in his absence, and cry again.

He calls. That day and the next. He calls. He calls. He is somewhere—there—somewhere, not here.

We could not stay as we were.

30   *Garage Sale*

Preston misses John, but, surprisingly, becomes helpful. Maybe Bruce has given him a talking-to. I don't ask. He helps Bruce carry furniture into the large space behind the garage that we always called "the storage room," although all we stored there were boxes of old school papers and dolls and a broken lawn mower. Christmas decorations. Once the kids, around 5 and 6 then, wandered into the space and opened the three-year old Christmas gingerbread house to share with their friends. The gesture was amusing at the time and yet I had been appalled that such a stale concoction could be digestible. We'd often reminisce about that funny event: the two of them and two or three neighborhood kids gnawing away on those broken chunks of hard gingerbread trimmed in plaster-like frosting.

Now we see that the storage room space can indeed accommodate a great amount: my two new chintz sofas, the steel and glass dining table with the big leather (or faux) dining chairs, the end tables from marriage #1, the white lamps and brass coffee tables and desk from marriage #2, my collages of playbills in frames, as well as the little color TV Doug had given me that he wouldn't take back, my sewing machine, old typewriter. We store my life.

Closest to the door we will add my bedroom set, which Susan plans to take when she finishes her senior year and gets her own apartment. She wants this piece of our original life, I think, and I am happy to have her use it. This storage area will be closed to the renters. *Renters.* I can't get used to the word. Strangers will be living in my house. It seems such a violation. Fortunately, I do not have the time or energy to think of anything except the tasks at hand: packing and sending boxes, tagging and lugging and labeling everything that we can put a price tag on.

Preston remains cooperative and useful and he and Bruce do most of the heaving and lifting. John's girlfriend Greta comes over, too; Susan and her friends pitch in. Perhaps we all want to linger around the house, all of us tagging, toting.

At the end of July the garage sale day is finally here. This is the day when we move everything onto the front lawn, dry with summer heat, and into the open garage, and then around to the side of the house. We create room arrangements on the lawn: the old dining set, the pine hutch, the kids' beds next to their desks. The biggest problems are those desks, those monoliths of wood that I'd taken such pride in providing. K.E. and I had moved them in her VW van from the high school's surplus room—the cost was $5 each for the big old teachers' desks—and lugged them, drawer by drawer, into each of the kids' bedrooms. There I painted them: brown with tan drawers for John; white with pink and green drawers for Susan. The kids were adolescents then.

Now it is the summer of 1986, and Bruce is hauling the desks into the sun. It's Saturday, early morning, and already cars are stopping by. Everywhere, even on the fringes of the lawn, are tables of knickknacks, dishes, pots and pans, sports equipment—all the trappings and detritus of three people who have lived in a house for twenty-one years.

The sale extends into the next day—and who knows what's left and what's done. The house is basically empty, except for the sofa bed in the rec room and two end tables. We will leave them behind. Marita, my good friend, wants Susan's chests (once mine and my sister's, unpainted then), so we will take them to her, along with Rosemary, the cat. The kids' cat. Another betrayal. ("I'll get her!" Susan says. "I'll get her as soon as I can.") I have the cash I earned from all this—around $1,000—in an envelope to buy necessary things in San Francisco. *What?* I think. That's it? *What have I done?*

John calls from Honolulu. He has no one immediately around, he says, "to bounce ideas off of." I want to say, If you're unhappy, come home. He senses this, and assures me that he's doing well, people are kind. The headmaster will make arrangements to deduct a portion of his salary to pay off a Harvard loan. His classes will begin soon, and he looks forward to students and staff.

Bruce takes Preston to the airport.

In the meantime, Susan has a final little party with her friends. She and I cry together, carp as usual, cry again. Barbara hosts Bruce and me for a farewell dinner and I am moved to tears, there too. We continue to work on the house—carting books, moving odd lamps and tables into the storage room, donating old clothes, dishes, glasses to Goodwill.

Susan drives the old Tercel, now hers, to her Dad's; then she'll drive to William Paterson College in North Jersey.

Bruce and I, alone, sleep on sleeping bags in the empty living room. I feel purged, cathartic. Bereft. Odd. It's done.

31   *Walking Away, August 1, 1986*

I sit in the passenger seat of my Ford Escort, year 85 ½ (the salesman stressed the "half" as though the fraction carried with it some essential new feature) and stare at the house I've lived in for twenty-one years. I admire the paint colors I'd refreshed it with a few years back, the blue exterior, the off-white trim, their names: Pottery, Vanilla. It's very hot in the car, and my pantyhose are sticking to my thighs, my striped summer dress is about to wilt.

That morning the Connollys, the renters, arrived, and I welcomed them.

They tell me they are excited about living here, and the wife exclaims that the house seems so big. It does look big: the cathedral ceiling, the wide expanse of blue carpet and rose colored walls. It looks huge to me, too. And enormously appealing.

A yearning to stay seems to push against my chest. "Do you want to walk through together?" I ask. For the next five minutes I tour the history of my life in the house:—its present empty spaces nothing I could have imagined just a month before when John took over the rec room, when Susan's room was filled not only with Susan, home for the summer, but with all her clothes and possessions, her furniture and friends.

At each turn Theresa Connolly exclaims, "I'd forgotten all these cheerful colors!" But she also looks mildly dismayed. "I miss seeing your furniture and things," she says. "They made it nice." We stand there. "But I have my own," she says. I've no idea what to do, what I am doing, really.

"Here are the keys," I say. I am an automaton, or actress playing a role. I shrug, wish them well, remind them that I posted local phone numbers on the bulletin board in my kitchen. I turn away to walk down my sidewalk (the possessive remains, asserts itself: my, mine) and join Bruce, who is standing at the car.

He and I wave to the renters, they to us. "That's it, then," I say, getting in. Bruce, now in the driver's seat, checks the map of Pennsylvania even though we know the turnpike is a straight drive—directly from Mt. Holly, New Jersey, where we're heading for his farewell party as their City Manager. The decision to leave has been made, of course, yet I can't recover from the fact that we've given up the company car, the good salary, the benefits that came with the new position a mere six months ago, given it all up. He is so excited about leaving for San Francisco that he has no misgivings about relinquishing the job. He finds the fact that he has acquired one reassurance that he can find another. There will be a luncheon in his honor, which is why I'm wearing my good patent heels and a dress on this stifling day, the first day of a 3,000-mile trip across the country.

"If we leave at two or so, we ought to be able to get as far as Ohio," Bruce says, folding the map and tucking it behind my passenger seat. The car is heavy. Under my front seat is a box of silverware; behind me, with all our suitcases, is his electric typewriter, a portable metal file cabinet containing files I think I will need, as well as a coffee maker, tent, sleeping bags, cooler, and—I added at the last minute, remembering camp sites from the previous two summers—a bucket and plastic dishes. We are laden with our portable life.

"Ready?" he says. He's handsome in his dress pants and shirt, no doubt a great deal warmer than I, but the air con is now on and Baroque music, Bach maybe, is playing on the radio—a rather grand orchestration to our departure. We pull forward, up Burnt Mill Road, the road I've traversed all these years going to school, getting gas at the corner and groceries in the little shopping center next to the gas station, to the red light where we set off, up Route 295 to our immediate destiny of a lunch.

I turn to him, this man I love, to his question of Ready? "I think so," I say, smoothing my dress, reaching for his hand that is always there and reassuring. Still, I feel I'm driving off the end of the universe as I know it.

32   *Advent of Adventure*

"One day down," he says ten hours later as we haul suitcases into the spartan setting of a Motel 6 in Youngstown, Ohio. He also immediately announces, "I want to use the bathroom." I've been living with him for a year and a half and know his rhythms. His bathroom retreats in the evening allow me a space of time to keep my journals.

"Give me five minutes first," I say. I am still in the dress and heels that I've been wearing all day. I've traveled 400 miles that way. I strip off that dress, those panty hose, wash myself up quickly and put on a light robe that I'd packed strategically at the top of one of the suitcases.

On the room's small table I've already placed the vase of flowers from the setting of the lunch buffet given in Bruce's honor. There I had milled around a room I'd never been in, with people I'd never met, people he didn't know that well either. I smiled and felt out of place, not belonging to the scene at all, as though I had a sign on my dress: "I'm A Great Adventurer Who Will Be Leaving All This Small-town Stuff Behind." Bruce's fellow employees shook his hand as though they'd been honored to know anyone such as he—brave enough (or foolish enough) to give up a great job to set off across the continent with no job at the other end. They insisted we take the flowers, vase and all. The arrangement had traveled wedged between us in that small, crowded car.

In the suitcase I also find our bottle of brandy and wait for him to emerge. How odd to sit here! I think of my friends: of Barbara's crying at the dinner she gave us; of Marita, whom I'd embraced; of Janet and my no longer having her constant comfort and companionship.

I wonder how I'll be able to deal with life without my friends. I am haunted by thoughts of Susan, by what she is doing, haunted by the image of her driving up the road in the Tercel, my waving from the sidewalk. I know she's at her dad's temporarily and will drive herself to college. But I feel I've stripped her of her real home. I have.

I hear the toilet flush in the adjacent room, the water running. I feel, in that barren motel room, that I am in someone else's life. How have I gotten here?

The bathroom door opens. "Hi, Sweetheart," he says. "Is my suit hanger still in the car?" I shrug: who knows? He folds his pants carefully over the room's only chair, takes the brandy and water I'm now offering him.

We stretch out next to each other on the bed. He reaches for my leg, patting it in reassurance, leans to kiss my cheek. "Well, we made it through Day One," he says.

I wake in the middle of the night, though, thinking that I have turned into the person that I feared he was when I met him: unsettled, tentative. How on earth can we begin anything again when we're 45 and 46? I'm back to the old *King Lear* question: are we wisemen or fools?

The next few days—driving along Chicago's Lake Shore, and walking around Madison, Wisconsin, traversing the rolling farmlands of Wisconsin and Michigan—keep me highly entertained. At a campsite on our second night of travel I place the vase of flowers on the picnic table next to the tent. The following night—the second campsite—I throw it away, flowers and vase and all, a gesture that signals mixed feelings: there's the relief of not having to worry about water spilling in the car, but the action also seems to be symbolic of tossing away the comforting accoutrements of life, a life of dressing for a lunch where flowers grace a table.

One morning, now Monday, August 4, I sit at a picnic table overlooking the Missouri River, somewhere in South Dakota, the day bright and blue with only a few clouds in the sky. I awoke so early I'd had the communal bathroom pretty much to myself, enabling me to make coffee using the one outlet there. At the picnic table I drink that coffe and smoke a cigarette, waiting for Bruce to return from the men's showers. We still have the tent to take down, the sleeping bags to roll up, everything to shove back into the Escort before we set off for the Badlands, the plan for the early part of the day, and then to Mt. Rushmore.

Seeing these storybook places I'd only heard about, making love with him in a strange motel or tent in the evening, keep at bay the foreboding sense of what I feel is my walking away from responsibility. I feel that Susan, even at almost-22, is unfinished. I tell myself I was married and had John when I was 22, but that doesn't change my feelings. No one left me.

Bruce joins me at the picnic table for coffee and we watch the river, the lush trees bordering it, and smile at each other. "It's going to be a good day," he says. I agree. With him anything seems possible, even what I am doing, almost watching myself doing it.

It was on our fifth night on the road that I felt I was failing at being an adventurer. We were somewhere on Big Horn Mountain, and that evening my hands were so frozen I could barely take off my shoes even though I was in the tent.

The flaps of the tent parted, and I gasped at the air that rushed in. Bruce crawled inside, folding his big frame into that small space.

"Cold out there tonight," he said. He reached for our bottle of wine. Even in a tiny space we kept our pleasures handy.

"Did you see the deer?" I whispered.

"What deer? There are probably lots out there." He handed his plastic glass back to me to hold as he realized he had the ritual out of order. With difficulty he pulled jeans from his long legs and unzipped one side of our double sleeping bags. His legs were cold against mine. "You're nice and warm," he said, taking his wine back, leaning on an elbow. The flashlight, propped in a corner, emphasized his cheekbones, his pronounced brow. "What deer?"

"There was one that stood in front of the tent. He just stood there, and I couldn't get in and I was freezing."

Bruce was amused. Shadows darted around the tent as he adjusted himself into our cocoon. "It's pretty damn cold," he said.

"If I have to go in the middle of the night—oh my god—and it's so cold out there—he might be there."

He laughed. "Honey, he's more afraid of you than you are of him. It's just a deer." He lit a cigarette, mine, too. Our routine. Smoke must have puffed out the two little screened flaps that served as "windows." We'd bought this somewhat bigger tent in New Jersey, just for this trip, to erect on nights of no rain. I longed for a motel. I longed for my own bed, the house I left.

That day we'd driven through the Black Hills to Sturgis where, to Bruce's thrill, there turned out to be a motorcycle rally. He'd heard about such an event taking place in Sturgis but was surprised to find out that we'd coincidentally arrived at that time. He loved the roaring of those engines, the designs of different "bikes," as he called them, pointing them out to me. That day in Sturgis I discovered his love for and knowledge of motorcycles, as I went on discovering things about him. Beyond Sturgis we drove through towns called Deadwood and Lead and through the forests and wildflowers and streams of Spearfish Canyon. Those adventures took us to this freezing campsite on Big Horn where there were no showers, not even toilets.

I sank deeper into the drafty warmth of the sleeping bag. "This is a desperate place, isn't it? I can't wash my hair at that pump! It'll turn to icicles."

"Desperate?" He chuckled at my choice of words and leaned over to kiss my forehead.

"Where are we?" I asked.

"Oh, somewhere on a mountain in Wyoming. It's great, isn't it? Hasn't it been?"

We put away our cocktail party gear—the ashtray, the wine, the glasses—tucked into the tent's corners, and settled into the sleeping bag, our rolled-up jeans serving as pillows. The quiet was almost deafening. I listened to it, felt his size, his warmth next to me. "I love you," I said.

"I love you. And it _is_ pretty damn cold." We snuggled into our cocoon, pulled up the zippers.

"What if. . .?"

"Shh," he said.

33   *Some Surprises*

That's the way it usually went: my fears, his assurances. The Big Horn campsite was so cold we had to finish dressing the next morning in the cramped car, teeth chattering as we took down the tent and tossed in our frozen toothpaste and toiletries, thawing out only at a roadside rest stop an hour or so later.

He'd mapped out the country and I followed his lead, enchanted by day by museums and natural wonders, resigned by night to the misery of camping, particularly at a KOA. KOA stood for Kampgrounds of America, probably because they featured a playground for children. They were a last resort with their long lines at communal showers, tents in close proximity to each other and often on a flat field, but they were the only place we could call ahead and actually reserve a spot—as we had to do that day of touring Yellowstone. We endured the long drive from the national park to that campground only to discover there were no restaurants or stores nearby. So: we pitched our tent and got back in the car.

Forty-five minutes later we finally spotted a roadside restaurant and drove up the gravel road to its perch on a hillside. "We're in Idaho now," I said. "That sign back there. We're staying in a Montana campground to visit a park in Wyoming and going to eat in Idaho."

He grunted amusement. He was hungry. "Well, we'll see," he said, getting out of the car and reaching for my hand to head up the ramshackle steps to the front door.

The place—somewhat rustic, lots of wood—was surprisingly redolent of herbs and freshly baked bread. We were seated and given menus in French, of all things, with translations. A party of eight arrived, all dressed up, as though celebrating a special occasion. The place turned out to be a French restaurant run by chefs who'd worked in San Francisco. What a thorough surprise—we exclaimed over our menu choices, ordered as though we had been living this way all along.

"The wine is great," Bruce said, lifting his glass to mine, touching their real-glass rims. He looked around the restaurant, pleased at our serendipitous discovery. Plates were set before us, warm baguette slices, soft butter. His glance of pleasure met mine. "I love you," he said. "I love you," I said. It was so true I could have abandoned my anticipated asparagus souffle right that minute and gone to bed with him. Then I thought of "bed:" the zipped-together sleeping bags in the almost-public tent.

I observed the women across the room in their flowing skirts, their flowered dresses, their smart handbags. I laughed, tilted my head in their direction. "I'll bet they're not returning to a KOA," I said to Bruce. He nodded amused acknowledgment, now busy cutting into his filet.

Who lives like this? To travel from a secure life on one side of the continent, to who knows what on the other side? To freeze on a mountain top then dine in a snug French restaurant in the middle of nowhere? Us, that's who.

The second day of Yellowstone Park (replete with Old Faithful) brought us to storms in Jackson, Wyoming. The rain was so heavy we could barely see through the cascades of water washing over our little Escort to detect "No Vacancy" signs blurrily aglow in motel after motel. Camping was of course out of the question, and we drove on in darkness brought on even earlier by the storm. Finally, Bruce found a motel well beyond our budget (I watched tensely as he ran in drenching rain to the office), and for a room so small we had to walk across the bed to get to the bathroom. But it was snug and warm and ours for the night against the tension of the storm outside.

I phoned Susan, who was still at her dad's house in Ocean City. "My mom's calling from Wyoming!" she shouted to someone else in the room, a stepsister? "I miss you terribly," she told me. We had been gone, Bruce and I, just over a week. I missed her, too. I missed my house. I missed their childhoods. I called John. He was staying with the headmaster while he searched for a place to live. "I can't talk," he said. "It's awkward here. Thanks for the call."

I set the receiver back in the cradle and took a deep breath.

"They're fine. They're all right," Bruce said, no doubt taking in my anxious face. He was stretched out on our big bed, hemmed in by cozy pine walls. The rain beat relentlessly outside, against the window, on our car. My hand still on the phone, as though the children (not children anymore!) were at the other end, I turned to him, "Why don't you worry?"

He looked surprised. "I don't know. Because they're okay." We knew Bruce Jr. was in San Bruno, California (just south of San Francisco), Scott in Ashland,Oregon, Preston still with his mother in Portland. "Oh, honey," he said. "They're old enough. All of them."

Yes, I knew that, but they were my kids. I had been three people all my adult life and had a hard time separating myself. It was the constant reassurance of him that kept me going. I felt a selfishness in seeing all those wonders by day and enjoying him by night. It had been two years since I met him, and I remained consistently happy, selfishly happy. We were together aiming for San Francisco, to a destiny I could not imagine, a life I could not imagine.

That night in Jackson I had a dream: *My Ford Escort, the car that Bruce and I have been driving across the country, has been run through the picture window of my New Jersey house. It remains lodged there, hovering above the bushes out front. When I turn to him in alarm, the dream-Bruce assures me: "No problem." The dream-me stares at the ruin of both things—house and car—and tries to accept that idea.* No problem. Maybe. In that snug motel—with its pine-paneled walls making it even more of a hideaway—I tried to tell myself that everything might still be fine.

I looked for signs of reassurance wherever I could find them, as I did at another campground, this time in Utah. At first it was only a morning and an outhouse buzzing with bees. I had no idea where we were—we endured, the previous evening, a bumpy dirt road for six very long miles to arrive at dusk to slabs of rocks and isolated spaces. Now, this hot morning, all I could see was an outhouse and pump—and bees. I'd tentatively placed my towel and a tube of Prell shampoo on a large rock before I ventured, ducking bees, over to the ugly outhouse structure. When I emerged, bees were swarming around the shampoo, too. I reached cautiously for a corner of the towel to shake them away and ran, in my unbuckled sandals, to the water pump.

I could see Bruce off to one side, almost small from where I was, or of ordinary size in relation to the tent, which seemed a boy's toy next to him. How had we fit in there last night? He was dipping a pan of water into our bucket (he'd hauled a bucket of water next to our site last evening), preparing to shave, which he would do at the picnic table pretending there was a mirror. The sight was sweet, and I remembered why I was here—wherever I was.

When I surveyed my surroundings in the other direction I gasped aloud. The view was incredibly beautiful: rock upon rock undulating into the distance, pinks and corals and deep reds against a bright and clear blue sky. There was no one in the world but us, it seemed, us in this Technicolor universe, with our little tent and, down a path, an outhouse buzzing with bees.

I turned to the pump and bent my head into the thick stream and screamed with the cold. The sun was hot, but what had I expected? I lathered and rinsed and then, with my washcloth, scrubbed my armpits and between my legs—the coldness there feeling rather good. With my head wrapped in the towel and grateful for the cleanliness I'd bestowed on myself, I gazed in another direction now, to see a flagpole jutting out of the layers of pink and red rock. A flagpole? There was something beyond all those gorgeous slabs after all, on the other side. Toweling my hair—which would dry in ten minutes in this sun—I rejoined Bruce and our campsite.

"Hi, Honey," he greeted. "Looks like we have some leftover cookies for breakfast. Two bananas. No coffee though." He had put away his razor and slicked back his hair. We look like shiny pennies, I thought.

"I saw a flagpole over there." I pointed and he turned. "I mean, maybe there's a ranger station we didn't see. Maybe there's an electric outlet." Bruce laughed at my joke. "So you're going to find it and make us coffee?" But I was already at the trunk of the car, lifting out the small cardboard box that contained our four-cup coffee pot. I grabbed a can of coffee and filter and said I would be back.

There was no one around. Weren't there other campsites? Stopping again at the pump to fill the decanter, I walked over a plateau of red rock to find the flagpole, rising out of nowhere, to look for a ranger station or something beyond. When I got closer, though, I saw that there was an actual electric outlet in the middle of the flagpole—just above the height of my head. I turned to signal to Bruce: *There's something here!* He started in my direction.

"Incredible!" he said when he got there. He held high the coffee maker with its short cord, and with the greatest of satisfaction we listened to its gurgling, and inhaled, among the pines and heated rocks, a distinct coffee aroma. In a few minutes, we set out our cookies and bananas, poured our coffee into mugs at our picnic table, and took in that magnificent view.

That morning in Kodachrome Basin, I considered that if we could make coffee at a flagpole in the middle of nowhere, everything might yet work out.

My resolve didn't last. The next night, somewhere beyond Bryce Canyon, we pulled into campgrounds among undulating sand dunes. Dune buggies buzzed and swooped in a near distance. A chilly drizzle had started. Bruce noted the stark change from the previous day, assessed my uneasiness. "I'll search for firewood," he told me, getting out of the car. "A fire will make you feel better."

A forlorn table sat next to the space where we would put up the tent. "I'll make sandwiches right here," I said, still in the car. I held up a can of tuna and an opener. He went off, a hunter on a mission, and I was touched as I watched him, through the car window, lurch into the oncoming darkness.

The sandwiches became a dismaying project, which I could have anticipated if I'd properly considered a closed-up car and an open can of tuna. Still, I mixed celery that I chopped on a Tupperware lid and tossed it into the Tupperware container with the tuna and mayonnaise, groceries we'd shopped for late that afternoon. I mourned for my kitchen at home and could not imagine another one anywhere. The fire—predictably since everything was damp—didn't light. We put up our tent anyway since there was no place else to go.

Bruce poured white wine, which helped, to have with our tuna sand-wiches. "It's all part of the adventure, honey," he said, and I reminded myself once again that there was a price to be paid for running away, for traveling from the one fascination like the Mormon Tabernacle to another like Capital Reef National Park in an afternoon, for being in love.

By day eleven real homesickness set in. What had brought it on so strongly? The scenery had been dazzling—and appalling, too. At one point we drove on a narrow bridge of a road between two precipitous canyons, condors swooping outside my passenger-side window, Bruce leaning forward, unable to talk. The tension was like a third person in the car with us, the road seemingly without end. We settled into a decent motel and it offered me some respite, some comfort. I lectured myself that other people have undergone great changes and adapted to them; certainly I can.

The Grand Canyon and one more comfortable motel created a sense of sanity again for me and I was chagrined, even disappointed in myself, that I couldn't be more resilient. Even reaching the kids didn't help since Susan reported fighting with her dad's wife and John cut short our call. Maybe it was the finality of the trip that had me panicked. What did we do when we reached the other end of the continent? Fall off?

Several bad motels after that served only to make me more frightened, more aware of the enormity of what I felt I'd done (aban-donment! The word that haunted me), forcing Bruce to be the constant consoler. The sites, I had to admit, had been dazzling: Mt Rushmore, the National Parks of Zion and Canyonlands and Bryce. However, a night in a motel where I feared walking on the floor, where children screamed through thin walls, led me to a minor despair.

Sitting at a small window near tears I preached the old litany to myself: *you wanted change, you wanted change, change takes courage.* From the stiff chair of that creepy room, I answered: *I know, I know. I didn't think it'd come to this.*

I couldn't face the motel bed. The screaming children quieted down; a few doors banged. I stared at the wall. Bruce emerged from the bathroom and stopped, taking me in. "What's wrong?"

My voice didn't seem to work. I had no right to cause him distress. I shook my head in denial, *Nothing.*

He nodded, poured us each a glass of wine in the plastic glasses we carried with us and stretched out on the bed. There was only one chair in the room. "Do you want the chair?" I managed to say.

"I'm fine. I'm good." He looked for a place to set his glass and saw that there were no end tables. He held the glass. He made amiable small talk, reviewing the sites we'd seen that day, the day before. His eyes were gauging my anxiety.

Even aware that he must get weary of my nit-picking, I wanted to take advantage of his comfort. He always offered comfort. Eventually I got to the big stuff: What will we do when we get there? (We'll figure it out.) What if we don't get jobs? (We'll get jobs. Why wouldn't we?) What if we don't like it? (You saw San Francisco. Why would we not like it?) I've never lived in a city. (You wanted to, didn't you? Isn't that what you said?) and so we go on. He knows the questions; I know the answers.

I wondered: if he whined and panicked each time a little rain fell, which is what it did profusely earlier this evening or we wouldn't have been so desperate for a motel room that we'd taken the only vacancy we could find, where on earth would we be?

34 *Final Days*

We reserved a camping spot somewhere in the desert: Lake Havasu. "Lake" sounded promising, particularly as we traversed arid Arizona. The air got hotter and closer, though, and the air con in the Ford Escort wilted against the record temperatures.

The campsite, labeled "primitive," which we knew, turned out to be just that. I had considered what we'd been doing among isolated red rock canyons or mountain pines or the flat fields of KOAs to be "primitive," but, as Bruce got out of the car to look around, I could see him almost fall over from the heat. "Primitive" here meant a spot in a field: no water, no nothing.

"We can't do that," I said, unnecessarily since he was already back in the hot car.

We found a motel, costing no more than we've paid for some of the skimpy ones we'd retreated to, which seemed, at that point, palatial to us. There was air conditioning! There were smooth white sheets, a table and two chairs. I thought I could dash across the lot to a laundromat, which I'd spotted, and he headed to the motel pool for a swim.

Reunited, we laughed as we drank our wine, cooled to room temperature by the air conditioning, and made sandwiches at our table. We'd rescued the ingredients from a cooler whose ice, purchased somewhere near the Grand Canyon, was now a tub of water. I could barely survive folding the clothes, I tell him, the laundry room was like a sauna. The pool water was too hot to swim in, he says. A joke.

But we are here now. Where were we? At London Bridge? Really? Here in Havasu?

We had been on the road for two weeks, skimping as much as we could, and now Bruce suggested that instead of heading to San Francisco the next day, we go to Los Angeles. I hadn't been there either, had I? Disneyland? What did I think? Of course, I wanted to do that; I wanted to avoid the end of the journey. I feared the end of the journey, feared looking for employment, feared the unknown.

I feared, as well, our initial landing in San Bruno where we will be "put up" for the night, an offer made by Bruce Jr., who was sharing a house with four or five other guys. I didn't want to be there. I even feared—this was crazy—moving out of our car where we'd "lived" for weeks. The car was familiar: I had belonged to it.

Yes, I agreed to L.A.—I even liked saying the initials—and we took off across the desert and mountains to this new destination. Bruce's mother had given us $40 as a travel gift, and we decided to spend it on Disneyland. When I called to tell her this, to thank her, she was surprised. "Disneyland? Of course, if that's what you two want." We could "do" the park for $40 then, our reward for traversing the country.

What an evening! We walked Disneyland's cheerful Main Street, went on the rides, even the Haunted House with its surprise gusts of air, and rode the boat through "It's a Small World," to his utter impatience with the relentless song and my enchantment with all the costumed dolls. The roller coasters were our favorites (we'd previously been to amusement parks in New Jersey and Pennsylvania), and these we rode over and over, screaming, arms raised high, collapsing in laughter at the end of each ride. We watched a Lionel Hampton concert, got sticky with cotton candy, stayed until midnight for the lighted Mickey Mouse Parade.

I escaped my fears, escaped myself, for the evening, although Disneyland inevitably reminded me of Florida's Disneyworld a seemingly lifetime ago with my then-children. I had to call them tomorrow. Tomorrow was a day when we would reach—almost—our San Francisco destination. Had John found a place to live? I knew Susan needed more tuition.

It had been a great day playing in the park, but tomorrow I would have to be an adult again.

Adjustments and Discoveries

35   *Arriving in San Francisco*

It was gracious of Bruce's twenty-four-year-old son, Bruce Jr., to offer us a place to sleep when we arrived in San Bruno after leaving Los Angeles. He shared a big house with four other young men and, since one of those housemates happened to be gone right then, Bruce Sr. and I were given the absentee's bed, a waterbed, where we churned and swooped most of the night. When the guy returned, we were told we were welcome to use the living room floor for our sleeping bags. Of course, neither of us could imagine doing that. Besides, for our one night's stay we'd brought our own toilet paper and our camping towels and went out for coffee because the kitchen was unapproachable with piled up dishes. We thanked our hosts and said no. We'd intended to head out anyway.

Bruce, the Master of Planning, suggested that instead of driving directly to San Francisco from San Bruno, we travel around the bay and enter San Francisco grandly, formally, across the Golden Gate Bridge. To do that, we had to take the San Mateo Bridge to the East Bay, drive north, then cross back west on the San Rafael Bridge. That positioned us north of the Golden Gate Bridge, from which vantage we could take in the grandeur of the entire scene in front of us: the bridge's huge orange pillars rising above the curve of the Marin Headlands, the expansive blue San Francisco Bay dotted with white sailboats, and the city's buildings, like a miniature stage set, arranged at the bay's far rim. "San Francisco!" Bruce announced, reaching for my hand. "We are here."

It was quite a thrill to ride over the bridge that morning, the sun literally beckoning us to a new world.

We had an immediate item of business—actually two parts of the same problem: where to sleep. We needed an apartment, our long-range goal, but would be unlikely to find one where we could stay that first night, so we needed a hotel, too. This was San Francisco—with its lovely Ritz Carlton and Mark Hopkins and other beautiful hotels—clearly not for us. Bruce suggested we cruise around the low-rent districts near downtown, where we eventually found a cheap hotel. We could take in a suitcase but had to leave all our possessions in the car parked on the street. That seemed vulnerable, but we had no choice.

We bought a newspaper and poured over the ads for apartments, which totally confused us. "Good weather?" we'd question about the ad. "Isn't it all the same city?" It would be much later when we'd learn that San Francisco contains within itself a number of climates—from the warm inner areas like the Mission District, to outer fogged-in Richmond, that is, any neighborhood's approximation to ocean, hills, valleys, bay.

The rentals were listed by Houses and then Apartments, which were also sub-divided: two bedrooms, one-bedroom, junior, studio, in-law. I wasn't sure what some of these meant, and their prices, as they had the previous summer, made my eyes widen and my stomach tighten. Bruce said maybe we should consider a "studio" apartment, a concept new to me at the time. Apparently a "studio apartment" designated a kitchen, a bath, and another room—a bedroom, one supposed. I could not picture such an arrangement. Where would one sit?

I had something else in mind, of course. I had space in mind, a place that would accommodate inviting John and Susan to stay with us during the holidays. Both Bruce and I had budget in mind. Different areas of the city commanded different prices, too, we saw, and right where we were, as we sat in a corner restaurant having lunch, seemed to be a somewhat affordable area.

"There are Vacancy signs on some of the buildings around here," Bruce noted. "Let's just start here." I was agreeable—I mean, weren't we close to downtown as well, Union Square? Why not? We spent the next few hours walking up steps or riding squeaking elevators, escorted by "building managers"—usually young—to an available unit. Each time I would inwardly cringe at the small space designated a "bedroom," where one could not envision a bed placed in it, a small closet in the corner. Or, kitchens they called "pull-man"—on a wall of one side of a room that was also a living room and bedroom? Often the paint was dull, the doors dark, the ceilings low. My spirits sank low, too. What were the possibilities?

In each case I could not place Bruce and me in the space let alone asking my children to join me: *Here's we are, kids. Sort of sad, isn't it?* We walked on. On Geary Street we finally found a unit I could live with—an upper floor, with newer carpeting covering (one could tell) uneven floors, but big enough with a real living room and real bedroom. The price, though! Far more than we wanted to pay. We walked down the hill a block and saw, on a corner, yet another apartment building. "Let's try this," Bruce said. "O'Farrell Street."

The ad was for a studio. "Oh no! I can't stand those." I recalled the several we'd seen.

"We're here anyway," Bruce said. "Why not check it out? The building looks good."

The small lobby had a stone fountain in its center, water actually gurgling, a terra cotta tile floor, rounded alcoves with vases. A young woman emerged from a corner office to take us up to the "studio," which turned out to be on the 7th floor. We walked from the elevator, with its folding brass door, past rounded archways to the unit available: a regular "hobbit hole" I thought immediately. One entered through an arched door, then through an interior entrance way and another arch into a fairly large room. On one side of the room, the ceiling framed another arch featuring what could be an eating area. A doorway led to the kitchen. On either side of that doorway were built-in bookcases. The kitchen was big—many cabinets, high and low, all white and gleaming, a big window at its end. The bathroom was respectable with a sliding glass door on the tub, a shower. There was a very big coat closet. But the *piece de resistance* was the "other closet"—the size of a small room, with shelves and a rod at one far end. What I thought immediately is "a guest—one of the kids—could sleep here!" I realized there was also enough room in the long entrance way to accommodate another sleeping bag or cot.

What truly sold me was the big room—it reached to tall windows at the far end. The entire place had been recently carpeted in a mauve-colored carpet, the walls freshly painted in off-white, and the woodwork done in a gleaming gray. It all looked so neat and tidy, spacious and inviting. The price—almost $700 a month (I'd been paying $350 for my N.J. mortgage) was a lot, but no more than anything else we'd looked at. And this place was inviting. I loved the arches of the entrance door and hall, the defined dining area. I could see, in that kitchen alone, places to put so much of the stuff we had carried, had sent.

Bruce and I smiled at each other. I nodded. "We'll take it," he said. That assent meant filling out papers and running credit checks on us—that might take a day or two, the young woman told us. There was no way to keep in touch, however, except for us to call her from a pay phone. We arranged a time we could do that—she suggested we make it late in the day. Bruce and I spent that evening in nervous anticipation, not helped by the rather sleazy hotel we'd purchased. We had to rise early to move the car so it wouldn't get ticketed.

That afternoon when we called, the credit check hadn't gone through yet; why didn't we call the next day, say at 10 in the morning? Of course, that meant finding another hotel—which we did, discovering that it was something like a bordello with its heavy red drapes, gold cords, too soft mattress. We got a parking ticket that night since we hadn't read the sign right.

At ten in the morning, in our rather bleak mood, we found a pay phone, and the woman said, yes, everything is all right; you can move into your apartment any time, today, if you want. We immediately switched to joy. We actually had a place to land! A home! We now had our own apartment. We would not have to "camp "—except for one night on our own carpet before we could buy a bed—nor would we have to search for yet another motel.

Years later, when I tell people that the apartment was on O'Farrell Street in the Tenderloin, their eyes will widen. They picture drug addicts sprawled on the sidewalk, cigarette butts and needles, mindless jaywalking, a predominant fear and caution not to even go there.

"It wasn't like that then," I say. And it wasn't. In 1986 the side-walks were clean and led straight downhill to Macy's and Union Square. The apartment was sparkling—all freshly painted and car-peted. New to me also was the fog that swept the city then in the evening, its cool air floating through those tall windows without an air conditioner whirring or even screens. There were no bugs. I was elated.

But somewhat spoiling my elation was Susan's situation. She missed me; she had a very difficult time living with her father and his wife. Their major weapon of coercion was blackmailing her about her tuition. If she didn't do such and such they wouldn't help, she said. I didn't think they helped to begin with. I fretted endlessly about abandoning her to them, to her own wits. For my selfishness.

And I did feel selfish. I was so happy there. I now loved the mauve-gray combination I once made fun of when it appeared in magazines and hotel lobbies as a popular color scheme. Now it was mine, it was ours. I was happy that the apartment had that one closet so huge I could offer it as a guest room to John, and an entrance way so extensive it could be Susan's area. I'd already set aside money to fly the kids here at Christmas, to fly them to our new home. Bruce and I were like children; we almost skipped along the streets: O'Farrell, Geary, Post—a strange site to picture in his case because he was big.

With our apartment secured, we went in search of Temp Agencies and got registered that same afternoon. I had received already, via Bruce Jr.'s mailing address, rejections from school districts that I inquired about while I was still in New Jersey. It seemed I needed something like a California credential in order to teach. No matter. I would do it. We would do it. After eighteen nights on the road, I felt a smidgen of security.

In addition to buying a bed—Bruce preferred a futon and frame, an idea new to me—we had to start hauling to our apartment the boxes I'd mailed to young Bruce's garage. This project took some energy and doing: parking the car temporarily in the street, lugging boxes and a mattress and its wooden frames across the lobby to the iron-gated elevator, then down the hall to our apartment. The futon was ingenious—a sofa by day, a bed by night. We now had the beginnings of furnishing a place to live.

In our second full week in San Francisco, here is the way life is going:

I walk home from my temp assignment at Smith Barney on California Street, thrilled at the high building that overlooks the Cable Cars, which clang and rattle on the street below. I relish the sidewalks with their coffee and sandwich shops, the smartly dressed people. Even the walk to go home through the downtown streets with all their stores is captivating: I'm in a city!

I enter our little apartment. Bruce, sitting at the table we bought at a garage sale a few days ago, looks up from his big yellow tablet. "Hi, Honey," he says. He pushes back his chair, stands, embraces me. "I'm pretty much through this application, I think. Maybe you'll check it?"

I feel his body, his solidness, lean against his height. Is there anything on earth that is any better than this? "Of course," I say. Then "Look!" Dangling by its string at my arm's length is an Eppler's Bakery box. "Rum cakes! I got them on my way home." He is pleased.

He makes coffee. We clear the table; I change my clothes. We spread newspapers on the new mauve carpeting so I can paint the used table and its chairs. We bought the paint yesterday, at Color World up the hill, in a gray hue that exactly matches the woodwork of our apartment. The other furnishings are our futon and cardboard tables and two small lamps we bought at Sears. A breeze wafts in the high windows at the far end of the spacious room. "These will dry quickly," Bruce observes of our table and chairs.

True. We'll have a dining set in a dining area by morning.

We clean up the paint, walk up to Edinburgh Castle on Geary, get beers and fish and chips, which, although they're wrapped in the newspapers in authentic London style, are actually fetched by a runner, we learn, who darts across the back alley to a Vietnamese shop that caters them. They're delicious. We talk to others at the huge bar about the varieties of ale, about which we know nothing. A bagpiper wheezes and squeaks his way through the crowd, an expectation here.

On our way home (home!) we stop at Safeway and get a jug of cheap wine to take back to the apartment where, together, we unfold the futon sofa's wooden frame to make up our bed for the night. We fall into it, into each other's arms.

"We're here," he says.

"Yes," I say. "Here."

"Home," he says. "Now."

"Yes," I say again. And fold myself into him.

That's the way it goes. Sometimes I think about all that furniture on my front lawn, the pieces I sold so cheaply to get rid of and that I now could use. My excitement of the new, however, overcomes any nostalgia or regret of the old. Over the next days we buy three unpainted chests which we haul into our apartment, piece by piece. These Bruce will have to "build," or reassemble, and I will paint them twice: once a dark green, which I think will be a good contrast and then, sick with my choice, repaint them all a mauve (back to Color World!) to match the rugs and feel much better.

We buy a wicker desk for the electric typewriter, which has traveled in the car with us, and a wicker chest to store blankets by day when our bed turns back into a sofa. In such a manner we have outfitted a home. It's our mutual home, in San Francisco. I am in love not only with the apartment, but with the entire city, which seems to glitter by day until the fog rolls in in the evening. I am in love with him.

"You're on a honeymoon," a hairdresser tells me when I've scheduled a much-needed appointment. He is returning to New Jersey after giving San Francisco a "try" for seven years. I have been exclaiming to him of my excitement to be here. He misses lawns and spaces, says the city is too expensive.

He makes me frown, to ponder, but not for long. In spite of the fact that I can't decide whether to renew my New Jersey car insurance or take out California insurance, in spite of the fact that we now have to pay a whopping (to me) $100 a month to get the car off the streets at night because we've gotten several parking tickets, that my new temp job is causing me severe gas pains and a headache from sitting for eight hours each day, or that I can't take the California test to qualify for a teaching credential for months, or that I miss the kids—in spite of all that, I like San Francisco.

I feel I'm a part of this city—feel a happiness in a partnership that I have never had before. How odd! At 45 years old, to have the experience of beginning. I am haunted by the kids and what they're doing, but mostly I am living in the present: guiltily, but there.

Bruce searches for planning jobs to apply for. We walk the neighborhood each evening after our dinner; on the weekends we drive to Sausalito, or Golden Gate Park to watch Shakespeare, or to picnic on the Marina Green. We are a team, as he has always said we were, and I am happy.

Until I can't reach John. Until Susan calls. Until I realize that her insurance runs out when mine does—part of my old plan—and Kaiser Medical has an eight-week wait for me. I tell her to pursue what she can there, feeling I've let her down once again. I have. I get another temp job that is equally boring but doesn't have the benefit of lunchtime on California Street, and pays a pittance. I wonder how I can live like this for very long. How do people do such meaningless work for years? Make so little?

But the weekends are free of lesson preps and responsibilities, and we explore the city. It will be months later, when I hear someone at the office say something about television, that I realize we don't have one. I am surprised by the little things I no longer have—the wicker bed tray, the crepe maker, the fondue set, baking pans, mixing bowls—struck by how much I've given away, how little I now own.

Bruce and I devote whole Saturdays to working on applications and resumes. We are determined. Our temp jobs range from enervating to insulting. For instance, I spend one entire day underground, in the bowels of a Wells Fargo bank, where I was to work the next two weeks relieving the woman whose position I would be temporarily replacing. I feel bad for her, for her sense of importance as she shows me around, and yet I cannot do this; I cannot live in this underground vault of a space for two weeks even though I need the money; I must risk calling the agency and saying No, I do not want that job, fearing they won't place me in another. Still, we accept the assignments that come our way. There are various temp agencies; we apply to each, take their tests. I make us dinner each evening.

Then it helps that Susan is pleased when, shortly after she returns to college, she's been assigned third grade for her student teaching, and John loves the school he's teaching at. At his temp job at Macy's Bruce finds an ad for tap dancing lessons. "I thought you'd like this," he said. "It says $5.00 a session."

I do like it; I'll do it. I'd sent my dancing leotards and shoes in one of those mailed boxes. I register for a literature course at Berkeley extension. I have got to justify my "leave of absence" from the high school in order to return. If I return. I picture that hot house, the flat streets I drove along every school morning for eighteen years, the faculty meetings in the library. I don't want the pull of money and security to be so strong I have to leave my heart here in San Francisco and go back to New Jersey.

36   *Coping*

In late September, six weeks after our arrival, I walked home up Van Ness Avenue from Ahmanson's Realty, where I had been hired as a secretary a few weeks before. I was relieved to have a "job," one I'd acquired through responding to want ads. I'd prepared several resumes: a teaching one, an "arts" one, and the "secretary" one. I'd actually been interviewed for an Arts Director position in a city that was an hour's drive away and realized the folly of what I had done during the interview, which I was totally incompetent at. The reliable secretary position I'd landed was a relief from the temp agencies. The company was in a big building near Aquatic Park. My only relief from the closeness and dullness of that job was the brief walk to Aquatic Park at noon to have lunch and view the Bay, which was always gorgeous. But even lunch hours were tedious. I was given a full hour and had nowhere to go. I had asked about shortening my lunch and thus my day, but that was not the way it was done. Hours were 8 to 12, then 1 to 5, period. At the high school we had twenty-minute lunches and too much to do, always. Walking home that September day, the late afternoon air as usual was clear; the sky as usual was cloudless. I loved everything about San Francisco so much: the scenery, our apartment, the weather. At the same time I fretted constantly over our lack of real income.

As I entered the apartment, entered its rounded archways, its mauve and gray and white colors that I absolutely loved, Bruce was sitting at one end of the futon-sofa, staring toward the windows. One hand was extended toward a mug of coffee on the cardboard side table, paused, as if he'd forgotten that that's what he was doing. The other hand, palm open, rested on the sofa, next to an open envelope, a folded piece of stationery. I could see its brief typed message.

I paused in the doorway. "Which one?"

"Oh." He turned to me. "Hi. The one in Manteca." I didn't move at first, in respect for his feelings. He said he thought he had a good chance and I agreed. "They want California experience. They say." I tried to reassure him that it would have been too far to travel—over an hour, more, and he didn't really want to do that. "It's a job," he said.

That much I knew. I too was crushed. I'd spent the afternoon during one of my many dull moments again reviewing how we would pay the bills with just my secretary salary—not much, but steady— and his temp job assignments, unsteady. I'd wondered, as I'd done many days before, how long we could go on holding things together.

He was trying to gauge my mood. He plunged in. "Sharon called. She needs the support money."

"We'll send it. We always do."

He looked mournful. I knew Preston's support money was important; I respected that Bruce thought so. I also resented the fact that if it weren't for me and the secretary job that bores me to death, we would not be able to send it. I'd been rehearsing, on my energetic walk home, telling Bruce that this possibly might not work out, the "this" being our experiment of San Francisco. I wouldn't mention such a thing now. "I didn't take the bus," I said. "I walked home. It's amazing that the weather is still so beautiful and it's almost October."

"Well," he said, standing up and refolding the letter into its envelope. "There's another ad I found. I'll work on that one tomorrow."

I nodded, retreated to the bathroom, washed my face. He was standing outside the door.

"I just realized I can't do that!" he said. "I'm laying rugs tomorrow."

I was drying my hands. "What? Rugs?"

"It's a two-day assignment. I agreed." He walked around me, closed the bathroom door behind him. I started dinner. I would reheat the spaghetti meat sauce from two days ago. I put on a pot (acquired through another garage sale) of water to boil, rummaged in the fridge for lettuce. I loved this kitchen, though, love its cozy efficiency; I felt I'd borrowed it from someone else, or it was on loan because it was "rented." I was also wondering—as I'd been for days— what to do about Christmas. How to buy gifts. With what. I had purchased John's and Susan's airline tickets to come out here. But what about gifts? Food for us all? Entertainment of some kind? I wanted to ask Bruce how he thought we'd do all that—his kids, our mothers.

Instead, I served the meal in silence. He ate in silence.

"Thanks, Honey," he said when we were finished. He started to pick up the dishes, then stopped, standing close to me. His presence, his physical presence next to me, reminded me of why we were here at all. I stood up and he set down the dishes to embrace me. We held that position for a full minute. I loved him. "I'll keep trying," he said.

"I know."

My tap classes are in a large studio, flanked by wall mirrors. They are not so much instructive "classes," since everyone can tap, but dance sessions. They delight and exhilarate. I love dancing with others, concentrating on the steps and combinations, love watching us in the large mirrors, our energy and synchronization, love the coordinated tapping sounds we produce together on the wooden floor. After an eight- hour day in that office with not enough to do, I come alive again in the tap studio.

Bruce is heartened, almost ebullient; he's gotten a second interview for a planning job in Santa Barbara. A second interview is most encouraging and suggests that a job offer could be in the waiting. The job—if he wins it—is a good one, a lucrative one. Isn't that what we want? Except that what we wanted was San Francisco, and Santa Barbara is hundreds of miles away.

I feel I've "settled" into our goal: this city. I have a job—dull as it is—but I have the tap troupe and the class I'm taking at the Berkeley extension. A few weeks before, we'd discovered an ad in the *Bay Guardian* for a "Shakespeare Reading Group," and found the organizer's apartment—his name was Dave—on the high area of San Francisco called Twin Peaks, another delightful discovery with its views of the entire city. What would Bruce's getting this job mean? Moving to Santa Barbara? Starting again?

That evening at the studio I tap away such a thought.

Almost as much as his actually getting the job, the immediate requirements of "a second interview" also upset me. He'll need the car to drive himself to Santa Barbara; he'll have to stay overnight, necessitating a motel, meals, gas. Just as we're barely managing.

I know he needs a job desperately, and I know he's been depressed about not finding one. Now I am depressed that this is what he has "found."

But he does leave in the morning, and I walk to work and back again. I fret—almost seethe—in his absence: I haven't struggled through all this to shift somewhere else, not where I want to be, lovely though Santa Barbara is. We'd stopped in San Barbara last summer on our then-vacation. I'd loved its symmetrical and many palm trees lining the park at the rim of the ocean, its Mission-style architecture, the Santa Barbara Mission itself. Santa Barbara was impressive at the time, as so much was. It was not a destination then, though, and to me still was not a destination after the excitement of settling into San Francisco.

We walk around the city the Saturday after Bruce's return from Santa Barbara, and I try to be somewhat cheerful, which isn't very difficult since his presence alone softens me. We attend a great concert at Davies Hall, where we'd acquired last-minute tickets, but, during the music, I'm thinking that if he gets this new job, I won't have the San Francisco Symphony handy this way; we won't have the San Francisco Opera. We've discovered that one can get same-day rush tickets for performances: $5 each for the symphony or $10 for standing room at the opera. A twenty-dollar weekend has become our entertainment budget.

On Monday, two days later, Bruce shows up at Aquatic Park where I am having lunch, where he knows I'll be. He's joined me there before. I am pleased to see him until I see his concentrated expression.

"I want to talk," he says, and his seriousness sounds ominous. "I don't know what to do."

He sits down next to me. I close my lunch bag, turn to him.

"You are really upset," he says, "and I am not sure why. I am trying—"

"I know!" I interrupt, and he pauses, politely acknowledging my interruption.

"—I am trying to find work. Today I've driven around to several places answering ads. I have more places to check out this afternoon—" He pauses again. I see his sadness, his sense of futility, and I despair at the fact that he's not his reassuring self. My recriminations for two days, while silent ones, were apparent to him.

"I probably won't get the Santa Barbara job. You don't want to go there, you've made that clear." His sadness is overwhelming to me.

"I—"

His eyes meet mine. That clear gaze stops me. The man has such insight always that I cannot argue; I am deeply affected by the way he's been affected. My seething in silence communicated only seething to him, judgment. He is a man who does not judge.

"It's okay," he says. "I'm not sure I want to go there either." We stare at the scenery—the blue bay, Alcatraz island. Voices of passersby fill our silence.

"I've been reluctant to take a job in the evenings," he says. "I don't want to leave you, ruin what we have together."

I shake my head, no I don't want him gone all the time I am home. I think of my evening tap troupe, though, my class. I say as much.

"They're only for an hour or two. You enjoy them," he says. "But maybe I should," he says, "find work in the evenings. It would help, wouldn't it?"

He stares toward the bay, probably taking in, as I am, the seemingly irrelevant sun flashing against the turquoise water, the views of Alcatraz and the Golden Gate Bridge gleaming before us, enticing us, mocking our moods. I feel despondent with his insight, his concern. "I love you," I say.

"Yes. Well. Of course that's mutual." He stands. Again he is silent.

I don't know whether to stand with him, suggest we walk? Even moving seems frivolous and dismissive. I don't know what to do.

"You've lost faith in me," he says.

That is what has wounded him. There is nothing I can say. After a long minute or two, I do stand next to him, put my arms around him. He always feels so big and reassuring in an embrace, which we hold only briefly; it's he who pulls away. "It's all right," he says. "I'm all right."

"Of course I'd go with you," I say. "We would go." My "but" lingers, unsaid, and he fills in. "We're too settled here," he says. "I can see that. And I probably won't get the job anyway."

He doesn't. The crisis is averted; his ego is not.

37   *Vacillations*

The tap studio advertises auditions for its San Francisco Tap Troupe, and I get accepted. The Tap Troupe is a group of ten gay men and five straight women who tap dance together in groups of ten or twelve. We wear tuxes to perform, sometimes with fishnet tights instead of trousers for us women. The rehearsals expand to two evenings a week. On another evening I attend the class I am taking through Berkeley Extension, something called New-Age Goddesses and Literature. My office job is so slow that when the boss isn't looking, I'm able to put together my class presentation on *Madame Bovary*, where I will explain that each character has a mythological counterpart—a silly discovery I've made, which pleases me. I realize how much I miss teaching and learning, how barren the days themselves can be.

On weekend evenings Bruce and I either walk to Davies Symphony Hall for rush-hour concert tickets ($5) or walk to the War Memorial Auditorium for standing room tickets for San Francisco Opera ($10). Once a week we drive to Dave's condo in Twin Peaks to meet with others in the Shakespeare Reading group. Dave's idea is to read Shakespeare plays together, with each of us taking parts, an idea that suits me just fine since it echoes those days in the Reed dorm with the seminar folks. Our first play has been *Richard III,* a play of many parts. Dave, our leader, gets to play Richard, and the other six or eight of us fill in all the other roles. I particularly enjoy the company of Karen and her friend Jane. Jane has written a play, and we drive to Berkeley to see it performed in a small venue. Karen is directing another play, which we also see. We are rich in experience; we walk the city streets, drive to Golden Gate Park, eat simply.

I've applied for the California Teaching Credential that will enable me to reach out for real teaching jobs; Bruce continues to apply for planning jobs. So far these have yielded nothing. Nevertheless, with Christmas coming, we walk down O'Farrell Street, where we live, to Macy's one late afternoon and purchase belts for his three sons, Christmas presents. I buy John a leather case and a book; I buy Susan a sweater and a Japanese doll—the cutest thing, I think— like a Madame Alexander doll, something frivolous, suggestive of San Francisco. What of our mothers? We settle on coasters with San Francisco scenes, one set each, to be mailed off. These simple gifts don't feel like much, but we're doing something.

Bruce is quiet. He hasn't done justice to his sons' Christmas, and he will not see them this holiday. I feel guilty that I will be bringing my own family into our apartment, increasing its occupancy from two to four. No wonder Bruce is brooding a bit. I'd already purchased round-trip tickets for John and Susan with money I'd set aside to do that, and also charged at Macy's floor futon cushions that unfold into beds for each of them.

We buy a tree from a local grocery store and set it up in front of our three tall bay windows. It's decorated with the lights and ornaments I'd sent last summer. Christmas dinner will be acquired mostly at Walgreen's. I'll buy two little canned hams, which I'll bake with cloves and mustard, and two boxes of Betty Crocker scalloped potato mix. Of course I'll augment that menu with other menus— making a meatloaf, baking cookies, and so on.

Finally, the days arrive: the 23rd when John flies in, and the 24th when Susan does. I am ecstatic. It has been so long. John has had a great semester, is truly loved by his students and wants to talk and talk about it. Susan wants to know how long she can stay.

The harmony is short-lived, however. Even with our "field trips" around the area—north along California's scenic coast, or into

Napa and wine country, we are not a relaxed family. Looking back, I can see why. John and Susan—in their early twenties—were forced to ride in the back seat of that Escort. John lectured us about smoking, got tired of being with everyone. Susan, overweight as usual, often bought herself extra snacks. Tensions flared, then subsided.

I take Susan to San Francisco Ballet's Nutcracker, which is a success, but then both kids renege on going to the Symphony, claiming they want time to themselves. Well, okay; I adjust to that idea, and Bruce and I go alone. New Year's Eve becomes a really good occasion for all of us. In 1986 San Francisco sponsored a "First Night" for New Year's Eve, allowing us, for $5 tickets, to have access to a number of venues and performances around the city—Bobby McFerrin, Tuck and Patty and several big bands—so we four trek to those. They're great shows; the evening is mild and clear. Back in the apartment we ring in the New Year with pizza and wine, replete with the paper hats and noisemakers I've bought. We end well.

Thus the New Year becomes 1987, numerals that sound awkward to me. John leaves, to both my relief and anguish; he's been tense and fussy and yet I can't stand parting with him again, my intellectual buddy for so many years. He calls, though, over the next few days. He's happy to be back in Honolulu and now tells me, "I miss you; I always miss you."

Things cannot be what they were; I need to accept that.

Susan stays around, as she wanted to, and Bruce is tolerant, earning my gratitude once again, as he acts the good sport. He drives the three of us to Santa Cruz, to Monterey, to Carmel, until, finally, the day comes when she leaves, too. I'm hoping that her friend Darlene will pick her up at the airport, that Susan will stay with her friend that night until she returns to college, that someone will take care of her.

I cry at the airport when we see her off; she and I had both cried when John left earlier. I cry back at the apartment because I don't know how I will ever be able to afford to fly them back here again if we stay. Those flights had been my "old" money. *If* we stay.

We are stretched well beyond our meager salaries.

I think about the good jobs Bruce and I gave up in New Jersey. Where I once complained that the high school demanded too much of me, I now see I had a position of creativity, variety, effectiveness. In addition, I earned almost four times what I'm earning in my office job that is boring to the point of numbness. If I returned to my old high school, it wouldn't be as Performing Arts chair—necessarily— but my teaching salary would be restored, and I'd have classes that demanded that I think and analyze and present ideas, deal with literature. The allure of such a situation is almost irresistible.

I consider my original plan to return to our old home: I can do that! But then I remember the dry lawn, the stifling heat, or, in other seasons, the frozen ground, the snow and ice, the windows thick with inside frost. I picture the street out front, cars constantly going by, the gas station at the corner, the flat cement shopping center. My friends—Barbara, Janet, Marita—write, and I miss them. I wonder if I miss them enough?

My "children" are not children. Susan, in spite of tears, seemed pretty independent at the end, taking herself to the science museum the last day because of a new lesson she was planning. It was I who had bought her a doll for Christmas. She'd looked confused at first, then said, "Mom, it's really cute," as though she didn't want to hurt my feelings. It was I who was clinging.

Bruce and I are alone again. Our apartment with just the two of us now seems spacious; San Francisco has been presented and accepted by my family, which suggests a sort of sanction to what we have been doing. In this new year, 1987, we resolve (not really, not formally) to keep at it, try harder. I concentrate on the California Credential—maybe if I can get back to lesson plans, talking about literature and writing, my days will have meaning. Bruce determines he can go beyond the search for a planning position and consider management jobs. In the meantime, we trudge back to what we've been doing.

The Summer Of 1987

San Francisco, California

38 *Opportunities and Agonies*

Good things happen. The Tap Troupe performs at eccentric and enjoyable venues. One such venue is the Tea Dance—a social for gay people. The entire group of us go—the Stage Band that plays the music we dance to, our Tap Troupe, even a vocalist. We perform a sort of floor show in the middle of the evening. Bruce, always open to new experiences—and this is surely one of them—attends, too, and I can be with him before and after I dance. Our Stage Band- and-Tap Troupe entertainment entourage is also booked at the Gift Center downtown for an awards event that Bruce can't attend since the audience is by invitation only. After the show I gather to take home to him some of the elegant refreshments that have been arrayed for us: jumbo shrimp, tiny quiches, dense chocolate brownies. The Troupe performs at a special dinner held at the San Francisco Zoo where banquet tents have been set up, replete with the platform that we dance on, and Jimmy Stewart is rumored to be a guest. That night I walk past flamingo ponds carrying my tap shoes and tux outfit, startled by the roar of a lion—or was it an elephant?—to a dressing room which turns out to be one of those movie-star trailers. I marvel at the novelty of what I am doing; who could have predicted this? A fundraiser for AIDS is held at the theater of the Palace of Fine Arts, one of San Francisco's great landmarks, and our entire Troupe, as well as a number of other performers, are gathered onstage for a finale where we sing "San Francisco, Open Your Golden Gate" while a fog machine swirls fake fog around us. These performances and venues are all quite thrilling, and I work hard at the tap routines, practicing on the tile floor of our kitchen in non-tap shoes.

I've inquired about a National Teaching Credential program and am invited to join the committee that meets at Stanford University to begin formulating plans for this credential. I wished there had been such a thing in place already so that my teaching experience in New Jersey would have instantly been honored in California. As it is, though, after taking several state-required tests, I finally receive from the state of California a Provisional credential, allowing me to be employed in the school systems, pending my taking several other courses: health, teaching reading. What a state system! This is on top of my master's degree and 20 years' experience. I send out around twenty letters of inquiry to various school systems whose addresses I found in the phone book in the library. One of the school districts—Alameda, a city across the bay—calls me and lines up an interview.

"I'll have to lie," I tell Bruce, "to be able to go. What can I tell Thomas?" Thomas is my boss at the real estate office—a really nice guy who, I think, wonders what I'm doing there in the first place. I like and respect him. It's not his fault the job is so boring. I'm even friendly with the other woman there, the "office manager," although she once had me retype 100 new envelopes so I could amend the "two spaces" I'd typed between state and zip code on the old envelopes to her insistent "one space between" on the new.

I lose sleep the night before the Alameda interview, rehearsing the phone call I'll have to make to the office in the morning. What can I say? An upset stomach? A twisted ankle? I almost don't go to the interview for fear of losing face with Thomas. Finally, I report pains in my shoulder; I should be all right by tomorrow. Surely I'll be in by then. Holding the phone, I blush to our apartment wall about my lie.

Bruce and I drive to Alameda, find the high school with time to spare. It's a large, sprawling L-shaped building that needs paint, squaring off a big lawn on which sits a Jet plane, a real plane. "There's a Naval Air Station at this end of the island," Bruce says. "Alameda is an island, basically. It's always interested me." Well, no surprise there. Everything interests Bruce.

Encinal High School hallways are wide, the ceilings high; huge windows along the halls look out across the football field to San Francisco Bay. The whole structure needs some attention. However, the interview goes well enough, even though I'm thrown off a bit when I'm asked if I'm accustomed to teaching students of other cultures (I think of two Korean students I once had in New Jersey) but, ultimately, I'm offered the job of filling in for a semester while another teacher is on leave.

I accept the position, even though the district will give me only six years' salary credit for my twenty years' experience; in addition, California salaries are not nearly as generous as New Jersey salaries. No matter—they will hire me, and I will be able to resign from the real estate company. I lose another night of sleep, composing and re-composing in my head a letter that I type in the morning and hand, guiltily, to Thomas.

He acknowledges my resignation with some perplexity, and I am free.

I'm assigned three 11th grade and two 10th grade English class-es—a rather thrilling prospect for me: this new/old odd school, its mix of races attending, the huge classroom I am to teach in. Windows on one side of the room look out to the jet plane on the lawn, and high windows on the opposite wall face the hall that, in turn, has views of the bay beyond. There's an outdoor swimming pool, a typical California high school feature, I learn.

Since I will need the car, we figure out a way for me to drop Bruce off in the morning at the new clerking job he's acquired—a small but steady paycheck at an investment company. I'll pick him up when I am finished in the afternoon. We'll work it all out.

"We always do," he says.

By June of 1987, four months later, and ten months after we'd arrived in San Francisco, the situation has become even better. The temporary semester I filled in for another teacher's sabbatical has ended, and I've been offered my own position for the coming school year. I now have a secure income, benefits. Bruce is still employed clerking and filing for a company that publishes a financial investment magazine. He likes the environment: the people, the setting. I like his setting, too. The company had taken over an old brick building, renovating its interior with open stairways and huge plants and plexiglass dividers, a gurgling fountain. It was located in what was called the "Dog Patch" part of the city, an area that eventually will be reconstituted with beautiful condos and restaurants, but at that time was more industrial, near ports of the San Francisco Bay.

We continue to walk to the ballet, to the opera, to the symphony, still by acquiring bargain rush tickets at the last minute. The clerks in our local convenience store know us. I've made a good friend at the high school, Helen; her husband, Joe, a witty and artistic man, is totally compatible with Bruce. The four of us have dinners together, attend events together.

Bruce and I have become part of San Francisco. Aren't we happy? In short: he is, and I am—mostly. All I have to do is sever my ties with New Jersey. It's true that I now have a teaching job. But it's a long day and requires a commute across the Bay Bridge. My opportunity to return to my former high school ends as of June 30. Before that date, I still have options. I can still return to a higher salary, to fewer than five long classes a day to teach. Can I do that? I think of the low brick building of the old high school, the dull drive through suburban streets to get there. I think of my house. Can I return to my house? The renters want to stay.

I feel I've betrayed my New Jersey friends. I've told Janet and Barbara and Marita I'd be gone only a year. Now will I tell them I have no idea when I'll ever see them again? I waver.

John has signed a contract for the next school year at Iolani, in Honolulu. He'll teach a summer school class as well; he is happy. But what of Susan? In May she graduated from William Paterson College and I didn't attend the ceremony. I'd given her an option: shall I fly there for the ceremony, or do you want me to buy you a ticket here? It's hard to believe that we faced such hard choices. She chose to come to San Francisco again. "Besides," she said, "Dad will be at graduation, and I don't think I need you both here at the same time." His attendance to her event was fine with her, but she did not want to live with him and his wife in Ocean City, New Jersey.

She cried over the phone, "I want a family!" meaning, I translated, *I want my home, you there.* "I don't know where to go." She had a friend she could stay with one weekend, maybe longer. She had no money for an apartment, and only a waitressing job at the Red Lobster—not near her dad's house. She'd felt lucky that Red Lobster had allowed her to switch locations from Paterson, where she'd worked part-time, to another of its franchises in Cherry Hill. So: even if she did agree to staying with her dad, she'd have to give up her job. And to keep her job, provide income until she could find a teaching position, she needed to be in or near our old neighborhood.

I suggested maybe she'd like to join us in San Francisco, move here, although I realized that Bruce and I did not have the space to accommodate her permanently, nor could I subsidize another apartment. She'd scoffed at the suggestion. "I don't have any friends in San Francisco! That was all your idea, not mine. I like it at home. Here."

Her situation was an enormous problem to me. My guilt was great. I'd never lived without my kids until leaving them so permanently. Could I return to the grimness of that New Jersey setting for Susan? How could I tell her I was not returning?

Guilt and money were the two biggest factors that held me back from resigning from the New Jersey high school. There was no doubt that I loved San Francisco, loved the arts immediately available to us, loved our apartment, loved Bruce. The contract for a year at Encinal High in Alameda, was just that: a year. It seemed a lark, but chances are I'd be re-hired. Thus, I considered *Staying versus Leaving:* yet another enormous decision facing me that early summer of 1987.

I made lists of pros and cons, once again:

- *In California*: I would have the long commute across the Bay Bridge every day;

- (*In New Jersey* a ten-minute drive through suburban streets of houses).

- *In California:* I would teach five classes of up to 35 students each, for 55-minute periods;

- (*In New Jersey* classes could not exceed 25 students, and English teachers were assigned only four classes of 45-minute periods).

- *In California:* I would be making $27,000;

- (*In New Jersey* I would be making $37,000. This point was a considerable one to agonize over, considering living costs.)

- *In California:* We had the beauty of San Francisco: the Bay, the Pacific Ocean, the parks, the bridges, the access to coastal towns, mountains. The arts at hand. The magnificent weather year-round.

- (*In New Jersey* we'd experience the heat and humidity of summer, the snow and ice and freezing temperatures of winter. We had Philadelphia, the Jersey shore, New York.)

- I tried to tip the balance in favor of staying in San Francisco until I added in Susan's emotions, added in the strain of our finances—which would be straining further as we searched for a different, larger, thus more expensive apartment. Unless Bruce got a good job. So, I had to add:

- *In California:* We needed a place with more space, which would cost us more. I would worry about what would become of Susan.

- (*In New Jersey* I had the large house; Susan could live with us; she'd have a home.)

What to do?

Was this whole project a success? Or a failure? I didn't want to return; I felt too guilty and frustrated to stay. There I was, or was not, agonizing once again.

39   The Letter

One day in mid-June Bruce, as usual, waited for me at the customary corner of 3rd and Mariposa Streets. He stood there, sun glinting off his glasses, tall and imposing in sports jacket, the good slacks and shoes he always wore. I experienced a fresh thrill of pleasure each time I picked him up after school, and today was no different. "Hi, Honey," he said automatically, getting into the car, and I leaned over to kiss his cheek.

We rode along, me making the usual banter about my day and the students, and him saying little until he turned to me. "I noticed that you didn't send that letter."

I knew what letter he meant. Finally making a decision - -I thought—I typed a letter of resignation to the New Jersey school system a few nights before. The letter was carefully and respectfully crafted, thanking the district for all the opportunities it had given me both in and beyond the classroom, noting my former superintendent, thanking the principal in particular. I read the letter over several times, pleased with my firmness, my phrasing. I typed an envelope and put a stamp on it and told myself I could mail it any time that week—or the next. As of this particular afternoon, the letter had been sitting on the desk for three days. Dropping it into the mailbox felt too much like an ax swing to my options in life.

"Is there any reason why not?" Bruce asked. "Why you haven't sent it?"

"I don't know," I said.

I parked the car in the garage—our rented space for it—and we walked in silence up the hill into the apartment, both of us passing by the envelope on the desk, neither of us saying anything. He put on a pot of coffee; I changed my clothes, got out my folders of student essays and settled myself at our table. I stared at the student papers—final essays on the hypocrisy of characters in *The Scarlet Letter*—but I was distracted with thoughts of my own. He had asked me why I hadn't sent the letter of resignation. I had said "I don't know." Was that an honest response?

I watched him as he poured himself a cup of coffee, seated himself at one end of the futon sofa, crossed his long legs, and stared toward the windows.

I was in love with this man because he did know. He knew that he wanted to be here, that he wanted to be with me. How could someone be so sure, confident in his decision? Was it because his "stakes" were lower than mine? I caught myself at that thought. Bruce did not reason economically. He was a believer in the idea that if you wanted something enough you would find a way. Was I his way? This city? I reminded myself, once again, that he was the only man I'd known who accepted me for everything I was, everything I did; he was always open to new ideas, adventures. He was bright and sexy. What on earth did I want beyond what I had sitting across the room from me this very minute?

I studied him, thinking. I knew that I had found everything that I had been missing. My children alone had remained a stable feature of my life that I felt I'd had some control over. Even there, it was difficult for me to realize that, as they became young adults, they wanted their own control, that it wasn't up to me to bestow happiness or security on them forever. Without them, could I ever feel complete? Could I actually be a permanent part of a partnership in a setting that to me seemed a temporary vacation?

I didn't know.

I had sung Bruce's praises for years, been grateful for him, feeling he brought to me something beyond a love interest. He represented a being who knew himself—when I thought about it, I recalled that that had been my original attraction to him. With him I had been forced to reckon with myself, come to terms with what had made me insecure, unhappy, tense, tentative, as well as what had made me happy. I had stopped "searching."

I sat at our gray-painted table, pen poised in my hand, and looked across the room at Bruce, who was still staring thoughtfully toward the windows. I realized I was living with a man I loved and who loved me. I had come so far from being that woman in heels scouting around Portland, Oregon, for one more place "to meet people." At that time I had wondered why I couldn't "belong somewhere." For two years I had belonged to him and now I—we—had established a sense of belonging here, in San Francisco. We had friends, jobs, the accessible arts.

I thought of another assignment I'd given to my students: Write an essay based on this line from a Pogo cartoon (it was a prompt borrowed from the UC Admissions system): *We have met the enemy, and they are us.*

Was I my own enemy? What more did I think I wanted?

From my seat at the table in our little studio apartment, my folder of essays in front of me, I watched Bruce across the room. Five minutes went by, and he was still looking toward the window. He hadn't touched his coffee. "Are you all right?" I asked.

He turned to me, his face serious, as though taking in the question. He didn't answer.

"You're so silent," I said.

I could almost see him gathering his thoughts, choosing his words. "I am depressed about your lack of faith," he said.

That phrase again! I felt a sudden weakness, my face flushing, and was relieved to be sitting across the room. "The letter," I said.

"Yes. I don't know what to do about your doubts and fears. I don't know why you have them."

I didn't know what to say. I couldn't again lament "abandoning" grown-up children or relinquishing career options. I couldn't say, my doubts and fears are my old friends—how can I let them go?

"I love you," he said. I thought then: he has put a paragraph together in his head. He has measured out what he wants to tell me. "We are all right," he said. "The adventure is working. We have jobs. We'll be moving soon to a bigger place. We are happy."

I knew all he said was true, and I almost cried. His gentle approach always gave me pause. He never got angry; he just sort of sank into contemplation.

"I don't understand you," he finished.

I sent the letter. Not that evening, nor the day after, but I sent it. That evening I said, "I haven't sealed the envelope."

He'd noticed that, too.

"Can I read it to you?"

"I was hoping you would," he said.

I read the words, feeling that I didn't know who had written this piece—a voice outside myself: *I am not returning.* He listened. "It's good," he said. "We're good. You know that."

Indeed, I did know that. I was alone when I walked it to the mailbox that weekend. Even standing at the mailbox, I hesitated. I mean, I opened the heavy drawer and let it close again, still clutching

273

the envelope. Why was it so difficult? It would only be the end of New Jersey, that life, that person. Persons, plural: Teacher, Leader, Director. I was cutting off some parts of myself. But the most important parts, that of Mother, Homemaker, Provider for family—those would end, too.

I startled myself. That conclusion wasn't exactly true. I had a whole new life to recreate here, and I was already recreating it, new roles along with the old.

I debated: If I returned, could I . . . well, live with myself? Could I say, I gave it a try, but it was all too different—and there was my daughter to think of. Was that my hesitation?

I caught myself at that last thought. Was I willing to give up my dream of being an adventurer, of forging a new life in this gorgeous place, in order to be on hand for a grown daughter? I pictured myself back in the house, staring at the road, the blank field across from it. I pictured having nowhere to walk but the local supermarket and drugstore, and even then I always drove since the road was well-traveled and had no sidewalk. I tried to see myself back in the low yellow brick building of the high school that I claimed was part of my "identity." I felt stifled even thinking of it. My former friends would be happy to see me, but my colleagues would just shrug, possibly thinking, *we knew she'd be back.* Would I smile and say, *I gave it the old college try, but, well, I missed you and—it's true, I'm back.*

Would Susan move back to her pink and green room in our house—for how long? Would she say in six months, "Mom, I found a job and I really want my own place. Staying here with you and Bruce makes me feel that I'm moving backwards." Then what?

Would Bruce return with me?

I didn't consider that part; I think I assumed he would go with me, assumed that if I had admitted to despair, Bruce would probably tolerate my decision to return to New Jersey. His disappointment would be palpable, but he would do it. I realized that I could not ask such a thing of him. I could not be emotionally beholden to his tolerance. He'd have to look for a job all over again, back at my mercy, my largesse. We would both know I hadn't the courage for change. Beyond worrying about his disappointment in me, in my lack of faith in "us," I wasn't sure that I could face my own sense that I had given up too soon, had failed myself. I couldn't even imagine packing up everything again, sending it all back, driving back across the country. How different, how defeating, deflating, all that would be! The process was awkward to even think about.

No, no, no. I could not do that at all. It had taken too much to get here, and Bruce was right: we were succeeding. We were happy. He was also right in not "understanding" me. I didn't understand me either. I had always wanted to live in such a place, have a man such as him, have the arts so accessible. I wanted to be the adventurer, the new person.

Isn't that what I accomplished? What we accomplished, together?

One more time I pulled the heavy mailbox drawer forward— and dropped the letter in.

40   *Finale*

In the Fall of 1987, a year after we arrived in San Francisco, we moved into a one-bedroom apartment Bruce had found for us. He followed leads in newspaper ads, checking out places beforehand. He enjoyed such scouting ventures. "I think you'll like this one," he'd told me, and he was absolutely right.

The building was an old Art-Deco style within walking distance of the War Memorial Opera House, Davies Hall. It was spacious, light-filled, with hardwood floors and big rooms and high ceilings, many closets, available parking. Its only drawback was a kitchen so small I could stand in one place and just rotate myself around to make dinner. There were no cabinets, just a few shelves to put dishes and glasses on, a sort of laundry-tub of a sink, a narrow stove. And yet, I have to add, during the San Francisco earthquake of 1989, plants toppled from our bookshelves in the living room, a lamp crashed to the floor, but nothing moved on those shelves in the kitchen. The glasses and dishes stayed as they were. How odd that was.

However, even before that, I was willing to forego the kitchen space for the graciousness and convenience of the rest of the apartment. Next to the tiny kitchen was a dining room with built-in cabinets that opened to a large living room. Our bedroom accommodated all we'd had in our studio apartment: the chests, our gray table and chairs, the futon bed. In addition, the bedroom had a lighted, walk-in closet. Another apartment "closet" held a fold-out bed and our wicker desk, creating a built-in guest room. And still there were closets, a central open foyer of a space.

Would anyone believe, though, that I left the O'Farrell Street studio apartment—our inviting hobbit-hole with its rounded doorways, its mauve and gray coziness—with a real sadness? It had been our landing place, our mutual nest, our first home. As we closed the door and I viewed its now empty space, I realized that every change was difficult for me, even this one, leaving an apartment of one-year duration. The image of Bruce and me setting down our wine glasses on one of our cardboard tables to dance to a song that had come on the radio, clinging to each other with the love and closeness we always felt, well, it had happened here, hadn't it? Owning nothing at the time, insecure about a future, dancing in a rented studio next to a rickety temporary table had been one of my happiest moments ever. I had to realize that this was a forever- me: always clinging to what worked, always both eager and reluctant to try the new.

He was not reluctant. We now had—thanks to his scouting—another mutual place—big and airy and able to absorb more furniture. Bruce was eventually promoted to a manager position in the research company he had been working for. It was a good promotion and one that made him happy and made things easier for us financially. I made Susan the "manager" of my New Jersey house and paid her the little salary I had been giving to a colleague in New Jersey. The renters were staying. I told her I could take the reserve of rent I'd accumulated and give it to her for an apartment. (I'd saved the reserve I'd been realizing each month toward repairs, etc.) She moved from staying with a girlfriend to her own small apartment near Cherry Hill on Labor Day, moved my old bedroom set from our house's storage area into that apartment.

She just had to find a real job, a teaching position, and was looking. I urged her to substitute, to go in the "back door," seize that kind of opportunity, the way I had done—which she eventually did. In the meantime, she worked long shifts at the Red Lobster. She made arrangements to have the rest of the furniture that Bruce and Preston had carried to the storage room the year before sent to us, which I paid for, depleting an old savings account I'd reserved for such an event. Bruce and I had the space to receive it, but how incongruous it was to see the matching chintz sofas again, the occasional tables from my past, both the gifted, framed posters: *Hamlet* that Doug had once given me, *Portland Jazz-1984*, that Bruce had sent. We had room for it all.

But before that furniture got there, Bruce and I were married. It was in September, 1987, a year and a month after we'd arrived in San Francisco. I took off that Friday from my Encinal High School position where I was now teaching my own classes of eleventh and tenth grade English. In two years I would become English Department Chair.

On our wedding day we dressed in our good clothes—him in his light brown suit, me in a new turquoise silk suit I'd bought at Ross in San Francisco. I remember the two of us sitting on the edges of our futon bed to put on our shoes, but do not remember whether we even bothered to fold the futon back into its sofa. We probably did. We'd already let our families know we were getting married. John and Susan were delighted—they both sent cards and Susan ordered balloons delivered as well. Each of our mothers was pleased.

That morning we walked from our new apartment to City Hall. Along Gough Street crowds had formed to greet Pope John Paul II, who was visiting San Francisco that day. I found the event to be an exciting coincidence and wanted to see both the Pope and the vehicle he was said to be traveling in called a Pope-Mobile. Bruce and I lingered with the crowd for ten or fifteen minutes, but had to leave, not wanting to be late for our appointment. The day was gorgeous, the pool in front of City Hall (there was a pool then) glittered in the sunlight. We walked across the square and treated ourselves to cinnamon buns, similar to those we'd eaten years before in Portland.

At City Hall it was such a surprise to me to see other "brides" waiting in the marble vestibules in bridal dresses, holding bouquets. Some even had gowned attendants. Dave, our reading-Shakespeare friend who was to be our witness, was right on time, too.

The ceremony was simple, performed by a judge in the high, lighted rotunda. Exchanging vows seemed such a natural thing for us to be doing, almost superfluous, as he placed a simple band on my finger next to the antique ring he'd given me two years before. Dave took pictures, which I was grateful for. I would send them to family later.

After the ceremony we celebrated with cocktails at Harry's Bar on Van Ness, and much later with the friend I'd made at Encinal and her husband—Helen and Joe. They brought a gift of wine glasses and wine and we toasted ourselves in the apartment among the celebratory balloons. We four went to dinner at an outdoor restaurant on Polk Street. I remember the day as "fun," happy from beginning to end. Such an event seemed an appropriate culmination of our year, of our commitments to new jobs, new friends, new apartment, the new city of San Francisco, and now, officially, to each other.

In that way we began a whole new phase of life that I could never have anticipated that summer day of 1984 when I first wandered around Portland, Oregon. That afternoon I had hesitated on the winding staircase of Harrington's Bar and Restaurant before deciding to sit down on a stool next to what seemed to me to be an interesting-looking stranger.

TWO PHOTOS: EARLY AND LATE

Jackie and Bruce, Summer, 1984, Oregon

Bruce and Jackie, Summer, 2018, San Francisco

EPILOGUE:
WHAT BECAME OF EVERYONE IN
THIS STORY?

Jackie continued to teach at both Alameda High Schools for seventeen years and was chair of the English department at each school. She then taught part-time at City College of San Francisco for another seventeen years. She occasionally teaches a course on Shakespeare for adult programs.

Bruce worked for the magazine company for ten years and, when they downsized, returned to selling cars, mostly Saabs, which he loved and was good at. Due to Bruce's research into Tenants in Common, he and Jackie acquired a beautiful Victorian flat in 1993. Several years later, the units converted into condos (under Bruce's supervision). He loved riding his motorcycle and reading poetry. He enrolled in poetry classes and wrote poems for years.

In 1995, Jackie sold the house in Cherry Hill, New Jersey, and purchased a second condo in San Francisco so "the kids would always have a home." It wasn't to be.

Jackie's daughter Susan died in October of 2010 of a heart attack. She was 45 and lived in Wilmington, Delaware, where she was a grade school librarian and had taught elementary school for nineteen years. Mother and daughter took a number of vacations together during their mutually free summers. Several times a year,

Jackie would return to the East Coast to visit Susan, but she has not been back to the New Jersey area since Susan's death.

Jackie's son John died of cancer in November of 2020 in San Francisco at the age of 57. He taught English for several years in both Honolulu and Japan, then acquired a master's degree in Transportation Planning from UC Berkeley and worked in that profession before returning, during his last few years, to teaching. He'd also received a degree in Religious Studies and remained a scholar his entire life. He was always close to Bruce and Jackie, living near them in the Bay Area for over twenty-five years.

Neither John nor Susan married.

Bruce died in their home, of cancer, in October of 2019. Several of his poems were read at the Memorial Service held at Bird and Berkett bookstore in San Francisco. Bruce and Jackie were married 32 years.

Bruce Jr., Bruce's oldest son, lives with his wife Andrea in Colorado. Scott, the middle son, shares his time between Ashland, Oregon, and Sayulita, Mexico. Preston is founder and CEO of BTI, a bicycle supply business in Santa Fe, New Mexico where he lives with his wife, Dominique. All sons remain adventurers, and Jackie stays in touch with them.

None of Bruce's or Jackie's children had children.

Jackie still lives in their San Francisco Victorian condo where she continues to frequent the arts and to travel.

She has never regretted the decisions she made.

ABOUT THE AUTHOR

Those Several Summers is Jackie Davis Martin's third major book. A memoir about losing her daughter, *Surviving Susan*, was released in 2012 and her novel *Stopgaps* came out in May of 2021. In addition, her short stories and essays have been published in anthologies, including *Modern Shorts, Love on the Road,* and *Road Stories,* as well as in print and online journals. Prizes for fiction were awarded by *New Millennium, On the Premises,* and *Press 53,* among others. She has taught writing and literature her whole life - - at high schools in New Jersey and California, and at City College of San Francisco. She regularly attends San Francisco's Ballet, Opera, Symphony, and Bay Area theater performances, as well as participates in writing communities and groups.